Jason Lefebvre
Paul Bertucci

SAMS
Teach Yourself
ADO.NET
in 24 Hours

SAMS

201 West 103rd St., Indianapolis, Indiana, 46290

Sams Teach Yourself ADO.NET in 24 Hours

Copyright © 2002 by Sams Publishing

International Standard Book Number: 0-67232-383-4

Library of Congress Catalog Card Number: 2001099191

Printed in the United States of America

First Printing: May 2002

05   04   03   02   4   3   2   1

Trademarks

Warning and Disclaimer

EXECUTIVE EDITOR
Michael Stephens

ACQUISITIONS EDITOR
Neil Rowe

DEVELOPMENT EDITOR
Kevin Howard

MANAGING EDITOR
Charlotte Clapp

PROJECT EDITOR
Elizabeth Finney

COPY EDITOR
Margaret Berson

INDEXER
Sandra Henselmeier

PROOFREADER
Leslie Joseph

TECHNICAL EDITOR
John Purdum

TEAM COORDINATOR
Lynne Williams

MEDIA DEVELOPER
Dan Scherf

INTERIOR DESIGNER
Gary Adair

COVER DESIGNER
Aren Howell

PAGE LAYOUT
Susan Geiselman

Contents at a Glance

Contents

About the Authors

JASON LEFEBVRE is vice president and cofounder of Intensity Software
(http://www.intensitysoftware.com), a software development company specializing
in Microsoft .NET development. Aside from software development, Jason is the coauthor
of *Pure ASP.NET* (Sams Publishing), the code-intensive reference to ASP.NET. In addition, Jason has written numerous articles for nationally known magazines such as *Visual
C++ Developer's Journal*, *Visual Studio Magazine*, and *MSDN Magazine*.

PAUL BERTUCCI is managing principal and founder of Database Architechs
(http://www.dbarchitechs.com), a database consulting firm based in San Francisco,
California, and with European offices in Paris, France. He has more than 20 years of
experience doing database design, data architecture, data replication, performance and
tuning, distributed data systems, data integration, and systems integration for numerous
Fortune 500 companies. He has authored numerous articles, standards, and courses such
as Sybase's "Performance and Tuning" course and "Physical Database Design" course.
Paul is a frequent conference speaker and regularly teaches database design, performance
and tuning, data modeling, OLAP, Supply Chain Management, and SQL courses. He has
worked heavily with .NET, MS SQL Server, Sybase, DB2, and Oracle, and has archi-
tected several commercially available tools in the database, data modeling, performance
and tuning, and data integration arena. He also was one of the primary authors for
Microsoft SQL Server 2000 Unleashed (Sams Publishing). Paul received his formal edu-
cation in computer science from UC Berkeley. He lives in northern California with his
wife, Vilay, and five children (the fifth came right in the middle of writing Chapter 19 of
this book—a boy!). Paul can be reached at pbertucci@dbarchitechs.com and by phone
at 925-674-0000.

Dedication

This book is dedicated to my nephew, Jerry, who reminds me what it's like to see the world with young eyes.—Jason Lefebvre

I would like to dedicate this book to my loving wife Vilay and our new son Donald. Even during delivery, we joked about when I was going to finish my chapters.—Paul Bertucci

Acknowledgments

I would like to thank the entire Sams team for making this book the best it can possibly be. Special thanks goes to our acquisitions editor, Neil Rowe, who kept us on task and made sure our deadlines didn't slip (much). Thanks also to the development editor on this book, Kevin Howard, who was understanding and patient as the table of contents underwent some last-minute changes, and also to John Purdum (technical editor) and Elizabeth Finney (project editor).

Special thanks to my business partner, Robert Lair, for shouldering more than his fair share of the burdens while this book was wrapping up. Thanks also to Mike Amundsen for helping me to properly gauge the multiple layers of "late" and to keep things in perspective.

And of course, the most special of special thanks goes to my family, for their support and to my friends, who've marvelously endured the strained relations caused by too much work and not enough play.**—Jason Lefebvre**

I would like to thank my family (Vilay, Juliana, Paul Jr., Marissa, Nina, and little Donny) for allowing me to encroach on months of what should have been my family's "quality time." I'm sure my children wonder if daddy ever sleeps. They see me working when they go to bed and they see me working when they wake up in the morning.

Special thanks must go to one of the most outstanding consultants I know, Martín Sommer. His help in digging through many technical and coding issues during the chapter creation process was invaluable.

Many good suggestions and comments came from the technical and copy editors at Sams Publishing, along with Jason Lefebvre, yielding an outstanding effort.**—Paul Bertucci**

Tell Us What You Think!

As the reader of this book, *you* are our most important critic and commentator. We value your opinion and want to know what we're doing right, what we could do better, what areas you'd like to see us publish in, and any other words of wisdom you're willing to pass our way.

As an Executive Editor for Sams Publishing, I welcome your comments. You can fax, e-mail, or write me directly to let me know what you did or didn't like about this book—as well as what we can do to make our books stronger.

Please note that I cannot help you with technical problems related to the topic of this book, and that due to the high volume of mail I receive, I might not be able to reply to every message.

When you write, please be sure to include this book's title and author as well as your name and phone or fax number. I will carefully review your comments and share them with the author and editors who worked on the book.

Fax: 317-581-4770

E-mail: feedback@samspublishing.com

Mail: Michael Stephens
          Executive Editor
          Sams Publishing
          201 West 103rd Street
          Indianapolis, IN 46290 USA

Introduction

ADO.NET is more than just the next version of ADO; to date, it's the most powerful set of data retrieval and data manipulation tools available. Using ADO.NET and the Microsoft .NET Framework, you can create powerful data-driven ASP.NET and Windows Forms applications. ADO.NET is much more robust and scalable "out of the box" than any of its predecessors.

Sams Teach Yourself ADO.NET in 24 Hours breaks ADO.NET into 24 bite-sized hours, each designed to present a single task-oriented ADO.NET topic. At the end of each hour you'll find a question-and-answer section, and a workshop consisting of a brief quiz and an exercise. The workshop is designed to test your comprehension of the current hour, as well as reinforce the concepts presented in previous hours.

As with most computer books, the topics are presented with progressively more difficulty. The book begins by presenting fundamental concepts such as the ADO.NET base objects, including the `DataSet` and `DataTable`. Then you'll see how to connect to your data source, retrieve data, and save that data back to the data source. Later hours build on the knowledge presented in earlier chapters to tackle topics such as stored procedures, data binding, error handling, and using Web services to send a `DataSet` to a remote application. In addition, extensive examples are presented in each hour so that the readers can sink their teeth into real-life code and reap the benefits of the concepts quickly. Practice makes perfect!

ADO.NET concepts apply to many different types of applications including Web forms and Windows forms. This book utilizes examples of both types. Though not required, to get the most out of this book you should be familiar with the rudiments of ASP.NET or Windows Forms. Some knowledge of T-SQL would also be helpful, but don't worry if you're a little rusty: Hour 3 provides a brief tutorial on building SQL statements, to get you up to speed even if you've never built a SQL query before.

Additionally, though no previous knowledge of ADO is assumed, several references are made throughout the book comparing ADO to ADO.NET. If you've developed applications in Visual Basic 6.0 or ASP using ADO, you should feel right at home learning ADO.NET.

Because ADO.NET is, at the most basic level, just a set of classes in the Microsoft .NET Framework, it is purely agnostic with regard to programming languages and development environments. Most of the examples in this book are presented in Visual Basic .NET only. However, whenever you see a set of code for the first time, the example will normally be followed by the same example written in C#. Likewise, many examples are presented as ASP.NET Web forms created using Notepad. However, the ADO.NET code can easily be stripped out of the Web form and placed into a Windows Forms application, and the reverse. In hours that cover Windows Forms applications, the examples are created in Visual Studio .NET.

Conventions Used in This Book

This 24-hour course uses several common conventions to help teach the programming topics included in this book. Here is a summary of the typographical conventions:

- Code listings, computer output, and code terms mentioned in the text appear in a special monospaced font.
- Words you type appear in a **bold monospaced** font.

HOUR 1

Introducing the Microsoft .NET Framework and ADO.NET

The Microsoft .NET Framework is one of the most significant technology shifts Microsoft has ever made, analogous to the release of Windows 95 when Windows 3.1 was the prevalent operating system. The new framework is more than just an upgrade—it's an entirely new platform enabling software developers to create new types of applications, mainly by offering developers new tools, such as Web services, a set of strongly typed programming languages that are syntactically identical whether used to program for the Web or for the desktop, a common language runtime, a set of framework classes encapsulating areas of common functionality, and a greatly improved data access model.

The Microsoft .NET Framework ships with a set of useful built-in classes. These classes contain many of the objects you'll use to create applications, both for the Web and for the desktop, such as all built-in Web controls, Windows forms controls, and collection objects. Several of these built-in classes comprise ADO.NET.

In this hour, you will learn the following topics:

- An overview of the ADO.NET namespaces
- An overview of the ADO.NET objects
- How to download and install the Microsoft .NET Framework Software Developer's Kit (SDK)

The Microsoft .NET Framework Class Library

You'll find a staggering amount of classes and methods inside the Microsoft .NET Framework. To organize the classes, they are placed within groups called *namespaces*. A namespace is simply a logical division, and can be as large or small as desired.

Any Microsoft .NET developer should become familiar with a free sample application from Microsoft called the .NET Framework Class Browser (see Figure 1.1), available online at http://www.IntensitySoftware.com/ClassBrowser. However, the class browser is part of the QuickStart tutorials published by Microsoft and should be available on any machine with the QuickStart tutorials installed. If you accepted defaults during the installations of the QuickStart examples, it should be installed locally at http://localhost/quickstart/aspplus/samples/classbrowser/vb/classbrowser.aspx. Much more than a set of static help pages, the class browser loads the namespaces at runtime to display their methods and properties. Thus, if you are running the class browser locally, you are assured of up-to-date information on the assemblies installed on your system.

The class browser shows you the list of Microsoft .NET Framework namespaces on the left side of your screen as seen in Figure 1.1. It is absolutely worth your time to become familiar with these namespaces and the classes they contain.

FIGURE 1.1

The Microsoft .NET Framework Class Browser application is used to browse the framework's built-in classes and methods.

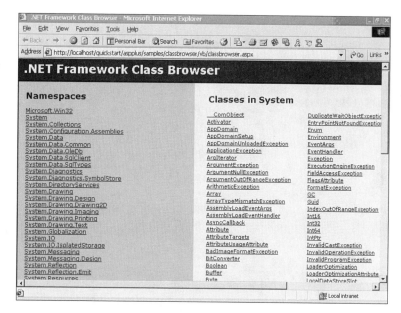

What Is ADO.NET?

ADO.NET is Microsoft's platform for data access in its new .NET Framework. Out of the box, ADO.NET is scalable, interoperable, and familiar enough to ADO developers to be immediately usable. By design, the ADO.NET object model and many of the ADO.NET code constructs will look very familiar to ADO developers.

At the most basic level, ADO.NET is a set of framework namespaces, specifically:

- System.Data
- System.Data.Common
- System.Data.SqlClient
- System.Data.OleDbClient
- System.Data.SqlTypes

The System.Data namespace contains many of the objects upon which ADO.NET is built. This is where you'll find the DataTable, DataSet, DataRelation, and DataView objects. Additionally, this is where ADO.NET constants are stored. For instance, the System.Data.SqlDbType class shown in Figure 1.2 contains all the Microsoft SQL data types.

FIGURE 1.2

*The
System.Data.SqlDbType
class contains constant
values for all the data
types in Microsoft SQL
Server version 7.0 and
higher.*

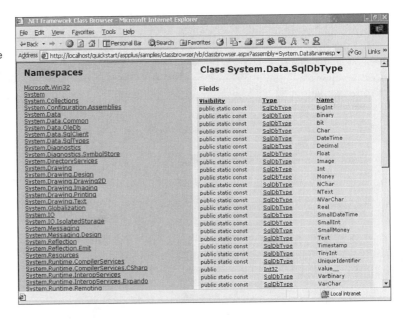

The `System.Data.SqlClient` namespace contains objects designed to work with a
Microsoft SQL Server database, version 7.0 and higher. This is where you'll find familiar objects such as `SqlCommand`, `SqlConnection`, and `SqlParameter` as well as new faces
such as `SqlDataAdapter` and `SqlDataReader`. If you're a SQL developer, this namespace
will be your sandbox for most of this book. The namespace uses a managed SQL
provider to work with the database. By working directly with SQL database APIs,
`SqlClient` bypasses ODBC (Open Database Connectivity) and OLE DB (Object
Linking and Embedding for Databases) entirely, offering a very robust and efficient
interface.

The `System.Data.OleDbClient` namespace is designed to work with any valid OLE DB
source. This includes data sources as varied as Oracle databases, Microsoft Excel files,
standard ASCII comma-delimited text files, and Microsoft Access files, as well as versions of Microsoft SQL Server prior to version 7.0. As mentioned earlier, if you're working with Microsoft SQL Server 7.0 or higher, the `System.Data.SqlClient` offers a much
better way to work with your data.

OLE DB, ODBC, and Managed Providers (Oh My!)

You've probably heard the terms OLE DB, ODBC, and managed provider
used when speaking of connecting to databases, but you might not know
how to distinguish each from the others.

1

Back in the dark ages (roughly 15 years ago), the prospect of retrieving data from a database was much more difficult than it is today. For each separate database type, you would have to learn that system's interfaces to retrieve any data. The interfaces of any given database system could be wildly different than any of the others because there were no standards.

By the late 80s, several vendors (including IBM and Microsoft) realized that it would be a good idea to offer programmers a standardized database interface. By factoring a standard interface from the mire of proprietary APIs used by the database system, programmers only had to learn one API instead. This standard API is known as ODBC.

OLE DB is much like ODBC, but based on COM (Component Object Model). OLE DB offers much better performance than ODBC, but it is only available to Microsoft-based solutions.

ODBC and OLE DB are both layers that exist between application code and the database. As such, they are not as fast as interfacing with the database system directly, in its language. The developers of ADO.NET created a namespace that works with Microsoft SQL Server (versions 7.0 and up) using its native APIs. Because the code connects directly to SQL Server and is managed by the framework, it's known as a managed provider.

Regardless of which method is used to connect to the database, ADO.NET provides a single interface for retrieving data. You don't need to worry about the underlying connection method.

The `System.Data.OleDbClient` namespace mirrors the `System.Data.SqlClient` namespace almost precisely. In fact, if you scan the classes in both, you'll notice that the class names differ only by their preface (for example, `SqlCommand` versus `OleDbCommand`). Fortunately, after you've worked with one namespace, you've learned how to use both.

ADO.NET Versus ADO

The relationship between ADO and ADO.NET is analogous to the one between Active Server Pages (ASP) and ASP.NET. Many of the object and method names are similar, but behind the curtains everything has been redesigned and improved.

For instance, the ADO data model was based on the recordset object. In essence, the recordset was a spreadsheet of data in memory. You were very limited in what you could do with a recordset of data. It was difficult to do advanced data filtering or combine two recordsets. Additionally, although it is possible to transmit an ADO recordset to a remote server, you must configure all firewalls between the two servers to enable the proprietary ports required for COM martialing.

Additionally, the remote server must know what an ADO recordset is—for all intents and purposes, this means that the remote server must be running a Microsoft operating system. Because of the limitations of the ADO recordset object, solutions based on ADO were likewise limited.

Microsoft has fixed these problems with ADO.NET. The centerpiece object of ADO.NET is the DataSet. The DataSet is an in-memory representation of data that provides a consistent relational programming model regardless of the data source. The DataSet contains a collection of DataTables, which are very much like recordsets in that each DataTable is a set of data. However, rather than just being a container for various DataTables, the DataSet can store relations and constraints pertaining to the DataTables! Not only can a DataSet mirror the relations and constraints in your data source, but you can add new ones as the logic of your application dictates. This gives you complete control of filtering and combining DataTables.

Additionally, DataSets (and the DataTables within them) are represented internally by strongly typed XML. Thus, at any point, it is possible to save a DataSet to XML. This might not seem like such a major point at first glance. However, this means that any platform that can parse XML—and I do not know of any platform that cannot—can retrieve data from an ADO.NET DataSet.

DataSets are easily transmitted to remote machines, as well. Web services are designed to transmit XML data via SOAP to remote machines. Because the DataSet is represented internally as XML, sending a DataSet to a remote server requires no special handling. The remote server could be running any platform that understands XML, such as Java-based solutions like IBM WebSphere. A WebSphere developer would only need to parse the XML.

SOAP (Simple Object Access Protocol) is an open standard that defines how objects should be packaged (via XML) and transported over TCP/IP (via port 80). The official SOAP specifications and other documents are available online at http://www.w3.org. Choose SOAP from the main menu.

The System.Data Namespace

The System.Data namespace contains most of ADO.NET's base objects, or the objects upon which ADO.NET relies to represent data retrieved from the data source. It also contains various supporting objects, such as many of the various ADO.NET exceptions (specific errors). Figure 1.3 shows how the various ADO.NET objects interrelate.

FIGURE 1.3
The ADO.NET object model is hierarchical.

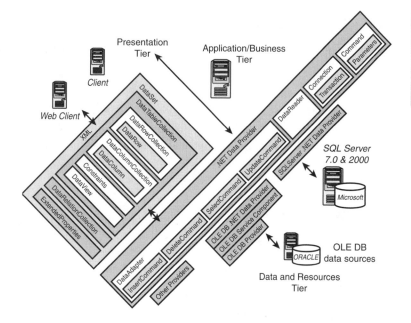

The `DataSet`

The `DataSet` object is the parent object to most of the other objects in the `System.Data` namespace. Its primary role is to store a collection of `DataTables`, and the relations and constraints between those `DataTables`. The `DataSet` also contains several methods for reading and writing XML, as well as merging other `DataSets`, `DataTables`, and `DataRows`.

The `DataTable`

The `DataTable` stores a table of information, typically retrieved from a data source. In addition to simply containing the various `DataColumns` and `DataRows`, however, the `DataTable` also stores metatable information such as the primary key and constraints.

The `DataRow` and `DataColumn`

The `DataRow` and `DataColumn` objects are at the bottom of the ADO.NET "food chain," so to speak. Ordinarily, you won't have to deal with these objects in an application. However, as you'll see later in this book, there are instances where it is useful to drill down to the actual columns and rows in a `DataTable`.

The `System.Data.SqlClient` and `System.Data.OleDb` Namespaces

As previously mentioned, the `System.Data.SqlClient` and `System.Data.OleDb` namespaces work with data sources. `System.Data.SqlClient` uses a managed provider to interact directly with Microsoft SQL Server version 7.0 and higher. `System.Data.OleDb` interacts with any valid OLE DB source. Though the namespaces are separate, the base objects function in nearly the same exact manner. Both namespaces contain `Connection`, `Command`, `DataAdapter`, and `DataReader` objects. Indeed, the namespaces almost exactly mirror one another.

The `Connection` Object

As you might have guessed, the connection object opens a connection to your data source. All of the configurable aspects of a database connection are represented in the `Connection` object, including `ConnectionString` and `ConnectionTimeout`. Also, database transactions are still dependent upon the `Connection` object.

The `Command` Object

The `Command` object performs actions on the data source. You can use the `Command` object to execute stored procedures, or any valid T-SQL command understood by your datasource. This is the object that performs the standard `SELECT`, `INSERT`, `UPDATE`, and `DELETE` T-SQL operations.

The `DataAdapter` Object

The `DataAdapter` object is brand-new in ADO.NET. The `DataAdapter` takes the results of a database query from a `Command` object and pushes them into a `DataSet` using the `DataAdapter.Fill()` method. Additionally the `DataAdapter.Update()` method will negotiate any changes to a `DataSet` back to the original data source. Unlike ADO, updating the original data source with modified data works reliably well.

The `DataReader` Object

The `DataReader` object is also brand-new in ADO.NET. The `DataReader` provides a very fast, forward-only view of the data returned from a data source. In most instances, to display a set of data in a Web or Windows form, this is the object you'll use, because there is very little overhead. No `DataSet` is created; in fact, no more than one row of information from the data source is in memory at a time. This makes the `DataReader` quite efficient at returning large amounts of data. You can think of the `DataReader` as a firehose that goes directly from the data source to the final destination. However, if you need to manipulate schema or use some advanced display features such as automatic data paging, you must use a DataAdapter and DataSet.

Installing the Microsoft .NET Framework

To follow along with the examples in this book, you'll need to install the Microsoft .NET Framework, or find a hosting company supporting .NET (Eraserver offers limited hosting for free at http://www.eraserver.net).

To download the Microsoft .NET Framework, navigate to http://msdn.microsoft.com/net. After downloading and running the executable install file, you still have a few additional steps to install the QuickStart tutorials.

After the SDK has completed installing, go to the Samples and QuickStart Tutorials entry in the Microsoft .NET Framework SDK program group, and follow the onscreen instructions. You will have to click one link to install the samples and another link to configure them.

Summary

In this hour, you've been introduced to the ADO.NET object model and read about some of the theoretical applications of ADO.NET. You saw how the DataSet object is the cornerstone of ADO.NET development. You also saw how the DataSet contains the DataTable that contains DataRows and DataColumns. Lastly, you downloaded and installed the Microsoft .NET Framework so that you can follow along with the examples in this book.

Q&A

Q If I install the Microsoft .NET Framework, will I still be able to build applications using ASP and Visual Basic 6.0?

A Absolutely! The Microsoft .NET Framework exists side by side with your other development platforms. You can even mix ASP and ASP.NET files within the same application! Likewise, Visual Basic applications are not affected at all.

Workshop

These quiz questions are designed to test your knowledge of the material covered in this chapter. The answers to the quiz questions can be found in Appendix A, "Answers to Quizzes."

Quiz

1. Name the most important root object in ADO.NET.

   a. The `DataTable`

   b. The `DataSet`

   c. The `DataAdapter`

2. True or false: ADO.NET represents all its objects internally using XML.

3. Which important ADO.NET namespace contains the `DataSet`, `DataTable`, and `DataRow`?

Exercise

After downloading the Microsoft .NET Framework SDK (location and details provided earlier in this hour), make sure to install the QuickStart samples provided in the framework. Spend some time using the QuickStart Class Browser application to become more familiar with the location of the built-in framework objects.

HOUR 2

Working with DataSets and DataTables

At the heart of the ADO.NET platform, you'll find the DataSet and DataTable objects. The DataSet operates just like an in-memory database. That is to say, the DataSet object can contain multiple DataTables, along with any relationships, constraints, and primary keys necessary to closely represent the data returned from the data source.

In this hour, you will learn the following:

- The basics of the database schema
- How to instantiate and manipulate the basic ADO.NET objects, such as the DataSet, DataTable, and DataColumns
- How to define the schema of a DataSet
- How to create and configure a new ASP.NET Web

Crash Course on Database Schema

In a database, such as Microsoft SQL Server, data is stored and organized in tables. Tables consist of a set of columns and a set of rows. The columns (also referred to as "fields") define what information you are storing about your object (such as name, description, color, and so on). The columns define how your data will look. This is referred to as the database *schema*. The rows (also referred to as "records") are your data—each row represents a group of columns of information.

A *primary key* is a column in your table that guarantees row-level accessibility. This sounds more complicated than it really is. Think of the data in a table organized like a spreadsheet. To access a particular row, the data provider needs to be able to distinguish that row from the rest in an efficient manner. The primary key is any field (or set of fields) that can be used to guarantee uniqueness. For instance, common examples of a primary key include:

- Identity field—A special automatically incremented number field that stamps each record added to the table with a unique number. No two records in the table will have the same value in the identity field.
- Social Security number—A field like this will work just fine so long as each person is listed only once in the table.

DataSet Overview

As mentioned, the `DataSet` object is the cornerstone of ADO.NET development. The `DataSet` contains a set of `DataTables`, as well as any relationships between those tables. Figure 2.1 shows the relationships between the objects within the `DataSet`.

> **Relationship**
>
> In a relational database, a relationship is a link between two entities (such as tables) that is based on attributes of the entities. For instance, if you have a table of customer information, you might link their `CustomerID` to the CustomerInvoice table, so that only valid customers in the database are invoiced.

If you are new to the Microsoft .NET Framework, some of the code in this hour might look intimidating at first. The good news is that the code in this hour is not required to understand the rest of the book. Most developers will never need to construct an entire `DataSet` from scratch, adding tables and creating the schema manually.

By working through this chapter, you will gain a much deeper understanding of how the DataSet and its component objects work. With this information, you will be able to more effectively debug ADO.NET programming problems.

FIGURE 2.1

The relationship between the various ADO.NET objects.

DataSet Object Model

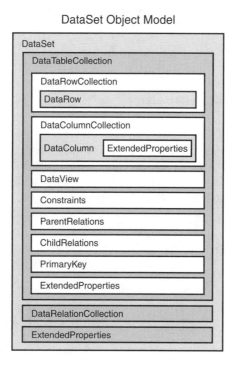

2

Creating DataSet Schema

In the next few sections, you'll see how to create a new DataSet and new DataTable. You'll also see how to manually create the DataTable schema using DataColumns. Finally, you will add some data to the DataSet using the DataRow object.

Instantiating a New DataSet

The first step to working with a DataSet is to create a new instance of a DataSet object. You can do this by using the following code in Visual Basic .NET:

```
Dim dsCompany as New DataSet()
```

or like this using C#:

```
DataSet dsCompany = new DataSet();
```

Adding a `DataTable`

When you have a `DataSet` object, the next step is to add a `DataTable`. The `DataTable` contains the columns and rows that make up the data you'll add later. To add a new table to the `DataSet`, you use the `Add()` method of the Tables collection in the `DataSet` object, as in the following line of Visual Basic .NET code:

```
dim dtEmployees as DataTable = dsCompany.Tables.Add("Employees")
```

or like this using C#:

```
DataTable dtEmployees = dsCompany.Tables.Add("Employees");
```

Notice how the "new" keyword is not used to add a new `DataTable` to the `DataSet`. The `Add()` method of the Tables collection in the `DataSet` object creates a new `DataTable`, adds it to the collection of tables inside the `DataSet`, and then returns the object, automatically.

Adding `DataColumns`

Now that you have a `DataTable`, it's time to define exactly what data the table will contain. For this example, the `DataTable` contains only three columns: EmployeeID, FirstName, and LastName. The EmployeeID is a standard identity field, which will also serve as the primary key. The FirstName and LastName columns will contain strings.

`DataColumns` are added to a `DataTable` in precisely the same way `DataTables` are added to `DataSets`. In this case, you will not need to refer back to the columns often, so you can just add the columns to the table and ignore the `DataColumn` objects that are returned from the `Add()` method. Listing 2.1 adds these three columns to the dtEmployees `DataTable` in Visual Basic .NET. Listing 2.2 performs the same actions in C#.

LISTING 2.1   Adding `DataColumns` to a `DataTable` in Visual Basic .NET

```
dtEmployees.Columns.Add("EmployeeID", Type.GetType("System.Int32"))
dtEmployees.Columns.Add("FirstName", Type.GetType("System.String"))
dtEmployees.Columns.Add("LastName", Type.GetType("System.String"))
```

LISTING 2.2   Adding `DataColumns` to a `DataTable` in C#

```
dtEmployees.Columns.Add("EmployeeID", typeof(int));
dtEmployees.Columns.Add("FirstName", typeof(string));
dtEmployees.Columns.Add("LastName", typeof(string));
```

The second argument of the Add() method in Listings 2.1 and 2.2 expects a data type. The Type.GetType() and typeof() methods return the proper data types that the Add() method wants.

When adding data later in the next few sections, the EmployeeID column should automatically generate a number for each new record added. To achieve this functionality, you must enter one additional line of code:

```
dtEmployees.Columns(0).AutoIncrement = true;
```

or in C#:

```
dtEmployees.Columns[0].AutoIncrement = true;
```

Adding and Removing Data

At this point, the schema of the DataSet is entered and you're ready to add some data. Recall that the column collection of the DataTable defines the schema, and the rows collection of the DataTable defines the data. In other words, to add data to our DataTable, all we need to do is add some rows to our DataTable: dtEmployees.

DataRows Contain Data

Adding rows to the dtEmployees DataTable is easy to do. First, you need to use the NewRow() method of the dtEmployees object. NewRow() returns a reference to a new row for your DataTable. Next, you must specify values for the columns in the newly created row. Lastly, you must add the row to the DataTable. Listings 2.3 and 2.4 demonstrate this by adding a few rows to our existing DataTable, dtEmployees.

LISTING 2.3   Adding Rows to the dtEmployees DataTable in Visual Basic.NET

```
'Create new row
Dim workRow as DataRow = dtEmployees.NewRow()
workRow("FirstName") = "John"
workRow("LastName") = "Fruscella"

'Create another row
Dim workRow1 as DataRow = dtEmployees.NewRow()
workRow1("FirstName") = "Leigh"
workRow1("LastName") = "Chase"

'Add new rows to the DataTable
dtEmployees.Rows.Add(workRow)
dtEmployees.Rows.Add(workRow1)
```

LISTING 2.4   Adding Rows to the dtEmployees `DataTable` in C#

```
//Create new row
DataRow workRow = dtEmployees.NewRow();
workRow["FirstName"] = "John";
workRow["LastName"] = "Fruscella";

//Create another row
DataRow workRow1 = dtEmployees.NewRow();
workRow1["FirstName"] = "Leigh";
workRow1["LastName"] = "Chase";

//Add new rows to the DataTable
dtEmployees.Rows.Add(workRow);
dtEmployees.Rows.Add(workRow1);
```

Creating and Configuring a New ASP.NET Test Web

Until now, you've probably taken it for granted that the code in this hour works. However, with just a few minutes of effort, you can verify that it works. By itself, ADO.NET code is not specific to Web forms or Windows forms. In fact, either can be used to test the code in this chapter. If you are handy with Windows forms using Visual Studio .NET or the tools inside the Microsoft .NET Framework SDK, feel free to plug the code in Listings 2.3 or 2.4 into a Windows form application.

The next section walks you through the process of setting up a new virtual directory in Windows 2000 and adding a Web form that can be used to test your code. Web forms were chosen because they are compiled automatically when they are first requested by a Web browser, thus saving you from having to manually compile a Windows form each time you need to test some code. When you save the file, ASP.NET knows to recompile the Web form the next time the file is requested.

Creating the Web Site

Installing a new Web site on a Windows 2000 machine is a straightforward process:

1. Make sure you are logged in as a user with administrative rights.

2. Locate (or create) a directory on your computer where you will place the files to be served by Internet Information Server (IIS, Microsoft's Web server that comes built into Windows 2000).

3. In the Administrative Tools program group, load the Internet Services Manager. Expand the entry for your computer. You should now see a screen much like Figure 2.2. If you do not have an entry for the Internet Services Manager, you probably do not have IIS installed. You can use the Add/Remove Programs entry in the Control

Panel to add the Windows 2000 IIS components. Please refer to your operating system manual for more details.

FIGURE 2.2

*Use the IIS adminis-
trative console to cre-
ate new virtual
directories and man-
age the Web sites on
your machine.*

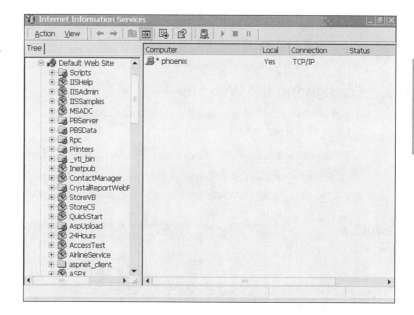

4. Expand the Default Web Site entry (which is installed by default). You should see a number of subentries.

5. Right-click on Default Web Site and select New Virtual Directory. The Virtual Directory Creation Wizard appears (see Figure 2.3). Click Next.

FIGURE 2.3

*The Virtual Directory
Wizard prompts you
for an alias.*

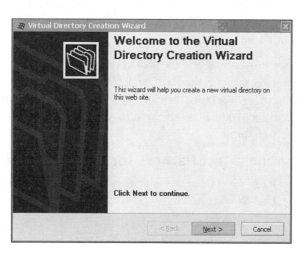

6. The wizard prompts you for an alias. Enter **24Hours** and click Next.

7. In the next screen, either type or browse to the directory you created in step 1 and click Next.

8. On the Access Permissions screen, leave Read and Run scripts checked and also check Browse. Click Next.

9. You have successfully added a new virtual directory to your Web site!

Configuring the Web Site

If you are concerned about security, you should change the default security settings for the new virtual directory.

1. Right-click on the 24Hours virtual directory under the Default Web Site.

2. Click on the Directory Security tab. Select the Edit button in the IP Address and Domain Name Restrictions dialog box as shown in Figure 2.4.

FIGURE 2.4

The IP Address and Domain Name Restrictions dialog box showing the virtual directory's properties.

3. Select the bottom bullet labeled Denied Access. Then click the Add button, enter **127.0.0.1**, and click the OK button. The 24Hours site can now only be loaded from the computer it is loaded on.

The site is now only available to users of your computer. If someone tries to access the site from a remote machine, they will be denied access. The site can be accessed by using either http://localhost/24Hours or http://127.0.0.1/24Hours. The site is currently empty, but you will be able to browse to the folders and files of the site after we add some Web forms.

Task: Creating a Test Harness for ADO.NET Code

Before you can test the code in this chapter, you must create a few pages that will contain the code. One page is needed for the Visual Basic .NET examples and another is needed for the C# examples.

1. Create two new files in the 24Hours directory named _24HoursVB.aspx and _24HoursCS.aspx. These files will be used as templates.

2. Place the code from Listing 2.5 into _24HoursVB.aspx and save the file.

3. Place the code from Listing 2.6 into _24HoursCS.aspx and save the file.

4. Create a copy of the _24HoursVB.aspx file and name it chapter2VB.aspx.

5. Create a copy of the _24HoursCS.aspx file and name it chapter2CS.aspx.

By repeating steps 4 and 5 of the previous task, you can use the _24Hours*.aspx files as templates for the examples in this book, unless otherwise noted. When you are done configuring these files, your directory will look like the one in Figure 2.5.

FIGURE 2.5

Setting up the example templates.

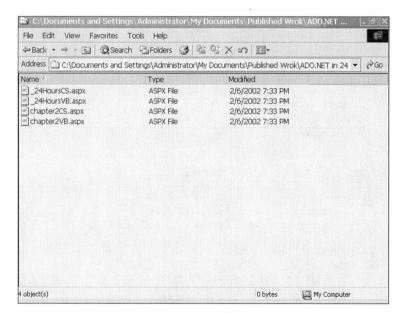

LISTING 2.5 VB.NET Code Test Harness

```
<% @Page Language="VB" Debug="true" %>
<%@ Import Namespace="System.Data" %>
<%@ Import Namespace="System.Data.SqlClient" %>

<HTML>
<HEAD>
    <LINK rel="stylesheet" type="text/css" href="24Hours.css">
    <!-- End Style Sheet -->

    <script language="VB" runat="server" >
```

LISTING 2.5   continued

```
Sub Page_Load(Source as Object, E as EventArgs)

    'Place VB.NET ADO.NET Code here

End Sub
</script>

</HEAD>
<BODY>

<h1>ADO.NET In 24 Hours Examples</h1>
<hr>

<form runat="server" id=form1 name=form1>
    <asp:Label id="msg" runat="server"></asp:Label>
    <asp:DataGrid id="myDataGrid" runat="server"></asp:DataGrid>
</form>

<hr>
</BODY>
</HTML>
```

LISTING 2.6   C# Code Test Harness

```
<% @Page Language="C#" Debug=true%>
<%@ Import Namespace="System.Data" %>
<%@ Import Namespace="System.Data.SqlClient" %>

<HTML>
<HEAD>
    <LINK rel="stylesheet" type="text/css" href="24Hours.css">
    <!-- End Style Sheet -->

    <script language="C#" runat="server" >
      void Page_Load(Object Source, EventArgs E)
      {

          //Place C# ADO.NET example code here

      }
    </script>

</HEAD>
<BODY>

<h1>ADO.NET In 24 Hours Examples</h1>
<hr>
```

LISTING 2.6   continued

```
<form runat="server" id=form1 name=form1>
   <asp:Label id="msg" runat="server"></asp:Label>
   <asp:DataGrid id="myDataGrid" runat="server"></asp:DataGrid>
</form>

<hr>
</BODY>
</HTML>
```

The Web forms in Listings 2.5 and 2.6 contain:

- A label Web control that will be used to display text messages
- A DataGrid Web control that will be used to display the contents of your DataSets

To test this hour's code, just place the code from Listing 2.3 into the VB.NET test harness in Listing 2.5 where it says "Place VB.NET ADO.NET Code here." All that remains is to connect the DataGrid to the DataSet. That can be achieved with two lines of code:

```
myDataGrid.DataSource = dtEmployees
myDataGrid.DataBind()
```

This instructs the DataGrid to use the dtEmployees DataSet as its data source and display it on the page when the page loads. Listing 2.7 contains the entire example in VB.NET. When you load the page, your results should look similar to those in Figure 2.6. For more information on the DataGrid Web control, please see Hour 11, "Using the Built-In ASP.NET List Controls."

LISTING 2.7   The Complete VB.NET Web Form Example

```
<% @Page Language="VB" Debug="true" %>
<%@ Import Namespace="System.Data" %>
<%@ Import Namespace="System.Data.SqlClient" %>

<HTML>
<HEAD>
   <LINK rel="stylesheet" type="text/css" href="24Hours.css">
   <!-- End Style Sheet -->

   <script language="VB" runat="server" >
      Sub Page_Load(Source as Object, E as EventArgs)
         'Create Principle Objects
         dim dsCompany as new DataSet()
         dim dtEmployees as DataTable = dsCompany.Tables.Add("Employees")

         'Create Columns
```

LISTING 2.7   continued

```
        dtEmployees.Columns.Add("EmployeeID", Type.GetType("System.Int32"))
        dtEmployees.Columns.Add("FirstName", Type.GetType("System.String"))
        dtEmployees.Columns.Add("LastName", Type.GetType("System.String"))

        'Create new row
        Dim workRow as DataRow = dtEmployees.NewRow()
        workRow("FirstName") = "John"
        workRow("LastName") = "Fruscella"

        'Create another row
        Dim workRow1 as DataRow = dtEmployees.NewRow()
        workRow1("FirstName") = "Santa"
        workRow1("LastName") = "Claus"

        'Add new rows to the DataTable
        dtEmployees.Rows.Add(workRow)
        dtEmployees.Rows.Add(workRow1)

        employees.DataSource = dtEmployees
        employees.DataBind()

    End Sub
  </script>

</HEAD>
<BODY>

<h1>ADO.NET In 24 Hours Examples</h1>
<hr>

<form runat="server">
   <asp:Label id="lblMessage" runat="server"></asp:Label>
   <asp:DataGrid id="employees" runat="server"></asp:DataGrid>
</form>

<hr>
</BODY>
</HTML>
```

The code in Listing 2.7 may appear a bit daunting at first. However, it's easier to understand the code if you analyze it in logical sections. The code in Lines 1–3 sets some global properties for the Web form. Specifically, Line 1 sets the language of the Web form to Visual Basic .NET and turns on debugging. Lines 2–3 load the `System.Data` and `System.Data.SqlClient` namespaces. This enables you to access objects such as the `DataSet` and `DataRow` in the server-side code.

FIGURE 2.6

The appearance of our test harness when loaded with the code from this chapter.

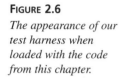

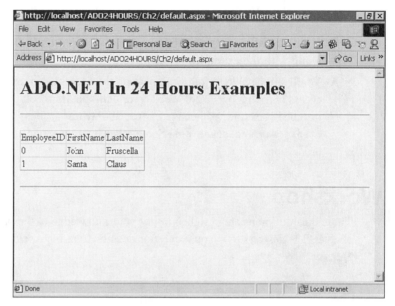

Lines 10–39 in Listing 2.7 are a block of script that executes on the server. The code consists of a single method: The Page_Load() event is automatically run whenever the page loads. Inside the Page_Load() event, lines 13–14 create new DataSet and DataTable objects. Lines 16–19 add some columns directly to the DataTable. These columns define the appearance of the data that is added next.

Lines 21–33 use the previously defined columns of the DataTable to add a few rows of data. Specifically, two new rows are created, configured, and then finally added to the DataTable object in Lines 31–33. Finally, the DataTable is bound to the DataGrid Web control, created on line 49. For now, don't worry about the details of databinding; the DataGrid just knows how to automatically loop through all the rows in the DataTable and display them on the page as in Figure 2.6.

Summary

In this hour, you've seen how to construct the schema of a DataSet from scratch. Then you added some data to the DataTable inside the DataSet. You also saw how to create a new ASP.NET Web with some sample Web forms that you can use for most of the examples in this book.

Q&A

Q I don't have access to a Windows 2000 Web server. Will I be able to follow along with the examples in this book?

A You'll still be able to follow along with the examples in this book, but you'll need access to a Windows 2000 Web server with the Microsoft .NET framework installed somehow. You can get a free 30-day test account at `http://www.eraserver.net`. Some other Internet service providers offer similar promotions.

Workshop

These quiz questions are designed to test your knowledge of the material covered in this chapter. The answers to the quiz questions can be found in Appendix A, "Answers to Quizzes."

Quiz

1. True or false: In a `DataTable` object, the `DataColumns` specify the table schema and the rows comprise the table data.

2. In your own words, describe the easiest way to add a `DataTable` to a `DataSet`.

Exercise

Create a Web form that builds a `DataSet` (with whatever schema you choose), adds some data to the `DataSet`, and then removes one of the records added.

HOUR 3

Using T-SQL: A Crash Course

ADO.NET enables you to connect to a data source and retrieve and manipulate data. However, ADO.NET doesn't actually gather the data itself. It simply sends a string to the data source with data processing instructions. The language used to communicate with the data source is known as T-SQL (Transact-SQL), which is a dialect of Structured Query Language (SQL).

Because you must provide ADO.NET with the proper T-SQL statements for data retrieval and manipulation, knowledge of T-SQL is an essential skill for any well-rounded developer. Hundreds of different kinds of T-SQL statements are available in a product such as Microsoft SQL Server. You can modify many aspects of the server itself, such as managing jobs, creating and maintaining databases, and other administrative tasks. This chapter provides a primer; you'll learn just enough about T-SQL to understand all the examples in this book.

In this chapter, you will learn how to do the following tasks:

- Retrieving data with the SELECT statement
- Adding data with the INSERT statement
- Modifying data with the UPDATE and DELETE statements
- Using some T-SQL built-in functions

Microsoft SQL Server and Microsoft Access both ship with a sample database called Northwind. This database will be used for the examples in this chapter. The Northwind access database is freely distributed. You can download it at http://www. intensitysoftware.com/ADO.NET/nwind.mdb. If you are using a default installation of Microsoft SQL Server, you'll see an entry in your program group for the Query Analyzer. You can launch this application, select Northwind as your database, and follow along with the examples in this chapter directly.

If you are using another data source, such as Oracle, you still should be able to follow along. Your database server probably ships with an application like Query Analyzer that you can use to enter database queries. Use that to enter the queries in the following sections.

Retrieving Data with SELECT

The SELECT statement is used to retrieve and filter data from your data source. Listing 3.1 shows the simplified syntax of the SELECT statement. Read from top to bottom, this statement says "select these columns from these tables where these search criteria are true." You can retrieve several column names from several tables, so long as you separate the column names by commas.

LISTING 3.1   The Syntax of the SELECT SQL Statement

```
SELECT
      column_names
FROM
      table_names
WHERE
      search_conditions
```

For instance, to retrieve all records from the Employees table, enter the following code in the query manager and press F5 or click the green Play button to execute the query:

```
SELECT * FROM Employees
```

This will return every single row and column in the Employees table. The results of your query will look much like Figure 3.1.

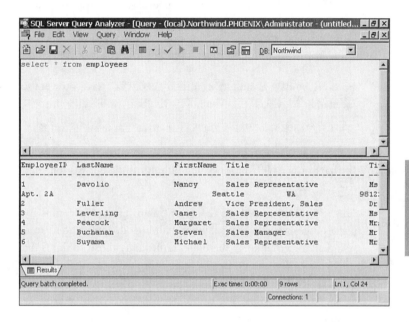

T-SQL is not case sensitive. SELECT * FROM Employees is syntactically identical to select * from employees. However, there is a convention to capitalize T-SQL keywords such as SELECT and FROM to distinguish them from table and column text.

Suppose you only want to return a single record; you want to return one employee based on his or her last name, for example. As you can see in Listing 3.1, the WHERE keyword enables you to filter the data based on any number of search criteria. The content of the search criteria itself is broad. However, most often, the values of various columns are checked. For instance, to return all employees from the database with the last name "King," you would use the following query:

```
SELECT * FROM Employees WHERE LastName = 'King'
```

Similarly, if you want to be even more specific and filter by the employee's first name as well, just add another condition to your query, as in the following SQL statement.

```
SELECT * FROM Employees WHERE LastName = 'King' and FirstName = 'Robert'
```

Strings in T-SQL are delimited by single quotation marks. If you attempt to use double quotation marks, an error will be returned by your data source. If you are filtering by a numerical field, there's no need for quotation marks at all.

Filtering by date is another common need. Let's say you want to return all employees hired after May 3, 1993. The query you build looks like this:

```
SELECT * FROM Employees WHERE HireDate between '5/3/1993' and getdate()
```

Notice that, like strings, dates in T-SQL are also delimited by single quotation marks. Getdate() is a built-in function that returns the current date and time in DateTime format.

Until now, we've used the wildcard "*" to select all columns for the table. This is fine for testing purposes, but not when building an application. Unless you are planning on using all the columns in the table, return only those columns that you plan to use in your application. You can do this by specifying the exact columns you need, separated by commas as shown in Listing 3.2.

LISTING 3.2   Specifying Columns in SQL Statements

```
SELECT
     FirstName, Lastname, Title
FROM
     Employees
WHERE
     HireDate between '5/3/1993' and getdate()
```

This greatly reduces the amount of data returned by the data source to your application. Because the bottleneck in many applications is the database server, any way to make your queries perform more efficiently is likely to make your application perform better.

In Microsoft SQL Server, all extra "white space" is ignored and does not affect processing. "White space" is defined as any character that does not generate a character on the screen. For instance, spaces, tabs, and newline characters are considered "white space." This enables you to format the appearance of queries however you want. Listing 3.2 separates the T-SQL commands from the actual table objects they use. Though the code takes up several more lines, it is easier to understand quickly.

This section only scratches the surface of what is possible with the SELECT statement. Microsoft SQL Server version 7.0 and higher ships with a terrific reference named SQL Server Books Online. This can be found in your SQL Server program group.

The online books are used on a daily basis by professionals everywhere (some might not admit to it), but new users might find it too terse to be very useful. In that case, there's certainly no lack of great books and Web sites devoted to the topic.

Adding New Data with INSERT

You can enter new data into the database by using the INSERT SQL statement. The syntax of the command is fairly simple. However, before building the query to add new data, you must know the schema of the table. Figure 3.2 shows the schema of the Categories table in the Northwind database.

FIGURE 3.2

The Microsoft SQL Enterprise Manager can display the schema of your database to help you build queries.

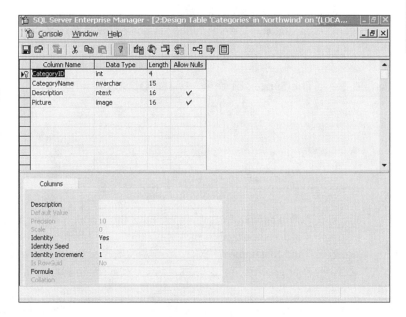

Notice that the table consists of four fields, including the CategoryID column. This field contains an integer that is automatically incremented for each new record added; we will not need to add a value with our query. Additionally, notice that the only required field in the table is CategoryName. The Description and Picture columns can both be left null. When executed, the statement in Listing 3.3 adds a new record into the category table:

```
INSERT INTO Categories
(
  CategoryName,
```

```
   Description
)
VALUES
(
   'Spam',
   'Spam and other canned-meat products'
)
```

The first line uses the keywords INSERT INTO to specify that we are inserting the data
into the Categories table. Then the first parenthesized section of code specifies the fields
into which we're putting our data. The VALUES keyword and the next parenthesized section enter the actual values in the same column order as the first section.

Modifying Data with UPDATE and DELETE

So far, you have seen how to retrieve and add data to the database. However, suppose
you would like to modify existing database rows. To modify data, you would use the
UPDATE SQL statement. A simplified version of the syntax of the UPDATE statement looks
like the code in Listing 3.3.

LISTING 3.3   The Syntax of the UPDATE SQL Statement

```
UPDATE
      table_name
SET
      column_name = expression
WHERE
      search_conditions
```

The specific example in Listing 3.4 explains the syntax quite well. After the statement in
Listing 3.4 is executed against the data source, any employee with last name of
"Peacock" and first name of "Margaret" as specified by the WHERE clause will be changed
to "Hogue" as specified by the SET clause of the statement. Figure 3.3 shows the change.

LISTING 3.4   Using the SQL UPDATE Statement to Change an Employee's Last
Name

```
UPDATE
      employees
SET
      LastName = 'Hogue'
WHERE
      LastName = 'Peacock' and
      FirstName = 'Margaret'
```

FIGURE 3.3

The value in the LastName column changes for the selected employee.

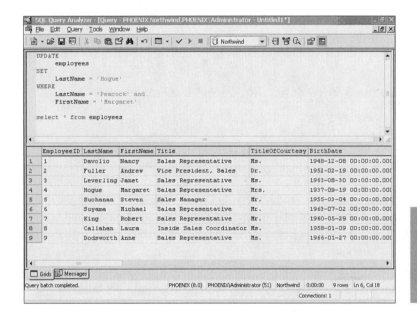

Be careful when using the UPDATE statement, particularly when working with live data. Remember that every row meeting the conditions of the WHERE clause in the statement will be updated. In fact, if you inadvertently do not include the WHERE clause in the statement, your query will affect every single row in the table!

It's also possible to update several fields at once. You only need to place commas between each segment as in Listing 3.5.

LISTING 3.5   Updating Multiple Columns in a Single UPDATE Statement

```
UPDATE
    employees
SET
    LastName = 'Hogue',
    Address = '11 Longfellow St.'
WHERE
    LastName = 'Peacock' and
    FirstName = 'Margaret'
```

Compared to updating database rows, deleting database rows is easy. Listing 3.6 shows the syntax of the DELETE SQL statement. It is the simplest query you have seen thus far. All you need to specify is the name of the table and the search conditions.

LISTING 3.6   Deleting Rows from the Employee Table

```
DELETE FROM
      table_name
WHERE
      search_conditions
```

To delete the employee with EmployeeID of 7, you use the query in Listing 3.7. Remember that if you are deleting only a single row, your search conditions must single out that row. Normally, the purpose of an ID field in a database table is to guarantee this uniqueness.

LISTING 3.7   Deleting Rows from the Employee Table

```
DELETE FROM
      employees
WHERE
      EmployeeID = 7
```

Using the Built-in SQL Functions

Hundreds of timesaving functions are built into Microsoft SQL Server. These functions enable you to perform all sorts of tasks such as working with dates and strings and performing mathematical calculations. Some of the most commonly used functions are described in this section. However, you can locate a list of all built-in functions by searching Microsoft SQL Server Books Online for "functions."

Working with Strings

Microsoft SQL Server ships with a number of functions that enable you to manipulate strings. For the most part, these string functions are similar to the ones used in Microsoft Visual Basic.

For instance, the Left() and Right()functions are nearly identical to their counterparts. They enable you to return part of a character string, from either the left or right end of the string, respectively. They have the following function definitions:

```
Left( string, value )
Right( string, value )
```

By calling the Left() function, and passing in 'She sells sea shells' as the string and 6 as the value, Left() returns 'She se'. Likewise, Right() with the same arguments returns 'shells'.

Sometimes, when working with strings, you need to convert the entire string to either uppercase or lowercase to compare two strings or to ensure that data is entered into a certain field in a standard way. The upper() and lower() methods perform exactly these tasks. The two methods accept the string to convert as a single argument.

Table 3.1 contains a list of some SQL string functions and their return values for a given string.

TABLE 3.1 String Functions at a Glance

Function Definition	Return Value for String: ' Gaiking Space Robot '
Len(*string*)	21
LTrim(*string*)	'Gaiking Space Robot '
RTrim(*string*)	' Gaiking Space Robot'
Reverse(*string*)	' toboR ecapS gnikiaG '
Lower(*string*)	' gaiking space robot '
Upper(*string*)	' GAIKING SPACE ROBOT '

Keep in mind that you can use string functions on other string functions that return strings. In other words, this is a perfectly legal set of calls that returns the length of a left and right trimmed string:

```
Len( LTrim( RTrim( string ) ) )
```

Working with Dates

In addition to the string functions, there are several invaluable date manipulation functions as well.

The DateAdd(*datepart, number, date*) function can be used to add a chosen unit of time to a particular date. The first argument, *datepart*, controls the part of the date you are adding. For a complete list of values for the *datepart* argument, see Table 3.2. *Number* is the amount of the chosen *datepart* you're adding to the *date*. For instance, in order to add two months to the current date, you can use the following:

```
DateAdd( m, 2, getdate() )
```

TABLE 3.2   Common Codes for Special Symbols and Syntax

Code	Symbol
Year	yy, yyyy
Quarter	qq, q
Month	mm, m
Dayofyear	dy, y
Day	dd, d
Week	wk, ww
Hour	hh
Minute	mi, n
Second	ss, s
Millisecond	ms

The functions Month(), Day(), and Year() are used to return the corresponding piece of a given date. For instance, Month('12/7/1952') returns 12, Day('12/7/1952') returns 7, and Year('12/7/1952') returns 1952. These functions can save hours of needless parsing of dates by hand.

One last function that is indispensable when working with dates is Datediff (*datepart*, *startdate*, *enddate*). This function returns the difference of two dates in units determined by the *datepart* argument. Fortunately, it also uses the codes shown in Table 3.2 for the values in its first argument.

Mathematical Functions

SQL Server contains a number of methods for working with numbers. You probably will never use most of them in a query (when was the last time you needed to compute the arctangent of a value as part of a query?). However, when you do need one of these methods, they are quite handy. Table 3.3 shows some math functions and their return values. For a complete list, please see Microsoft SQL Server Books Online.

TABLE 3.3   SQL Server Math Functions

Function	Description
Abs(*expr*)	Returns the absolute positive value.
Cos(*expr*)	Returns the cosine.
Exp(*expr*)	Returns exponential value.
Log(*expr*)	Returns natural logarithm.

TABLE 3.3 continued

Function	Description
Pi()	Returns the value of Pi.
Rand(*[seed]*)	Returns a random number. The seed is an optional argument giving Rand() a start value.
Sin(*expr*)	Returns the sine.
Square(*expr*)	Returns the square.
Sqrt(*expr*)	Returns the square root.
Tan(*expr*)	Returns the tangent.

Summary

In this hour, you've seen the four most often used SQL queries: SELECT, INSERT, UPDATE, and DELETE. You also saw how some of these queries run against the Northwind database on Microsoft SQL Server. Lastly, you saw some built-in SQL Server methods that make working with strings, dates, and numbers much easier.

Q&A

Q Where can I learn more about writing SQL queries?

A A great book for learning SQL syntax is *Sams Teach Yourself SQL in 10 Minutes Second Edition*. This book focuses on the queries themselves and avoids delving deep into database theory and database design. If you are interested in database theory as well, *Sams Teach Yourself Microsoft SQL Server 2000 in 21 Days* might be more appropriate for you.

Q If strings are delimited by the ' (single quote) character in SQL, how do you enter the single quote character into a database field programmatically?

A This is referred to as "escaping" the special character. Simply enter two single quotes instead of one. For instance, SQL Server will recognize the text "it''s" as "it's".

Workshop

These quiz questions are designed to test your knowledge of the material covered in this chapter. The answers to the quiz questions can be found in Appendix A, "Answers to Quizzes."

Quiz

1. Which of the following SQL commands enables you to create new entries in a database table?

   a. `INSERT`

   b. `ADD`

   c. `CREATE NEW RECORD`

   d. `UPDATE`

2. Which portion of a SQL query is used to filter the number of records returned?

Exercise

Write `SELECT`, `INSERT`, `UPDATE`, and `DELETE` queries for the Customers table in the Northwind database. Verify that your queries work by running them in the Query Analyzer application (SQL Server only).

HOUR 4

Adding Relationships to DataSets

In Hour 2, "Working with DataSets and DataTables," you saw how to use a DataSet to represent your data. You saw how DataTables are analogous to tables in a database. In the last hour, you saw how to use the four major SQL query commands to work with data in a database.

This hour extends the concepts in both Hour 2 and Hour 3 by first discussing database relationships, and then by showing how to create these relationships in a DataSet.

In this hour, you'll learn

- What a database relationship is
- How to use a database relationship
- How to use the Join operator
- How to use the DataSet Relations collection to add a relationship between two DataSets
- How to use the DataRelation to retrieve data

Database Relationships and Constraints

Before discussing how to create data relations inside a `DataSet`, it makes sense to explain how relationships function inside a relational database system such as Microsoft SQL Server. If you are already familiar with relational databases, you might want to skip ahead to the section entitled "The `DataRelation` Object."

Relationships

Suppose you have to store information about customer orders inside a database. You might choose to use a database schema like the one shown in the database diagram in Figure 4.1. There are five tables in this diagram, and they are all related to the main Orders table. Notice the lines connecting the tables together. Each of these lines represents a relationship in the database.

> Each of the relationships in Figure 4.1 are "one to many." Notice how each relationship has an infinity symbol on one terminating end and a key on the other. The table connected via the infinity symbol may contain multiple entries from a column in the other table. For instance, the CustomerID field of the Orders table may only contain entries from the CustomerID field of the Customers table. It can contain the same CustomerID as many times as required (one per order per customer, in fact). If you try to enter a value in the CustomerID field of the Orders table that is not also present in the Customers table, you will receive an error.

This is done mainly to avoid duplicating data. Rather than storing redundant customer data in the Orders table, you only need the CustomerID, which you can then use to retrieve that customer's information later, when you need it. (For information on retrieving the customer information, see the section titled "The `Join` Operator.")

If you are using Microsoft SQL Server 2000, creating a relationship between two tables is easy:

1. Create a new database diagram in your database by right-clicking on Diagrams and selecting New Database Diagram as in Figure 4.2. You are presented with the Create Database Diagram Wizard. Click Next.

2. Add all the tables from the left to the tables in the new diagram, on the right side. Select Next and then Finish to complete the wizard. You will see a screen much like Figure 4.3.

FIGURE 4.1

A database diagram of the built-in Microsoft SQL Server Northwind database

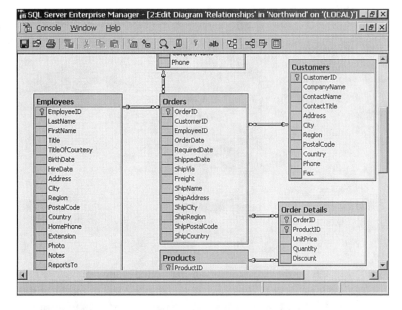

FIGURE 4.2

The Create Database Diagram Wizard assists in setting up a new database diagram.

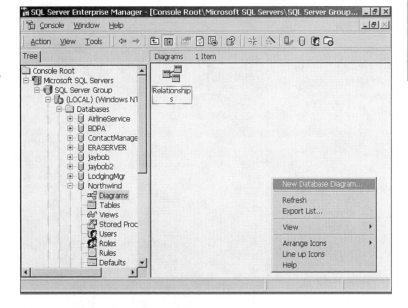

3. Right-click anywhere on the white background of the diagram window and select New Table. Name the new table EmployeeAwards.

FIGURE 4.3

*After the Create
Database Diagram
Wizard completes, you
will see a screen like
this one.*

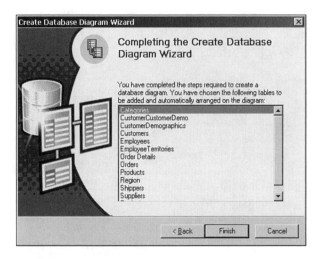

4. Create the new table according to the values entered in Figure 4.4. When you are
   done, right-click on the grey box to the left of the AwardID column. Select Set
   Primary Key. A primary key must be present in both tables participating in a relationship.

FIGURE 4.4

*Creating a new data-
base table inside the
diagram utility.*

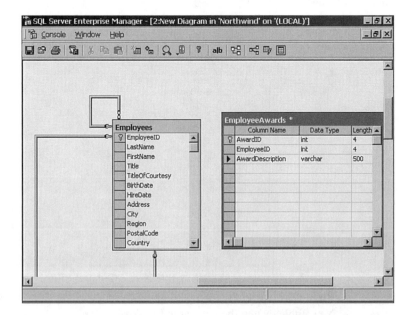

5. Next, click and drag the box to the left of the EmployeeID column of the Employees table and drag it on top of the EmployeeID column of the EmployeeAwards table. You are presented with a screen like the one in Figure 4.5.

FIGURE 4.5

After dragging and dropping the new relationship, you are presented with the Create Relationship screen.

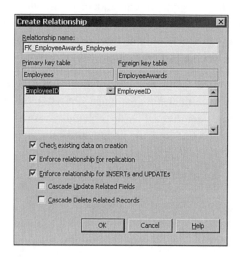

6. Select OK and you are done. Notice that the graphical representation of the relationship is added to the diagram, as seen in Figure 4.6.

FIGURE 4.6

The relationship between the two tables appears.

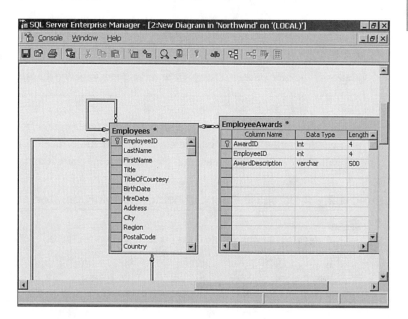

Now, if an employee wins an award, you can track it in the EmployeeAwards table.

The `Join` Operator

The only problem with using this type of data model is that whenever you need to retrieve records with columns from both tables, you must perform a join operation. The join operation enables you to select columns from two or more tables linked together by a relationship like the one you've just created.

There are a number of different kinds of join operations you can perform. Listing 4.1 displays the syntax to perform an inner join. An inner join will return records from two tables with matching records determined by the columns chosen for the join. For other types of joins, please refer to your database documentation.

LISTING 4.1   The Syntax of the `Join` Operator

```
SELECT
     column_names
FROM
     table_a
     INNER JOIN table_b on
     table_a.column = table_b.column
WHERE
     search_conditions
```

The join operation essentially lets you add columns from another table to your current resultset based on the values in a common field. Syntactically, the query in Listing 4.2 and the query in Listing 4.3 are exactly the same.

For instance, suppose you want to retrieve all customer orders from the Orders table and also get their titles and phone numbers at the same time. The queries in Listings 4.2 and 4.3 will both retrieve the same data, one with a join, one without.

LISTING 4.2   A Database Query Utilizing the Join Operator

```
SELECT
     Orders.*, Customers.ContactTitle, Customers.Phone
FROM
     Orders
     INNER JOIN Customers on
     Customers.CustomerID = Orders.CustomerID
```

LISTING 4.3   A Multitable Database Query Not Utilizing the Join Operator

```
SELECT
    Orders.*, Customers.ContactTitle, Customers.Phone
FROM
    Orders, Customers
WHERE
    Customers.CustomerID = Orders.CustomerID
```

Constraints

Constraints are basically just rules about the contents of a database field. For instance, Figure 4.7 shows a constraint present in the Employees table of the Northwind database. This ensures that no one enters a future date in the birthdate field.

FIGURE 4.7

A constraint present in the Employees table of the Northwind database.

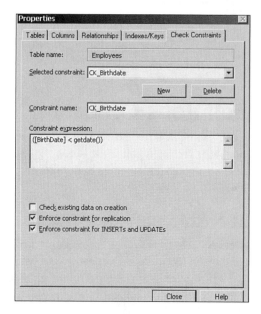

The DataRelation Object

As you've seen in Hour 2, "Working with DataSets and DataTables," the ADO.NET DataSet object can almost precisely mirror data returned from the data source. This includes all the data relations and constraints present in the database as well as the data itself!

In other words, within the DataSet itself, you can create relationships, just like the ones you saw earlier inside SQL Server. After the relationships are set up, you can retrieve relationship-based information without having to write a database query.

New Functionality with the DataSet**!**

In addition to giving you great power and flexibility when working with data retrieved from a database, ADO.NET also enables you to retrieve data from two completely different data sources (such as a Microsoft Excel file and a standard comma-delimited text file), create relations, and then navigate those relationships. Essentially, you can apply the power of a relational database system to such disparate data sources as XML files and Microsoft Excel files, without first importing the data to a relational database like Microsoft SQL Server.

The next few sections show you how to use the Relations collection of the DataSet to create relations between two or more DataTables.

The DataSet Relations Collection

The DataSet contains a collection of DataRelation objects named, appropriately enough, DataRelationCollection. This collection stores all DataRelations for the DataTables in your DataSet. There's no practical limit to the number of relationships you can add to a DataSet.

Adding a Relationship Between Two DataTables

Adding a relationship between two DataTables is straightforward. You can simply add a new DataRelation object to the Relations collection of your DataSet as in Listing 4.4. The first argument to the Add() method is the name of the relationship. The second argument contains the parent DataColumn. The third argument contains the child DataColumn of the relationship.

The parent is defined as the column in the relationship that is a primary key. The other column is said to be a foreign key, and is also referred to as the child. The child column may contain as many values from the parent column as desired (even repeating the same value). Think of it this way: One employee can work on multiple projects; one customer can make multiple orders. In these cases, the employees and customers are the parents and the projects and orders are the children.

LISTING 4.4   Adding a Relationship between two DataTables in a DataSet

```
dsCompany.Relations.Add("DataRelationName", _
    dsCompany.Tables("Table1").Columns("PrimaryKeyColumn"), _
    dsCompany.Tables("Table1").Columns("ForeignKeyColumn"))
```

For instance, suppose you have two tables in your DataSet:

1. The first table named Customers contains a list of your customers, with a column named CustomerID set as the table's primary key.

2. The second table named Orders contains a list of your customers' orders, using a CustomerID column to keep track of which customer made which order. (In other words, the CustomerID in this table will become the foreign key, after the DataRelation is added.)

> The primary key column does *not* need to have the same name as the foreign key column. Often, however, the two do share the same column name.

Adding a DataRelation to this table ensures that the CustomerID field of the Orders table contains only CustomerIDs from the Customers table. If you try to add a CustomerID to the Orders table that is not also present in the CustomerID field in the Customers table, you will receive an error (this applies to both tables in a database and DataTables in a DataSet). Listing 4.5 shows how to create a relationship between a Customers DataTable and an Orders DataTable using this example.

LISTING 4.5   Adding a Relationship between Two DataTables in a DataSet

```
dsCompany.Relations.Add("CustomerOrders", _
    dsCompany.Tables("Customers").Columns("CustomerID"), _
    dsCompany.Tables("Orders").Columns("CustomerID"))
```

After you have added a relationship between the Customers DataTable and the Orders DataTable, you can easily retrieve all orders for a particular CustomerID without writing a SQL query. This is referred to as "navigating" a relationship.

Navigating DataSet Relationships

When you have a DataRelation between two DataTables, you can retrieve all child rows in the table with the foreign key for a particular row in the parent table by using the

GetChildRows() method of the DataRow object. Building on the example from the previous section in Listing 4.5, the following code shows how to use the GetChildRows() method:

```
dsCompany.Tables("Customers").Rows(0).GetChildRows("CustomerOrders")
```

For the customer in the first row of the Customer DataTable, the preceding code returns any orders they have listed in the Orders table. It does this by using the CustomerOrders DataRelation name passed to it as its only argument. So, if the first customer has a CustomerID of 0, any rows in the Orders table that have a CustomerID of 0 are returned.

You can see a complete example using all of the concepts from this hour in Listing 4.6. This is a very long code listing, but it is also easily broken down into pieces that you have seen before, specifically in Hour 2, "Working with DataSets and DataTables." Because Listing 4.6 is so long, only the Visual Basic .NET code is provided. The C# code is available online at http://www.sams.com.

Listing 4.6 builds a DataSet with two DataTables, creates a relationship between those two tables, and then steps through each row of the parent DataTable displaying each child row in the child table. In this case, the code will display a list of employees (the parent DataTable) and a list of the projects each employee is assigned to (the child DataTable). Keep in mind that the only new code in Listing 4.6 is the code with a grey background.

LISTING 4.6 Adding a Relationship between Two DataTables in a DataSet

```
<% @Page Language="VB" Debug=true%>
<%@ Import Namespace="System.Data" %>

<HTML>
<HEAD>
    <LINK rel="stylesheet" type="text/css" href="24Hours.css">
    <!-- End Style Sheet -->

    <script language="VB" runat="server" >
      Sub Page_Load(Source as Object, E as EventArgs )
          ' Create Principle Objects
          Dim dsCompany as new DataSet()

          ' Create new datatables
          Dim dtEmployees as DataTable = GenerateCompanyDataTable()
          Dim dtProjects as DataTable = GenerateProjectDataTable()

          ' Add new datatables to the dataset
          dsCompany.Tables.Add( dtEmployees )
          dsCompany.Tables.Add( dtProjects )
```

LISTING 4.6 continued

```
' Create Relationships between tables in datasets
dsCompany.Relations.Add("EmployeeProjects", _
        dsCompany.Tables("Employees").Columns("EmployeeID"), _
        dsCompany.Tables("Projects").Columns("EmployeeID"))

    ' Bind to a datagrid to see DataTable data
    employees.DataSource = dtEmployees
    employees.DataBind()

    ' Bind to a datagrid to see DataTable data
    projects.DataSource = dtProjects
    projects.DataBind()

    Dim strBuilder as new StringBuilder()
    Dim EmployeeRow as DataRow
    Dim ProjectRow as DataRow

    ' Display Employees and the projects they are currently
    ' Assigned to
    for each EmployeeRow in dtEmployees.Rows
       strBuilder.Append("<BR>" + "**************************" + "<BR>")
       strBuilder.Append("EmployeeID: " + _
            EmployeeRow("EmployeeID").ToString() + "<BR>" + _
            "EmployeeName: " + EmployeeRow("FirstName").ToString() + _
            " " + EmployeeRow("LastName").ToString() + "<BR>")
      for each projectRow in EmployeeRow.GetChildRows("EmployeeProjects")
        strBuilder.Append("<b>Currently working on:</b> " + "<BR>" + _
                        "ProjectID: " + _
                        projectRow("ProjectID").ToString() + "<BR>" + _
                        "ProjectName: " + _
                        projectRow("ProjectName").ToString() + "<BR>")
      next
    next

    lblProjects.Text = strBuilder.ToString()
End Sub

public Function GenerateCompanyDataTable() as DataTable
    'Create Principle Objects

    Dim dtEmployees as new DataTable("Employees")

    'Create Columns
    dtEmployees.Columns.Add("EmployeeID", Type.GetType("System.Int32"))
    dtEmployees.Columns.Add("FirstName", Type.GetType("System.String"))
    dtEmployees.Columns.Add("LastName", Type.GetType("System.String"))
```

4

LISTING 4.6   continued

```
'Make the first column autoincrementing
dtEmployees.Columns(0).AutoIncrement = true

'Create column array
Dim dcPrimaryKey(2) as DataColumn

'Place EmployeeID in the column array
dcPrimaryKey(0) = dtEmployees.Columns("EmployeeID")

'Set the primary key for the table using the column array
dtEmployees.PrimaryKey = dcPrimaryKey

    'Create new row
    Dim workRow as DataRow = dtEmployees.NewRow()
    workRow("FirstName") = "John"
    workRow("LastName") = "Fruscella"
    dtEmployees.Rows.Add(workRow)

    'Create another row
    Dim workRow1 as DataRow = dtEmployees.NewRow()
    workRow1("FirstName") = "Santa"
    workRow1("LastName") = "Claus"
    dtEmployees.Rows.Add(workRow1)

    Return dtEmployees
End Function

public Function GenerateProjectDataTable() as DataTable
    'Create Principle Objects
    Dim dtProjects as DataTable = new DataTable("Projects")

    'Create Columns
    dtProjects.Columns.Add("ProjectID", Type.GetType("System.Int32"))
    dtProjects.Columns.Add("EmployeeID", Type.GetType("System.Int32"))
    dtProjects.Columns.Add("ProjectName", Type.GetType("System.String"))
    dtProjects.Columns.Add("ProjectDescription", _
                            Type.GetType("System.String"))

    'Make the first column autoincrementing
    dtProjects.Columns(0).AutoIncrement = true

    'Create column array
    Dim dcPrimaryKey(2) as DataColumn

    'Place EmployeeID in the column array
    dcPrimaryKey(0) = dtProjects.Columns("ProjectID")
```

LISTING 4.6 continued

```
            dcPrimaryKey(1) = dtProjects.Columns("EmployeeID")

            'Set the primary key for the table using the column array
            dtProjects.PrimaryKey = dcPrimaryKey

            'Create new row - Assign EmployeeID 2 to this project
            Dim workRow as DataRow = dtProjects.NewRow()
            workRow("EmployeeID") = 1
            workRow("ProjectName") = "Landslide"
            workRow("ProjectDescription") = "Super secret Web services project."
            dtProjects.Rows.Add(workRow)

            'Create new row - Assign EmployeeID 1 to this project
            Dim workRow1 as DataRow = dtProjects.NewRow()
            workRow1("EmployeeID") = 0
            workRow1("ProjectName") = "Avalanche"
            workRow1("ProjectDescription") = "Super secret user control project."
            dtProjects.Rows.Add(workRow1)

            Return dtProjects
        End Function

    </script>

</HEAD>
<BODY>

<h1>ADO.NET In 24 Hours Examples</h1>
<hr>

<form runat="server" id=form1 name=form1>
    <asp:Label id="lblMessage" runat="server"></asp:Label>

    <p>
    <strong>Employees:</strong><br>
    <asp:DataGrid id="employees" runat="server"></asp:DataGrid>

    <p>
    <strong>Projects:</strong><br>
    <asp:DataGrid id="projects" runat="server"></asp:DataGrid>

    <p>
    <asp:Label id="lblProjects" runat="server"></asp:Label>
</form>

<hr>
</BODY>
</HTML>
```

4

Let's examine this code in depth. Notice that there are two methods, `GenerateCompanyDataTable()` and `GenerateProjectDataTable()`, that create and configure the `DataTables` for our example. Hour 2 covers the details of all the code in these two methods. Each method returns a `DataTable` back to the `Page_Load` event, where the new and interesting code exists.

The `Page_Load` method outputs a list of employees and their projects in the following sequence:

1. A new `DataSet` is created, and two new `DataTables` are created from the two methods that generate tables and then added to the `DataSet`.

2. A new `DataRelation` object is added to the Relations collection of the `DataSet` object. The `DataRelation` is named "EmployeeProjects" and is set up with the EmployeeID column of the Employees table as the parent and the EmployeeID column of the Projects column as the child.

3. The two `DataTables` are bound to `DataGrid` Web controls so that we can see the values they contain.

4. Two `for-next` loops are used to display all child rows for each parent row. Specifically, this will display each employee along with each assigned project. The `StringBuilder` object is used to build a string to place into the label Web control to display the information in a Web form.

If you run the code in Listing 4.6, you should see a screen much like the one in Figure 4.8.

FIGURE 4.8

Listing 4.6 displays a list of employees and their projects by navigating the EmployeeProjects `DataRelation`.

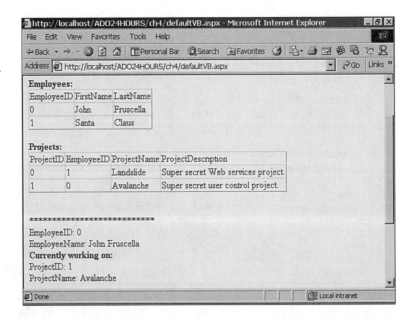

Summary

In this hour, you saw how to create relationships using Microsoft SQL Server. Then you saw how to retrieve information from the related tables using the SQL join operator. The DataRelation object and the Relations collection were then covered in depth and parallels made between the DataSet relations and relationships in SQL Server.

Q&A

Q Is it possible to still use regular join operations with the dataset?

A Yes, in fact you will still use joins in your database queries to retrieve data. Retrieving data first into DataSets, setting up relationships, and then navigating the relationships is much slower than simply using a join operation and letting your data source assemble the records for you. However, there are many instances (such as the case with varying data sources) where the DataRelation object comes in very handy.

Workshop

These quiz questions are designed to test your knowledge of the material covered in this chapter. The answers to the quiz questions can be found in Appendix A, "Answers to Quizzes."

Quiz

1. If a relationship is created between two tables, what values are permitted in the foreign key column?

2. What happens if I attempt to delete a record from a parent table with dependent rows in a child table?

Exercise

Using the example in Listing 4.6 as a base, create a Web form for an airline that does the following:

1. Create a Flight DataTable to store flight information (with whatever schema you choose) including which customers are booked for which flights.

2. Create a Customer DataTable to store customer information (with whatever schema you choose).

3. Link the two DataTables by DataRelations. By using the GetChildRows() method, display a list of flights and the customers booked to each flight.

Hour 5

Connecting to a Data Source

In Hour 2, you saw how to work with DataSets by creating a few DataTables and manually adding columns and rows. This is a terrific way to learn how DataSets work. However, most often data is retrieved from a database and used to populate a DataSet, automatically creating a copy of the database schema and adding the requested data.

However, before you can retrieve anything from your database using ADO.NET, you must create and open a connection to the database using the Connection object. The Connection object uses a database connection string to locate and connect a data source. The exposed properties and methods of the Connection object have changed very little since the days of ADO 2.6.

This hour discusses the properties, methods, and various uses of the `Connection` object. Specifically, at the end of this hour, you will know how to

- Use the `Connection` object to connect to your data source
- Identify all important parts of a connection string
- Build a connection string for your data source

The `Connection` Object

The `Connection` object is the way ADO.NET's built-in data providers connect to a data source. There are two `Connection` objects that ship with the ADO.NET: `OleDbConnection` and `SqlConnection`. As you might have guessed, the `OleDbConnection` object is used to create a connection to any valid OLE DB data source and the `SqlConnection` object is used to connect to Microsoft SQL Server versions 7.0 and up.

Just as in ADO, ADO.NET uses connection strings to connect to various data sources. The next section discusses connection string syntax and gives you several examples enabling you to connect to several types of databases.

Anatomy of a Connection String

A connection string is a semicolon-delimited set of name-value pairs that define the various properties of a database connection. A connection string can have several properties or as little as one property, depending on the requirements of the data source.

The connection properties are specified through a string rather than through a set of individual connection object properties so that the properties can remain highly configurable. Each OLE DB data provider may require setting special connection string properties. It would be difficult to encompass all these properties by specifically enumerating them as a set of built-in properties of the `Connection` object. Therefore, the connection string is used because additional name-value pairs can easily be added.

Connection strings specify a wide variety of information, such as the type of OLE DB provider you are using for your connection to the database (if you are using the `OleDbConnection` object), database user information, and security information. Here's a sample connection string enabling you to connect to a Microsoft Access database using the standard admin password and the Microsoft Jet drivers:

```
"Provider=Microsoft.Jet.OLEDB.4.0;Data Source=FilePath;Jet OLEDB:
User Id=admin;Password=;"
```

OLE DB Data Providers

As previously stated, when using the `OleDbConnection` object and the `OleDb` namespace, you are actually connecting to an OLE DB data provider. Therefore, with a few minor exceptions, connection strings in ADO.NET are the same as the ones used in ADO. When creating an OLE DB source connection string in ADO.NET, you must use the `Provider` keyword. The `Provider` keyword specifies the OLE DB provider you are using to connect to your data.

Specifying User Information

When you're specifying user information for OLE DB providers, the username is normally specified by the User Id and the password by the Password key. However, you can also specify your user name with UID and password with PWD.

Connection Object Methods and Properties

The `Connection` object has several methods and properties. Most of the properties of the `Connection` object are read-only, set when the connection string is specified. These include properties such as `Database`, which contains the name of the database you're working with, and `Provider`, which contains the name of the OLE DB provider you're using to connect to your data. You already know the `ConnectionString` property of the `Connection` object. The following sections discuss the commonly used methods.

The `Open()` Method

The `Open()` method of the `Connection` object opens up a connection to your data source. Because database connections are a very expensive resource memory-wise, you should only call the `Open()` method just before you're ready to retrieve the data. This ensures that the connection is not open any longer than it needs to be.

The `Close()` Method

Immediately after you are done retrieving data, you should call the `Close()` method of the `Connection` object. This closes the connection to the database. However, opening and closing a connection to the database is time-consuming. When performing a number of calls to the database in quick succession, it's normally best to leave the connection to the database open.

5

Make sure to always call the Close() method. When the Connection
object is recycled by the framework garbage collector, connections to the
database are not automatically closed. You can use the State property of the
Connection object to test whether the Connection object is open or
closed.

Connecting to Various Data Sources

It would be impossible to include code to connect to all the possible kinds of databases.
The next section shows you how to connect to Microsoft SQL Server versions 7.0 and up
using the managed SQL provider in the System.Data.SqlClient namespace and also
how to connect to various OLE DB data sources using the System.Data.OleDb namespace.

SQL Server

When using the managed SQL provider, do not specify the Provider keyword in your
connection string. In fact, the only connection string properties you're likely to need are
the ones in Table 5.1.

TABLE 5.1   SQL Connection String Options

Connection String Property	Description
Initial Catalog	Specifies the database you're connecting to
Server	Specifies the server you're connecting to
User ID	Specifies the user ID you're using to make the connection
Password	Specifies the password for the user you are using to connect to the database

Listings 5.1 and 5.2 show how to connect to a Microsoft SQL database and open and
close a connection.

LISTING 5.1   Connecting to SQL Server in C#

```
SqlConnection conn = new
        SqlConnection("Initial Catalog=Northwind;Server=(local);UID=sa;PWD=");
conn.Open();
conn.Close();
```

LISTING 5.2 Connecting to SQL Server in Visual Basic .NET

```
Dim conn as SqlConnection = New _
        SqlConnection("Initial Catalog=Northwind;Server=(local);UID=sa;PWD=")
conn.Open()
conn.Close()
```

> Don't forget to include or import the `System.Data.SqlClient` namespace into your project or Web form before attempting to use its objects, including the `Connection` object.

OLE DB Data Sources

The key to connecting to an OLE DB data source is using a properly formed connection string. OLE DB providers exist for almost every type of data imaginable. The Internet provides a wealth of connection string information for various OLE DB providers.

The following page contains a wealth of OLE DB connection strings: `http://www.able-consulting.com/ADO_Conn.htm`. However, if you do not find one for your data source, there are also hundreds of other well-written lists of connection strings on the Internet; a quick Internet search should enable you to find one that will allow you to connect to your database.

The following sections show you how to use ADO.NET to connect to some common OLE DB providers: a Microsoft Access database, as well as an Oracle database.

Microsoft Access Database

The code in Listings 5.3 and 5.4 shows how to connect to a Microsoft Access database using the Microsoft Jet OLE DB provider.

> The backslash character ("\") is a special character when used in a string in C#. Therefore, if you need to enter a single backslash, as in the path in Listing 5.3, you must use two backslashes together, which C# interprets as a single backslash. This is called "escaping" the special character.

5

LISTING 5.3   Connecting to a Microsoft Access Database in C#

```
OleDbConnection conn = new OleDbConnection(
                       "Provider=Microsoft.Jet.OLEDB.4.0;" +
                       "Data Source=c:\\nwind.mdb;" +
                       "User Id=admin;" +
                       "Password=;" );
conn.Open();
conn.Close();
```

LISTING 5.4   Connecting to a Microsoft Access Database in Visual Basic .NET

```
Dim conn as OleDbConnection = New OleDbConnection( _
                       "Provider=Microsoft.Jet.OLEDB.4.0;" + _
                       "Data Source=c:\nwind.mdb;" + _
                       "User Id=admin;" + _
                       "Password=;" )
conn.Open()
conn.Close()
```

Oracle Database

Connecting to an Oracle database is straightforward. The code in Listings 5.5 and 5.6 will connect to an Oracle database using the OLE DB provider provided by Microsoft.

LISTING 5.5   Connecting to an Oracle Database in C#

```
OleDbConnection conn = new OleDbConnection( _
                       "Provider=OraOLEDB.Oracle" + _
                       "Data Source=DataBasename" + _
                       "User Id=username;" + _
                       "Password=password;" );
conn.Open();
conn.Close();
```

LISTING 5.6   Connecting to an Oracle Database in Visual Basic .NET

```
Dim conn as OleDbConnection = New OleDbConnection( _
                       "Provider=OraOLEDB.Oracle" + _
                       "Data Source=DataBasename" + _
                       "User Id=username;" + _
                       "Password=password;" )
conn.Open()
conn.Close()
```

ODBC (Open Database Connectivity)

Though there is no ODBC .NET provider included with the Microsoft .NET Framework SDK, you can download one for free at http://www.microsoft.com/data. You can use this provider to connect to any valid ODBC source. Though ODBC is usually not an optimal choice, if you are unable to find a managed or OLE DB provider for your data source, you most likely will be able to find an ODBC driver.

You can use the following code to create a new instance of the ODBC `Connection` object:

```
Dim conn as OdbcConnection = New OdbcConnection("dsn=myDSN;UID=myUid;PWD=;")
```

The preceding `OdbcConnection` object is using a DSN (Data Source Name) to connect to the data source. A DSN provides a layer of abstraction in connecting to your ODBC data source. By creating a DSN, you specify the details of the connection in one location. This enables you to just enter the name of the DSN and any user authentication information in your connection string. To create a DSN for your ODBC data source, follow these steps:

1. In your computer's Control Panel, locate the ODBC Data Source Administrator. The name of the Control Panel applet differs between operating systems, but in all cases the name contains "ODBC." In Windows 2000, it's the Data Sources (ODBC) icon in the Administrative Tools folder. When the ODBC Data Source Administrator is running, click on the System DSN tab. Your screen will look like the one in Figure 5.1.

FIGURE 5.1

The ODBC Data Source Administrator.

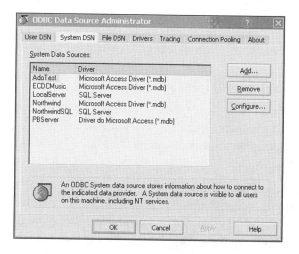

5

2. Click the Add button to add a new System DSN. On the next screen, you're prompted to choose the ODBC driver that the DSN will use to connect to your data source. Choose the appropriate ODBC driver.

3. The next screen is specific to the ODBC driver chosen. If you chose the Microsoft Access driver in step 2, you're presented with the screen in Figure 5.2. After filling out all required fields for your data source, a new DSN is added to your system, which you can then reference from your application. Keep in mind that if you deploy your application to another machine, you will need to re-create the DSN on that machine in order for your code to work.

FIGURE 5.2

Adding an ODBC connection to a Microsoft Access database.

Do not use an ODBC DSN to connect to your data source if a managed provider or OLE DB provider is available. The latter two options will give you the best performance.

Connection Pooling

Opening a connection to the database is an expensive operation in the form of both time and memory. If you had to open and close a connection to the database each time it was required by your application, the performance of your application would deteriorate, particularly if there are many concurrent users.

Luckily, both the OLE DB and managed SQL providers in ADO.NET automatically provide connection pooling. Connection pooling creates persistent connections to the database that can be shared, as needed. If a connection attempt is made and all connections are currently in use, another connection is added to the pool.

A separate pool is created for each unique connection string. If two connection strings differ by even a single character, two separate pools are created.

Summary

In this hour, you've learned how to use the ADO.NET Connection object to connect to various types of data sources. You've seen all the important elements of a connection string, and how to build connection strings for both the managed SQL provider and the OLE DB provider. You also saw several specific examples demonstrating how to connect to various data sources.

Q&A

Q Is it possible to use the Connection object in ADO.NET to send queries to the database as you could in ADO?

A Nope. This functionality has been removed, by design. To query the database, you must create a Command object, which is covered in depth in the next hour.

Q My data source has a managed provider, an OLE DB provider, and ODBC drivers. Which one should I use?

A Typically, the best option in terms of both speed and reliability is to use the managed provider. Your next best bet is to use the OLE DB provider. If everything else fails, use the ODBC .NET provider as you saw in this hour.

Workshop

These quiz questions are designed to test your knowledge of the material covered in this chapter. The answers to the quiz questions can be found in Appendix A, "Answers to Quizzes."

Quiz

1. Describe the difference between the SqlConnection and OleDbConnection objects.

2. True or false: If you do not call the Close() method of the Connection object, the connection to the database will be automatically closed before the object is destroyed by the garbage collector.

5

Exercise

Practice using the OleDbConnection (and SqlConnection, if you have a SQL Server system available to you) to connect to various data types.

HOUR 6

Retrieving Data from the Data Source

In the last hour, you saw how to use the `Connection` object to connect to several different types of data sources. This hour focuses on using the `Command` object to retrieve data from the database, which uses the `Connection` object to provide database connectivity.

In this hour, you will learn how to do the following tasks:

- Instantiate and use a `Command` object to retrieve data from a data source
- Use a `DataAdapter` object to place the results of a query into a `DataSet`

The `Command` Object

The `Command` object enables you to execute queries against your data source. However, in order to retrieve data, you must know the schema of your database as well as how to build a valid SQL query. In Hour 3, you learned how to build SQL queries to retrieve and modify data. You will now have the opportunity to apply that knowledge as you use the Command object.

> The SqlCommand object must be used in conjunction with the SqlConnection object. If you attempt to attach a SqlCommand to an OleDbConnection, you will get an error from the compiler. The converse is also true: OleDbCommands cannot be used with the SqlConnection.

Associating Connection Objects with Command Objects

Before creating a Command object, you should create a Connection object. Remember that a Command object is useless without a Connection object to provide communication to the database. Recall from Hour 5 that to create an instance of the Connection object, you use the following code:

```
Dim myConnection as new SqlConnection("Connection string")
```

or in C#:

```
SqlConnection myConnection = new SqlConnection("Connection string");
```

Similarly, to create a new Command object, you can simply use the new keyword and pass no arguments:

```
Dim myCommand as new SqlCommand()
```

or in C#:

```
SqlCommand myCommand = new SqlCommand();
```

However, there's one additional step if you use this method to create a new command. You must associate the newly created Command object with the Connection object. You can do this by using the Connection property of the Command object. Listing 6.1 shows how this is done.

> Most of the examples in this hour use the Northwind database. Therefore, to follow along, simply provide a connection string to the Northwind database in your datasource, if it is present. If you are using SQL Server, your connection string will be similar to the ones used in the examples of this hour.

LISTING 6.1   Instantiating the Command and Connection Objects

```
Dim myConnection as new SqlConnection("Initial Catalog=Northwind;
                                Server=(local);UID=sa;PWD=")
Dim myCommand as new SqlCommand()

myCommand.Connection = myConnection
myCommand.CommandText = "SELECT * FROM Employees"
```

The last line of Listing 6.1 specifies the command text that contains a query to pass to the database. Note that this line only specifies the query; it does not execute the query. We're almost ready to query the database and retrieve some data! But first, you'll have an opportunity to optimize the code in Listing 6.1 to make your life easier.

Overloaded Constructors Save Time

Figure 6.1 shows the Microsoft Class Browser entry for the SqlCommand object. Notice the very first section entitled 'Constructors.' This section shows you the various ways you can instantiate the Command object. Notice that you can specify the command text and Connection object when you instantiate the new Command object, rather than doing it line by line later. The code in Listing 6.1 can be reduced to the code in Listing 6.2.

FIGURE 6.1

The .NET Framework Class Browser entry for the SqlCommand object.

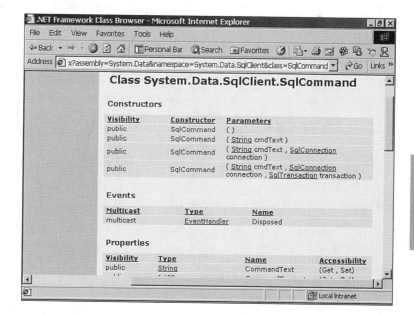

6

LISTING 6.2 Using Overloaded Constructors to Reduce Code Size

```
Dim myConnection as New SqlConnection("Initial Catalog=Northwind;
                                      Server=(local);UID=sa;PWD=")
Dim myCommand as New SqlCommand("SELECT * FROM Employees", myConnection)
```

Filling a DataSet with the DataAdapter

The Command object executes a query against a database. Alone, it can't place the results into a DataSet. This is where the DataAdapter object comes into the picture. One of the DataAdapter's jobs is to fill a DataSet with the results of a query. You can learn more about the DataAdapter in Hour 8, "Using the DataReader and DataAdapter."

The DataAdapter object is instantiated in a very similar fashion to the Command object:

```
Dim myAdapter as New SqlDataAdapter( myCommand )
```

or in C#:

```
SqlDataAdapter myAdapter = new SqlDataAdapter( myCommand );
```

Notice that you pass the existing Command object you're working with to the new DataAdapter object you're creating. This tells the DataAdapter which Command object will be used to query the database.

DataAdapter Fill() Method

As previously stated, the Fill() method of the DataAdapter takes the results of a database query and pushes them into a DataSet. Therefore, before you call the Fill() method, you must create a new DataSet to hold the results of the query. Additionally, you must open your connection to the database before calling the Fill() method. Listing 6.3 shows the complete code required to connect to the database and retrieve the results of the query into a DataSet.

LISTING 6.3 Retrieving a DataSet Using the DataAdapters Fill Method

```
SqlConnection conn = new SqlConnection("Initial Catalog=Northwind;
                                       Server=(local);UID=sa;PWD=;");
SqlCommand cmd = new SqlCommand("SELECT * FROM Employees", conn);

SqlDataAdapter adapt = new SqlDataAdapter(cmd);
DataSet dsEmployees = new DataSet();

conn.Open();
adapt.Fill(dsEmployees,  "Employees");
conn.Close();
```

> The Fill() method of the DataAdapter object cannot be found in the
> class browser under either the SqlDataAdapter or OleDbDataAdapter
> entries. That is because it is defined in the
> System.Data.Common.DbDataAdapter class instead. You can find all of
> the overloaded Fill() method definitions there.

You have several options to verify that the code in Listing 6.3 is actually retrieving data. You could create a Windows form application that opens the Employee DataTable in the dsEmployees DataSet and loops through the rows of data and outputs the values of specific columns. However, the easiest way to test this code is to use a Web form, as you did in Hour 2, "Working with DataSets and DataTables."

Place the code in Listing 6.3 into a Web form named hour6.aspx using the techniques at the end of Hour 2. Then, to view the Web form, you can navigate your browser to http://localhost/ADO 24Hours/hour6.aspx, if you followed the directions in Hour 2.

LISTING 6.4   Viewing the Contents of a DataSet in C#

```
<% @Page Language="C#" %>
<%@ Import Namespace="System.Data" %>
<%@ Import Namespace="System.Data.SqlClient" %>

<HTML>
<HEAD>
    <LINK rel="stylesheet" type="text/css" href="Main.css">
    <!-- End Style Sheet -->

    <script language="C#" runat="server" >
      void Page_Load(Object Source, EventArgs E)
      {
         SqlConnection conn = new SqlConnection("Initial Catalog=Northwind;
                                        Server=(local);UID=sa;PWD=;");
         SqlCommand cmd = new SqlCommand("SELECT * FROM Employees", conn);

         SqlDataAdapter adapt = new SqlDataAdapter(cmd);
         DataSet dsEmployees = new DataSet();

         conn.Open();
         adapt.Fill(dsEmployees, "Employees");
         conn.Close();

         employees.DataSource = dsEmployees;
         employees.DataBind();
      }
```

6

LISTING 6.4   continued

```
        </script>

</HEAD>
<BODY>

<h1>Creating a DataSet</h1>
<hr>

<form runat="server" id=form1 name=form1>
    <asp:DataGrid id="employees" runat="server"></asp:DataGrid>
</form>
<hr>

</BODY>
</HTML>
```

LISTING 6.5   Viewing the Contents of a DataSet in VB.NET

```
<% @Page Language="VB" %>
<%@ Import Namespace="System.Data" %>
<%@ Import Namespace="System.Data.SqlClient" %>

<HTML>
<HEAD>
        <LINK rel="stylesheet" type="text/css" href="Main.css">
        <!-- End Style Sheet -->

        <script language="VB" runat="server" >
        Sub Page_Load(Source as Object, E as EventArgs)

            Dim conn as New SqlConnection("Initial Catalog=Northwind;
                                        Server=(local);UID=sa;PWD=;")
            Dim cmd as New SqlCommand("SELECT * FROM Employees", conn)

            Dim adapt as New SqlDataAdapter(cmd)
            Dim dsEmployees as New DataSet()

            conn.Open()
            adapt.Fill(dsEmployees, "Employees")
            conn.Close()

            employees.DataSource = dsEmployees
            employees.DataBind()
```

LISTING 6.5 continued

```
        End Sub
        </script>

</HEAD>
<BODY>

<h1>Creating a DataSet</h1>
<hr>

<form runat="server" id=form1 name=form1>
   <asp:DataGrid id="employees" runat="server"></asp:DataGrid>
</form>
<hr>

</BODY>
</HTML>
```

 The C# and VB.NET code in Listings 6.3 and 6.4 are very similar. In fact, minor language-specific nuances of syntax aside, the code is identical and performs exactly the same.

The Web form in Listing 6.4 uses a Web control known as the DataGrid to display the DataSet. The DataGrid object is instantiated in a tag inside the server-side form toward the end of the listing. The DataGrid generates an HTML table built from the data sent to it.

Your ADO.NET code is inserted into the Page_Load method, which runs every time the Web page is loaded. In order to "wire up" the data to the DataGrid, the DataSource property of the DataGrid is set to dsEmployees. The last step required to display the DataSet on the page is to call the DataBind() method of the DataGrid control. After the Web form in Listing 6.4 is loaded, you'll see results very similar to those in Figure 6.2.

The unformatted DataGrid results aren't very pretty. However, it is very easy to configure the DataGrid control to display data in a format more pleasing to the eye. For more information on formatting the DataGrid control, see Hour 12, "Formatting ASP.NET List Controls."

6

FIGURE 6.2

Binding the results of a database query to a DataGrid Web control.

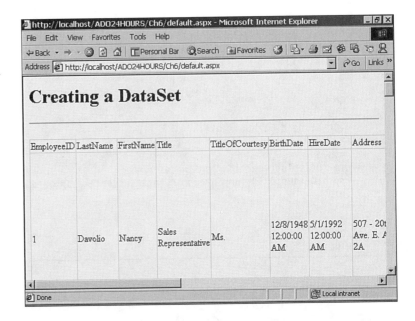

Retrieving a Single Value from the Database

Sometimes, you only need to retrieve a single value from the database, instead of a record or set of records. In this case, though you could use the methods described earlier in this hour to retrieve the value, the Command object provides a better way. Instead of using the DataAdapter object to place the results into a DataSet, you can call the ExecuteScalar() method of the Command object directly. This returns just the single value that you've queried from the database.

The code in Listing 6.5 shows this method of retrieving a single value. There are only three major changes from the example in Listing 6.4. First, the database query uses the Count() SQL function to return a count of all the records in the Employees table. Second, rather than using a SqlDataAdapter to fill a DataSet, the ExecuteScalar() method of the Command object is used. Lastly, a label is used to display the output instead of a DataGrid. When the example in Listing 6.5 is loaded, it will look like Figure 6.3.

LISTING 6.6   Retrieving a Single Value from the Database Using ExecuteScalar()

```
<% @Page Language="C#" %>
<%@ Import Namespace="System.Data" %>
```

LISTING 6.6   continued

```
<%@ Import Namespace="System.Data.SqlClient" %>

<HTML>
<HEAD>
    <LINK rel="stylesheet" type="text/css" href="Main.css">
    <!-- End Style Sheet -->

    <script language="C#" runat="server" >
      void Page_Load(Object Source, EventArgs E)
      {
          int recordCount;

          SqlConnection conn = new SqlConnection("Initial Catalog=Northwind;
➡ Server=(local);UID=sa;PWD=;");
          SqlCommand cmd = new SqlCommand("SELECT count(*) FROM Employees",
➡ conn);

          SqlDataAdapter adapt = new SqlDataAdapter(cmd);
          DataSet dsEmployees = new DataSet();

          conn.Open();
          recordCount = (int)cmd.ExecuteScalar();
          conn.Close();

          result.Text = recordCount.ToString();

      }
    </script>

</HEAD>
<BODY>

<h1>Retrieving a Single Value</h1>
<hr>

<form runat="server" id=form1 name=form1>
    The number of employees in the employee table:<br>
    <asp:Label id=result runat="server"></asp:Label>
</form>
<hr>

</BODY>
</HTML>
```

6

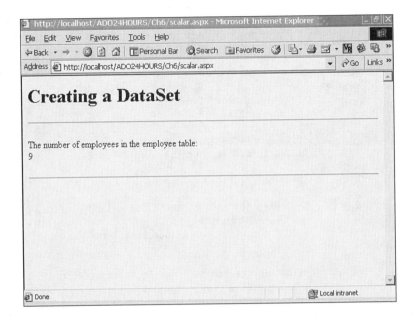

Summary

In this hour, you've seen how to use the ADO.NET Command object to query your data source and retrieve data. You saw how to associate the Command object with a Connection object and a DataAdapter object. You used the DataAdapter to fill a DataSet with the data retrieved from a database query and then display the data. Then you saw how to display the results in a Web form.

Q&A

Q How do I manually step through the results of a query as I used to do using the recordset object in ADO?

A There are several options available to do this. First, you could use a DataReader object, which offers a forward-only, read-only view of the data returned from the database. The DataReader is covered in much more detail in Hour 8, "Using the DataReader and DataAdapter." Additionally, you could also fill a DataSet using the DataAdapter and then manually step through each row in the Rows collection outputting whatever column values you want.

Q I'm unable to locate the Fill() method of the SqlDataAdapter object in the Microsoft Class Browser. What am I doing wrong?

A The Fill() method can be found in the System.Data.Common namespace in the DataAdapter class. The specific DataAdapters in each managed provider (such as the SqlDataAdapter) derive from this base class. To oversimplify a bit, this means that the specific DataAdapters have access to the properties and methods created in this base class.

Workshop

These quiz questions are designed to test your knowledge of the material covered in this chapter. The answers to the quiz questions can be found in Appendix A, "Answers to Quizzes."

Quiz

1. Which method of the DataAdapter object is used to place the records returned from a query into a DataSet?

2. What steps must you perform before being able to use a Command object to retrieve data from a data source?

3. True or False: You should use an OleDbConnection with a SqlCommand in order to retrieve data from Microsoft SQL Server using OLE DB drivers.

Exercise

Use the Class Browser application to examine the constructors of the DataAdapter object. See if you can simplify the code in this chapter even more by using different ways of instantiating the DataAdapter. Hint: If you pass a query as the first argument, the DataAdapter will implicitly create a Command object. Also practice executing various queries against your data source and viewing the results in a Web form.

6

HOUR 7

Modifying Database Data

As you saw in the preceding hour, the Command object is used in conjunction with the DataAdapter object to retrieve records from your data source and place them into a DataSet, which can then be displayed or manipulated. However, suppose you want to insert data, delete data, or perform any other valid action on the database that doesn't return any records. For this, you can use the ExecuteNonQuery() method of the Command object.

The ExecuteNonQuery() method executes a SQL statement against your data source. In this hour you'll see how to apply the SQL statements from Hour 3, "Using T-SQL: A Crash Course," to

- Insert new data into the database
- Delete data from the database
- Modify data in the database

The examples in this hour again use ASP.NET Web forms to provide concrete, real-life examples showcasing ADO.NET code. However, the ADO.NET code works just as easily with Windows forms.

Using ExecuteNonQuery()

The ExecuteNonQuery() method of the Command object is used to send a SQL command to the data source for processing. Any SQL command you want to send to the data source that will not return any data (or more specifically, any data that you don't plan to use) should be sent using the ExecuteNonQuery() method.

In the next several sections, you'll see how to use the ExecuteNonQuery() method to insert, delete, and modify data.

Inserting New Data

Recall from Hour 3, "Using T-SQL: A Crash Course," that inserting new data into your data source is done using the SQL INSERT statement. One of the easiest ways to add data to a table in your data source is to build the INSERT statement dynamically and then send it to the data source using the ExecuteNonQuery() method of the Command object.

Gathering the information to put into the database is highly dependent on your application, of course. The example in Listings 7.1 (VB .NET) and 7.2 (C#) use a Web form to collect the information from the user and send it to some server-side code that builds the INSERT statement and sends it to the database.

> Directly connecting to a data source from your presentation layer is referred to as *two-tier development*. This is a quick-and-dirty development method for small applications or quick applications with a short life span that will require little or no maintenance. Two-tier applications generally do not scale very well, and because all of the source code for the application is in the presentation tier, there are some additional security risks. To learn more about using ADO.NET in more advanced development methods such as N-tier development, see Hour 21, "Optimizing Data Access Using Tiered Development," and Hour 22, "Modifying Data in an N-Tier Application."

LISTING 7.1   Dynamically Building a SQL Statement Adding Records to a SQL Database

```
<% @Page Debug="true" EnableViewState="false" %>
<%@ Import Namespace="System.Data" %>
<%@ Import Namespace="System.Data.SqlClient" %>

<HTML>
<HEAD>
    <LINK rel="stylesheet" type="text/css" href="Main.css">
```

LISTING 7.1 continued

```
<!-- End Style Sheet -->

<script language="VB" runat="server" >
  Sub Page_Load(Source as Object, E as EventArgs)

    if IsPostBack and Page.IsValid then

        Dim conn as new SqlConnection( _
            "Initial Catalog=Northwind;Server=(local);UID=sa;PWD=;")

        'Build the SQL string
        'Use StringBuilder object for better performance
        Dim strBuilder as new StringBuilder()

        strBuilder.Append("INSERT INTO Employees ")
        strBuilder.Append("(FirstName, LastName, Title, HireDate) VALUES(")
        strBuilder.Append("'" + Request("txtFirstName") + "',")
        strBuilder.Append("'" + Request("txtLastName") + "',")
        strBuilder.Append("'" + Request("txtTitle") + "',")
        strBuilder.Append("'" + Request("txtDateHired") + "')")

        Dim sSQL as string = strBuilder.ToString()

        Dim cmd as SqlCommand = new SqlCommand(sSQL, conn)

        conn.Open()
        cmd.ExecuteNonQuery()
        conn.Close()

        txtFirstName.Text = ""
        txtLastName.Text = ""
        txtTitle.Text = ""
        txtDateHired.Text = ""
    end if

    LoadData()

  End Sub

  private Sub LoadData()

    Dim conn as SqlConnection = new SqlConnection( _
        "Initial Catalog=Northwind;Server=(local);UID=sa;PWD=;")
    Dim cmd as SqlCommand = new SqlCommand( _
      "SELECT FirstName, LastName, Title, HireDate FROM Employees", conn)

    Dim adapt as SqlDataAdapter = new SqlDataAdapter(cmd)
    Dim dsEmployees as DataSet = new DataSet()
```

7

LISTING 7.1   continued

```
                conn.Open()
                adapt.Fill(dsEmployees, "Employees")
                conn.Close()

                employees.DataSource = dsEmployees
                employees.DataBind()

        End Sub
    </script>

</HEAD>
<BODY>

<h1>Adding a Record to the Database</h1>
<hr>
<asp:Label id=msg runat=server />
<form runat="server" id=form1 name=form1>
    <asp:DataGrid id="employees" runat="server"></asp:DataGrid>
    <br>
    Add a new record:<br>
    <table>
    <tr>
        <td>First Name: </td>
        <td><asp:textbox runat="server"
                    id="txtFirstName" EnableViewState="false">
            </asp:textbox></td>
        <td><asp:RequiredFieldValidator runat="server"
                ControlToValidate="txtFirstName"
                InitialValue=""
                ErrorMessage="You must enter the first name."/></td>
    </tr>
    <tr>
        <td>Last Name: </td>
        <td><asp:textbox runat="server" id="txtLastName"></asp:textbox></td>
        <td><asp:RequiredFieldValidator runat="server"
                ControlToValidate="txtLastName"
                InitialValue=""
                ErrorMessage="You must enter the last name."/></td>
    </tr>
    <tr>
        <td>Title: </td>
        <td><asp:textbox runat="server" id="txtTitle"></asp:textbox></td>
    </tr>
      <tr>
        <td>Date Hired: </td>
        <td><asp:textbox runat="server" id="txtDateHired"></asp:textbox></td>
    </tr>
    </table>
```

LISTING 7.1   continued

```
    <input type="submit" id=submit1 name=submit1>
</form>
<hr>

</BODY>
</HTML>
```

LISTING 7.2   C# Code Used to Add Records to a SQL Database

```
<script language="C#" runat="server" >
    void Page_Load(Object Source, EventArgs E)
    {
        if(IsPostBack && Page.IsValid)
        {
          SqlConnection conn = new SqlConnection(
              "Initial Catalog=Northwind;Server=(local);UID=sa;PWD=;");

          //Build the SQL string
          //Use StringBuilder object for better performance
          StringBuilder strBuilder = new StringBuilder();

          strBuilder.Append("INSERT INTO Employees ");
          strBuilder.Append("(FirstName, LastName, Title, HireDate) VALUES(");
          strBuilder.Append("'" + Request["txtFirstName"] + "',");
          strBuilder.Append("'" + Request["txtLastName"] + "',");
          strBuilder.Append("'" + Request["txtTitle"] + "',");
          strBuilder.Append("'" + Request["txtDateHired"] + "')");

          string sSQL = strBuilder.ToString();

          SqlCommand cmd = new SqlCommand(sSQL, conn);

          conn.Open();
          cmd.ExecuteNonQuery();
          conn.Close();

          txtFirstName.Text = "";
          txtLastName.Text = "";
          txtTitle.Text = "";
          txtDateHired.Text = "";
        }

        LoadData();
    }

    private void LoadData()
```

7

LISTING 7.2   continued

```
    {
        SqlConnection conn = new SqlConnection(
            "Initial Catalog=Northwind;Server=(local);UID=sa;PWD=;");
        SqlCommand cmd = new SqlCommand(
          "SELECT FirstName, LastName, Title, HireDate FROM Employees", conn);

        SqlDataAdapter adapt = new SqlDataAdapter(cmd);
        DataSet dsEmployees = new DataSet();

        conn.Open();
        adapt.Fill(dsEmployees, "Employees");
        conn.Close();

        employees.DataSource = dsEmployees;
        employees.DataBind();
    }
</script>
```

Most of the preceding code is provided to give you some context in a realistic usage of
ADO.NET. The ADO.NET code exists inside the <script . . .>   </script> tags.
Let's analyze this code in detail step by step:

```
Dim conn as new SqlConnection( _
    "Initial Catalog=Northwind;Server=(local);UID=sa;PWD=;")
```

1. This code creates a Connection object that will be used to connect to the database
    server. In this example, we're connecting to the standard Northwind database on a
    SQL server. For more information about connecting to a database, see Hour 5,
    "Connecting to a Data Source."

```
'Build the SQL string
'Use StringBuilder object for better performance
Dim strBuilder as new StringBuilder()

strBuilder.Append("INSERT INTO Employees ")
strBuilder.Append("(FirstName, LastName, Title, HireDate) VALUES(")
strBuilder.Append("'" + Request("txtFirstName") + "',")
strBuilder.Append("'" + Request("txtLastName") + "',")
strBuilder.Append("'" + Request("txtTitle") + "',")
strBuilder.Append("'" + Request("txtDateHired") + "')")

Dim sSQL as string = strBuilder.ToString()
```

2. This block of code creates a StringBuilder object used to concatenate the SQL
    query string that we're going to send to the database server. We use the
    StringBuilder object because it performs string concatenation much more quickly

than applying the "+" operator to strings. The SQL query string can be built using any technique you prefer, so long as you have a well-formatted SQL query when you are done.

```
Dim cmd as SqlCommand = new SqlCommand(sSQL, conn)
```

3. Then we create a new Command object by passing it the SQL string we've just built and the Connection object from step 1.

```
conn.Open()
cmd.ExecuteNonQuery()
conn.Close()
```

4. We open the connection to the database, send the query to the database server where it will be executed, and then close the connection to the database. Notice that the connection is opened at the very last possible moment before we need it and then closed as soon as we're done. This is done because database connections are a relatively expensive resource.

```
txtFirstName.Text = ""
txtLastName.Text = ""
txtTitle.Text = ""
txtDateHired.Text = ""
```

5. This last set of code just prepares the objects on the Web form to add another record. The LoadData() method in Listing 7.1 is code you have seen before. It simply retrieves the set of employees to display on the Web form.

Deleting Data

Deleting data in a two-tier environment is done much the same as in the example in the preceding section. You build a SQL DELETE string dynamically, based on the item a user selects. The Web form in Listing 7.3 displays a ListBox Web control loaded with data from the Northwind Employees table. The C# server-side code is provided in Listing 7.4. If the user selects an item in the ListBox and clicks the Submit button, the record is deleted from the database.

LISTING 7.3 Dynamically Building a SQL Statement to Delete Records from a SQL Database

```
<% @Page Debug="true" %>
<%@ Import Namespace="System.Data" %>
<%@ Import Namespace="System.Data.SqlClient" %>

<HTML>
<HEAD>
    <LINK rel="stylesheet" type="text/css" href="Main.css">
    <!-- End Style Sheet -->
```

7

LISTING 7.3 continued

```
<script language="VB" runat="server" >
  Sub Page_Load(Source as Object, E as EventArgs)

    LoadData()

  End Sub

  Sub cmdDelete_OnClick(Source as Object, E as EventArgs)

    Dim selectedEmployee as Int32 = Int32.Parse(Request("lstEmployees"))

    if selectedEmployee > 0 then

      Dim conn as SqlConnection = new SqlConnection( _
          "Initial Catalog=Northwind;Server=(local);UID=sa;PWD=;")

      'Build the SQL string
      Dim sSQL as string = ("DELETE FROM Employees " + _
              "WHERE EmployeeID = " + selectedEmployee.ToString())

      Dim cmd as SqlCommand = new SqlCommand(sSQL, conn)

      conn.Open()
      cmd.ExecuteNonQuery()
      conn.Close()
    end if

    LoadData()

  End Sub

  Sub LoadData()
    Dim conn as SqlConnection = new SqlConnection( _
        "Initial Catalog=Northwind;Server=(local);UID=sa;PWD=;")
    Dim cmd as SqlCommand = new SqlCommand( _
      "SELECT FirstName + ' ' + LastName as Name, EmployeeID" + _
      " FROM Employees", conn)

    Dim adapt as SqlDataAdapter = new SqlDataAdapter(cmd)
    Dim dsEmployees as DataSet = new DataSet()

    conn.Open()
    adapt.Fill(dsEmployees, "Employees")
    conn.Close()

    lstEmployees.DataSource = dsEmployees
    lstEmployees.DataMember = "Employees"
    lstEmployees.DataTextField = "Name"
```

LISTING 7.3   continued

```
            lstEmployees.DataValueField = "EmployeeID"
            lstEmployees.DataBind()
        End Sub
    </script>

</HEAD>
<BODY>

<h1>Deleting a Record</h1>
<hr>

<form runat="server" id=form1 name=form1>
    <asp:Label id=msg runat=server /><br><br>
    <asp:ListBox id="lstEmployees" EnableViewState="true" runat="server">
    </asp:ListBox>
    <br>
    <asp:Button id="cmdDelete" OnClick="cmdDelete_OnClick"
                Text="Delete" runat=server/>
</form>
<hr>

</BODY>
</HTML>
```

LISTING 7.4   C# Code Without Web Form Used to Delete Records from a SQL
Database

```
<script language="C#" runat="server" >
    void Page_Load(Object Source, EventArgs E)
    {
        LoadData();
    }

    void cmdDelete_OnClick(Object Source, EventArgs E)
    {
        int selectedEmployee = Int32.Parse(Request["lstEmployees"]);

        if(selectedEmployee > 0)
        {
            SqlConnection conn = new SqlConnection(
                "Initial Catalog=Northwind;Server=(local);UID=sa;PWD=;");

            //Build the SQL string
            string sSQL = ("DELETE FROM Employees " +
                        "WHERE EmployeeID = " + selectedEmployee.ToString());

            SqlCommand cmd = new SqlCommand(sSQL, conn);
```

7

LISTING 7.4   continued

```
                conn.Open();
                cmd.ExecuteNonQuery();
                conn.Close();
            }

        LoadData();
    }

    private void LoadData()
    {
        SqlConnection conn = new SqlConnection(
                "Initial Catalog=Northwind;Server=(local);UID=sa;PWD=;");
        SqlCommand cmd = new SqlCommand(
          "SELECT FirstName + ' ' + LastName as Name, EmployeeID" +
          " FROM Employees", conn);

        SqlDataAdapter adapt = new SqlDataAdapter(cmd);
        DataSet dsEmployees = new DataSet();

        conn.Open();
        adapt.Fill(dsEmployees, "Employees");
        conn.Close();

        lstEmployees.DataSource = dsEmployees;
        lstEmployees.DataMember = "Employees";
        lstEmployees.DataTextField = "Name";
        lstEmployees.DataValueField = "EmployeeID";
        lstEmployees.DataBind();
    }
</script>
```

If you recall from Hour 3, in order to delete a record from the database, you only need to uniquely identify the record you want to delete in the WHERE portion of your DELETE query. In this example, the ListBox is populated with the name (which is visible) and EmployeeID (which is hidden from the user). In this case, and in most cases, the ID field uniquely identifies the record we want to remove. The EmployeeID value is passed from the ListBox to the SQL query, which is then applied to the database, removing the record. The only differences between this example and the one provided in Listings 7.1 and 7.2 are the way the data is displayed and collected on the Web form, and the exact syntax of the SQL query.

Modifying Data

Modifying data using two-tier methodology is done in much the same way as the other examples in this chapter. You build an UPDATE SQL string dynamically based on user selections and then pass the string to the data source where it is executed. However, the example in this section provides a new twist.

Rather than displaying a Web form to the user, the example in Listing 7.5 (VB .NET) and Listing 7.6 (C#) exists as an intermediate form. This Web form is called from other pages that pass information to it along the query string. The Web form accepts the input, creates an UPDATE string, sends it to the SQL database, and then returns to the calling page. This is a nice way to segregate functionality needed by more than one Web form in an application.

> There are a number of different ways to modify data. The two-tier example in Listing 7.5 is one of the easiest. In Hour 8, "Using the DataReader and DataAdapter," you'll learn how to use the DataAdapter object to automatically apply data changes back to the database.

LISTING 7.5   Dynamically Building a SQL Statement to Update Records in a SQL Database

```
<% @Page Debug="true" %>
<%@ Import Namespace="System.Data" %>
<%@ Import Namespace="System.Data.SqlClient" %>

<HTML>
<HEAD>
    <LINK rel="stylesheet" type="text/css" href="Main.css">
    <!-- End Style Sheet -->

    <script language="VB" runat="server" >

      Sub Page_Load(Source as Object, E as EventArgs)

          Dim EmployeeID as Int32 = Int32.Parse(Request("EmployeeID"))

          Dim firstName as string = Request("FirstName")
          Dim lastName as string = Request("LastName")
          Dim title as string = Request("Title")
          Dim hireDate as string = Request("HireDate")

        if EmployeeID > 0 then

          Dim conn as SqlConnection = new SqlConnection( _
                "Initial Catalog=Northwind;Server=(local);UID=sa;PWD=;")

          'Build the SQL string
          Dim sSQL as string = "UPDATE Employees " + _
```

7

LISTING 7.5 continued

```
                                    "SET " + _
                                    "FirstName='"" + firstName + "', " + _
                                    "LastName='" + lastName + "', " + _
                                    "Title='" + title + "', " + _
                                    "HireDate='" + hireDate + "' " + _
                                    "WHERE EmployeeID = " + EmployeeID.ToString()

            Dim cmd as SqlCommand = new SqlCommand(sSQL, conn)

            conn.Open()
            cmd.ExecuteNonQuery()
            conn.Close()

            'Return to the previous page
            Response.Redirect( Request.ServerVariables("HTTP_REFERER") )

        end if

    End Sub

    </script>

</HEAD>
<BODY>

<h1>Updating Database</h1>
<hr>

<p>
Since this page is designed to process data and then return where
it came fom, this UI should never display unless we're debugging.</p>

<form runat="server" id=form1 name=form1>
    <asp:Label id=msg runat=server /><br><br>
</form>
<hr>

</BODY>
</HTML>
```

LISTING 7.6 C# Code Without Web Form Used to Update Records in a SQL Database

```
<script language="C#" runat="server" >

    void Page_Load(Object Source, EventArgs E)
```

LISTING 7.6   continued

```
    {
        int EmployeeID = Int32.Parse(Request["EmployeeID"]);

        string firstName = Request["FirstName"];
        string lastName = Request["LastName"];
        string title = Request["Title"];
        string hireDate = Request["HireDate"];

    if(EmployeeID > 0)
    {
        SqlConnection conn = new SqlConnection(
            "Initial Catalog=Northwind;Server=(local);UID=sa;PWD=;");

        //Build the SQL string
        string sSQL = "UPDATE Employees " +
                        "SET " +
                        "FirstName=" + "'" + firstName + "', " +
                        "LastName=" + "'" + lastName + "', " +
                        "Title=" + "'" + title + "', " +
                        "HireDate='" + hireDate + "' " +
                        "WHERE EmployeeID = " + EmployeeID.ToString();

        SqlCommand cmd = new SqlCommand(sSQL, conn);

        conn.Open();
        cmd.ExecuteNonQuery();
        conn.Close();

        //Return to the previous page
        Response.Redirect( Request.ServerVariables["HTTP_REFERER"] );
    }
    }
</script>
```

Summary

In this hour, you've seen how to use ADO.NET to manipulate data. Specifically, you saw how to add new records to the database, delete records from the database, and update existing records using standard two-tier development practices.

7

Q&A

Q Can the `Command` object apply any SQL query to the data source?

A Yep! The `Command` object can be used to send just about any command to your data source. However, whether or not the command is understood is completely up to the data source. In other words, you can send an Oracle-specific command to Microsoft SQL Server, but you'll most likely receive an exception at runtime.

Workshop

These quiz questions are designed to test your knowledge of the material covered in this chapter. The answers to the quiz questions can be found in Appendix A, "Answers to Quizzes."

Quiz

1. What is the purpose of the `ExecuteNonQuery()` method of the `Command` object?

2. True or false: Using the `ExecuteNonQuery()` method to execute a query that returns data will result in an exception error being thrown from the data layer.

Exercise

Given that the SQL command to create a new table in your data source is

```
CREATE TABLE TableName
    (
    Field1 int,
    Field2 varchar(50),
    Field3 int
    )
```

Using the examples in this hour as a guide, create a Windows form or Web form that will enable you to create a database table. The table name and field names should be dynamically named based on user input.

HOUR 8

Using the DataReader and DataAdapter

In Hour 6, "Retrieving Data from the Data Source," you saw how to use ADO.NET to connect to a data source, fetch some records, place them into a DataSet using the DataAdapter, and display them on a Web form. In this hour, you'll see an alternative—and in many instances more efficient—method of retrieving data. Specifically, in this hour, you'll learn how to

- Bind the DataReader object to Web controls
- Step through the results of a DataReader object
- Determine when to use a DataAdapter versus a DataReader

DataReader Versus DataAdapter

In Hour 6, you saw how to use the Command object in conjunction with the DataAdapter object to retrieve records from the database and place them into a DataSet. The DataSet was then bound to a Web control such as the

`DataGrid` and displayed in a Web form. The code in Listing 8.1 is a review of the ADO.NET code required to perform these tasks.

LISTING 8.1 Retrieving Records with the `DataAdapter`

```
<script language="VB" runat="server" >
   Sub Page_Load(Source as Object, E as EventArgs)
       Dim conn as New SqlConnection("Initial " + _
           Catalog=Northwind;Server=(local);UID=sa;PWD=;")
      Dim cmd as New SqlCommand("SELECT * FROM Employees", conn)

      Dim adapt as New SqlDataAdapter(cmd)
      Dim dsEmployees as New DataSet()

      conn.Open()
      adapt.Fill(dsEmployees, "Employees")
      conn.Close()

      employees.DataSource = dsEmployees
      employees.DataBind()
   End Sub
</script>
```

 If you are placing the code from Listing 8.1 into a Web form, do not forget to import the `System.Data` and `System.Data.SqlClient` namespaces at the top of your Web form.

To use the `DataAdapter`, you must create a `DataSet`, as shown in line 7 of Listing 8.1. The `DataSet` is then passed to the `DataAdapter` in line 10, where it is filled with records from the database. In lines 13 and 14, the `DataSet` is then bound to a Web control in order to display the data as shown in Figure 8.1.

There is one problem with this method of retrieving data: The `DataSet` object exists in memory and contains all rows returned by your query. Suppose that you are retrieving a large number of records from the data source. For the brief amount of time it takes to bind the data to your form and send it to the user, you have a potentially large amount of memory consumed by the `DataSet`.

If you are only retrieving small `DataSets` on a low-traffic site, this probably won't be of much concern. However, as the number of concurrent users of your application increases, the more important this issue becomes.

FIGURE 8.1

The appearance of a Web form with bound Web controls.

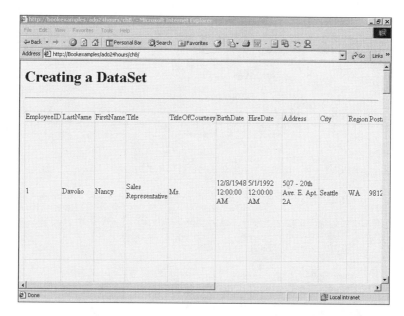

Like the DataAdapter, the DataReader object is designed to retrieve records from the data source. However, unlike the DataAdapter, the DataReader never has more than a single database record in memory at any given time. It does this by opening a forward-only, read-only stream of data from your data source.

If you think of your data source as a water reservoir, you could envision the DataAdapter method of returning records as a man running back and forth between the source and destination with buckets (albeit very quickly). The DataReader is more like a firehose.

Instantiating the DataReader

The DataReader is very easy to use. To get an instance of the DataReader object, you call the ExecuteReader() of the Command object, rather than using the DataAdapter. The ExecuteReader() returns a new instance of a DataReader object ready to display data starting at the first record returned. The code in Listing 8.2 (VB .NET) and in Listing 8.3 (C#) shows how to get a DataReader object.

LISTING 8.2 Getting an Instance of the DataReader in Visual Basic .NET

```
Dim conn as New SqlConnection("Initial Catalog=Northwind;" + _
                    "Server=(local);UID=sa;PWD=;")
```

LISTING 8.2   continued

```
Dim cmd as New SqlCommand("SELECT * FROM Employees", conn)

Dim reader as SqlDataReader

conn.Open()
reader = cmd.ExecuteReader()
```

LISTING 8.3   Getting an Instance of the `DataReader` in C#

```
SqlConnection conn = new SqlConnection("Initial Catalog=Northwind;" +
                                       "Server=(local);UID=sa;PWD=;");
SqlCommand cmd = new SqlCommand("SELECT * FROM Employees", conn);

SqlDataReader reader;

conn.Open();
reader = cmd.ExecuteReader();
```

In Listings 8.2 and 8.3, line 1 instantiates a new connection object. Line 3 creates a new object of type `SqlDataReader`. The connection is then opened and a new `SqlDataReader` object is created using the `ExecuteReader()` method.

This is significantly easier than retrieving a `DataSet`! Now that you know how to get a `DataReader`, it's time to see what the `DataReader` can do. In the next few sections, you'll see how to use the `DataReader` to step through database records and bind to Web controls.

Binding `DataReader` Results to a Web Control

The most common use for the `DataReader` is to bind it to Web controls, much in the same way as you'd bind a `DataSet`. Other than the fact that you've eliminated overhead by not creating a `DataSet`, binding to a `DataReader` is almost exactly the same as binding to a `DataSet`. The code in Listing 8.4 demonstrates how to bind the `DataReader`. When run, this Web form will appear identical to the one in Figure 8.1. Notice that in line 22, the `DataReader` object is passed directly to the `DataSource` of the `DataGrid` Web control.

LISTING 8.4   Data Binding the `DataReader` Object to a Web Control

```
<% @Page Language="VB" %>
<%@ Import Namespace="System.Data" %>
```

LISTING 8.4 continued

```
<%@ Import Namespace="System.Data.SqlClient" %>

<HTML>
<HEAD>
    <LINK rel="stylesheet" type="text/css" href="Main.css">
    <!-- End Style Sheet -->

    <script language="VB" runat="server" >
      Sub Page_Load(Source as Object, E as EventArgs)

        Dim conn as New SqlConnection("Initial Catalog=Northwind;" + _
                              "Server=(local);UID=sa;PWD=;")
        Dim cmd as New SqlCommand("SELECT * FROM Employees", conn)

        Dim reader as SqlDataReader

        conn.Open()
        reader = cmd.ExecuteReader()

        employees.DataSource = reader
        employees.DataBind()

        conn.Close()

      End Sub
    </script>

</HEAD>
<BODY>

<h1>Creating a DataReader</h1>
<hr>

<form runat="server" id=form1 name=form1>
    <asp:DataGrid id="employees" runat="server"></asp:DataGrid>
</form>
<hr>

</BODY>
</HTML>
```

Just as with the DataAdapter method of retrieving data, you should close your connection to the database as soon as you can. Because the DataReader requires an active connection to the database while it is data binding, you should close the connection to the database just after the data-binding

> statements. In addition, when you are done reading records from the
> DataReader, you should call the Close() method of the DataReader to save
> system resources.

Because the DataReader supports the IEnumerable interface, it can be bound directly to
the DataSource property of a Web control or any other control that supports data
binding.

Stepping Through Data with the DataReader

The DataReader offers more granular control of database records than just data binding,
however. By using the Read() method of the DataReader object, you can step through
each record of the resultset individually. This is akin to the old days of stepping through
each record in a recordset using ADO. This gives you the ability to process each record
with as much precision as you need.

Listing 8.5 demonstrates how to use a DataReader to pull back data and retrieve individ-
ual fields. This example uses some interesting DataReader methods, such as
GetOrdinal(), to facilitate the retrieval of the information. When run, the example in
Listing 8.5 (VB .NET) and Listing 8.6 (C#) will look like Figure 8.2.

LISTING 8.5   Retrieving Database Fields Using the DataReader in Visual Basic .NET

```
<% @Page Language="VB" %>
<%@ Import Namespace="System.Data" %>
<%@ Import Namespace="System.Data.SqlClient" %>

<HTML>
<HEAD>
    <LINK rel="stylesheet" type="text/css" href="Main.css">
    <!-- End Style Sheet -->

    <script language="VB" runat="server" >
      Sub Page_Load(Source as Object, E as EventArgs)

          Dim conn as SqlConnection
          conn = New SqlConnection("Initial Catalog=Northwind;" + _
                                   "Server=(local);UID=sa;PWD=;")
          Dim cmd as SqlCommand
```

LISTING 8.5 continued

```
cmd = New SqlCommand("SELECT EmployeeID, FirstName, " + _
                     "LastName, HireDate FROM Employees", conn)

Dim reader as SqlDataReader

conn.Open()
reader = cmd.ExecuteReader()

Dim strBuilder as StringBuilder = New StringBuilder()

Dim First_Name__Ordinal as Int32 = reader.GetOrdinal("FirstName")
Dim Last_Name__Ordinal as Int32 = reader.GetOrdinal("LastName")
Dim Hire_Date__Ordinal as Int32 = reader.GetOrdinal("HireDate")
Dim EmployeeID__Ordinal as Int32 = reader.GetOrdinal("EmployeeID")

while (reader.Read())
   strBuilder.Append( _
       reader.GetInt32(EmployeeID__Ordinal).ToString() + " " + _
       reader.GetString(First_Name__Ordinal) + " " + _
       reader.GetString(Last_Name__Ordinal) + " " + _
       reader.GetDateTime(Hire_Date__Ordinal).ToString() + _
       "<br>" )
end while


output.Text = strBuilder.ToString()

reader.Close()
conn.Close()

End Sub
</script>

</HEAD>
<BODY>

<h1>Stepping through records with the DataReader</h1>
<hr>

<form runat="server" id=form1 name=form1>
   <asp:Label id="output" runat="server"></asp:Label>
</form>
<hr>

</BODY>
</HTML>
```

LISTING 8.6   Retrieving Database Fields Using the `DataReader` in C#

```csharp
<% @Page Language="C#" Debug="true" %>
<%@ Import Namespace="System.Data" %>
<%@ Import Namespace="System.Data.SqlClient" %>

<HTML>
<HEAD>
    <LINK rel="stylesheet" type="text/css" href="Main.css">
    <!-- End Style Sheet -->

    <script language="C#" runat="server" >
      void Page_Load(Object Source, EventArgs E)
      {
         SqlConnection conn = new SqlConnection("Initial Catalog=Northwind;" +
                                       "Server=(local);UID=sa;PWD=;");
         SqlCommand cmd = new SqlCommand("SELECT EmployeeID, FirstName, " +
                                  "LastName, HireDate FROM Employees", conn);

         SqlDataReader reader;

         conn.Open();
         reader = cmd.ExecuteReader();

         StringBuilder strBuilder = new StringBuilder();

         int First_Name__Ordinal = reader.GetOrdinal("FirstName");
         int Last_Name__Ordinal = reader.GetOrdinal("LastName");
         int Hire_Date__Ordinal = reader.GetOrdinal("HireDate");
         int EmployeeID__Ordinal = reader.GetOrdinal("EmployeeID");

         while (reader.Read())
         {
            strBuilder.Append(
                    reader.GetInt32(EmployeeID__Ordinal).ToString() + " " +
                    reader.GetString(First_Name__Ordinal) + " " +
                    reader.GetString(Last_Name__Ordinal) + " " +
                    reader.GetDateTime(Hire_Date__Ordinal).ToString() +
                    "<br>" );
         }


         output.Text = strBuilder.ToString();

         reader.Close();
         conn.Close();

      }
    </script>

</HEAD>
```

LISTING 8.6   continued

```
<BODY>

<h1>Stepping through records with the DataReader</h1>
<hr>

<form runat="server" id=form1 name=form1>
    <asp:Label id="output" runat="server"></asp:Label>
</form>
<hr>

</BODY>
</HTML>
```

In the example in Listing 8.5, the standard ADO.NET objects are created and initialized with the database query in lines 12–23. Then, in line 24, a new `StringBuilder` object is created that will be used to build the SQL query string. Lines 26–29 use the `GetOrdinal()` method of the `DataReader` to locate the ordinal of the various fields in the resultset retrieved from the database. It's faster to retrieve the ordinal values once than to force ASP.NET to locate the values each time they're needed. Line 31 uses the `Read()` method to load the first record in the resultset and begin a loop. Lines 32–37 use the appropriate data retrieval methods to build a string to display in the Web form. Figure 8.2 shows how this example looks when loaded in a Web browser.

FIGURE 8.2

The appearance of the Web form in Listing 8.5 when loaded.

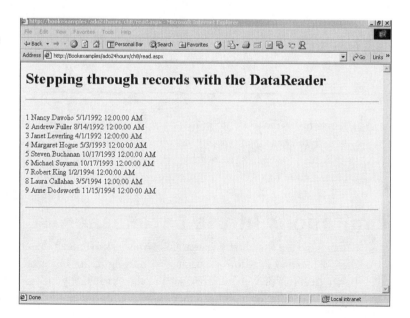

The `SqlDataReader` contains a number of methods for retrieving values from the fields in the data source. In fact, each different field data type has its own method for extracting data. The most common data retrieval functions for the `SqlDataReader` are listed in Table 8.1.

These methods all accept the integer ordinal of the location of the field within the record. Because the ordinal could change, or might be difficult to locate, the example in Listing 8.5 uses the `GetOrdinal()` method of the `DataReader` object. By passing the field name to the `GetOrdinal()` method, you can return its ordinal location within the array. By placing that value into a variable, you can simplify your code quite a bit.

TABLE 8.1 Data Retrieval Methods of the `DataReader` Object

Method	Field Type
GetBoolean()	Bool
GetByte()	Byte
GetChar()	Char
GetDateTime()	DateTime
GetDecimal()	Decimal
GetDouble()	Double
GetFloat()	Float
GetGuid()	Guid
GetInt16()	Int16
GetInt32()	Int32
GetInt64()	Int64
GetString()	String

The records in the example in Listing 8.5 are enumerated using a `WHILE` loop in conjunction with the `Read()` method of the `DataReader` object. The `Read()` method advances the `DataReader` to the next record and returns true or false, depending on whether or not there are more records.

Limitations of the `DataReader`

Though the `DataReader` is faster and carries less overhead than binding to a `DataSet`, there are some limitations associated with using it. For instance, if you plan to use the paging features of Web controls, such as the `DataGrid`, you'll need to handle the data paging yourself. For more information, please see Hour 12, "Formatting ASP.NET List

Controls." Additionally, it's not possible to sort, filter, or manipulate the data while using a DataReader, since it is read-only and forward-only.

Summary

In this hour, you've seen a comparison of the DataAdapter and DataReader objects. You saw how the DataReader object opens a fast, read-only, forward-only view of the data from your data source. The DataReader object's methods were explained in detail. Lastly, you saw some of the pitfalls associated with the DataReader.

Q&A

Q If I have to update data changed by the end user, is it better to use a DataReader and apply the changes myself, or should I use the DataAdapter and the associated hit in performance?

A This is a close call and depends very much on the requirements of your application. If you need to squeeze out every last bit of performance, you'll want to use the DataReader and perform manual updates. Otherwise, the benefits gained by using the DataAdapter object to automatically reconcile changes to the data will far outweigh the performance gains of the DataReader object.

Workshop

These quiz questions are designed to test your knowledge of the material covered in this chapter. The answers to the quiz questions can be found in Appendix A, "Answers to Quizzes."

Quiz

1. True or false: There is little overhead associated with the DataReader object.
2. What is the key difference between the DataReader and DataAdapter?

Exercise

Create either a Web form or Windows form that steps through a resultset of all customers in the Northwind database. Place the customers with last names beginning with A–M in one column and place the remaining N–Z in another.

HOUR 9

Binding Data to List Controls

The focus of this chapter will be on the requirements, from the ADO.NET perspective, for binding data to various controls such as ListControls and DataGrids. Data binding is necessary to link the Web or Windows form's UI controls to the data that is retrieved from a data source. When the control is activated or initiated, an underlying manager goes about initiating whatever was bound to the control (for example, a data retrieval using a SqlDataAdapter that fills a DataSet that is bound to a DataGrid). The whole binding mechanism does all of the heavy lifting of mapping the control to the data (like a DataSet, DataTable, and so on). What you will see is that if you know how to bind data to a ListBox control, you will also know how to bind data to a ComboBox control, and so on. The Web applications you develop will tend to use read-only list controls with rare update situations. The Windows Forms applications you develop, on the other hand, will be more DataSet-oriented and usually have much more update logic. The basic data binding approach is the same whether you are doing list controls for a Web server or Windows form.

In this hour, you will learn the following topics:

- What is meant by binding data to controls
- How to bind data to `TextBox` controls
- How to bind data to `ListBoxes` and `DataGrids`
- An example of a Master/Detail(parent/child) data binding requirement

Binding Data to Controls

List controls are components that provide certain UI capabilities such as a data list or data grid. There are two base classes for controls. These are `System.Windows.Forms.Control` (client-side Windows Forms controls) and `System.Web.UI.Control` (ASP.NET server controls). All controls in the .NET Framework class library derive directly or indirectly from these two classes.

Remember, these controls provide UI capabilities, but they do not populate data from a data source. This is done by binding data from a data source to a list control. In ADO.NET, you can bind not just to traditional data sources, but to almost any structure that contains data. You still have to create connections and data adapters to populate the data structures you choose to work with (datasets, arrays, and so on). Using data binding far outweighs having to code the retrieval and mapping of data to a control manually (the way we had to do in the olden days).

Simple Data Binding

When you only need to have a control display a single value, like that of a `TextBox` control, this limited usage is referred to as "simple data binding." Simple data binding is the ability to bind a control to a single data element (such as a value in a column in a `DataSet` table). There are tons of simple data bindings going on in applications—by far the most common data binding you will see.

Complex Data Binding

When you need to display and manipulate more than one data element at a time, like that in `ListBoxes` and `DataGrids`, this extended usage is referred to as "complex data binding." Complex data binding is the ability to bind a control to more than one data element and more than one record in a database.

`BindingContext` and `CurrencyManager` Objects

Any data source—whether it is an array, a collection, or a data table that you bind a control to—will have an associated `CurrencyManager` object that will keep track of the position and other bindings to that data source. So, you might have one CurrencyManager object keeping track of several text boxes because they are all bound to the same data table. This means that the data in each of the text boxes that are bound to the same data source will show the right data at the right time (the data that belongs together).

Of course, there will be multiple CurrencyManager objects if there are multiple data sources. Then there is a BindingContext object that sits on top of all the CurrencyManagers. It is this BindingContext object that manages all of the CurrencyManager objects for a Windows form that you are developing.

Data Binding Scenarios

Virtually every application you develop will be a candidate for using data binding if the applications must access some type of data source for information or have to manipulate data from a data source. Typical scenarios might be

1. Any report or printed document that must be generated from a data source and formatted into columns of lists.

2. Data entry forms that use text boxes, drop-down lists, and so on.

3. Parent and child data relationship of any kind such as you would find with customers and their orders, orders and their order details, parts and related accessories, and so on. These types of data fit nicely into DataGrid representations.

Class Hierarchies Relevant to Data Binding

Text box controls—Used to display, or accept as input, a single line of text. Can also support multilines.

- System.Windows.Forms.TextBox class

  - System.Windows.Forms.DataGridTextBox subclass

  - •System.Web.UI.WebControls.Textbox class

List controls—Enable you to display a list of items to the user that the user can select by clicking.

- System.Windows.Forms.ListControl class

  - System.Windows.Forms.ComboBox subclass

  - System.Windows.Forms.ListBox subclass

- System.Web.UI.WebControls.ListControls class
    - System.Web.UI.WebControls.CheckBoxList subclass
    - System.Web.UI.WebControls.DropDownList subclass
    - System.Web.UI.WebControls.ListBox subclass
    - System.Web.UI.WebControls.RadioButtonList subclass

DataGrid controls—Used to display data in a scrollable, tabular grid.

- System.Windows.Forms.DataGrid class
- System.Web.UI.WebControls.DataGrid class

Simple Data Binding in Windows Forms

Let's quickly step through an example that will display a Customer ID, Company Name, and Contact Name from the Customer table in the Northwind database supplied in Microsoft SQL Server. More specifically, you will be creating a few TextBox controls on a form and binding the Text property on these TextBox controls to the Customers data source. Then, you will create a button that will activate the data retrieval and display the data to the form. This is simple binding.

Create a New Project in VS .NET

1. Create a new project in VS .NET by choosing File, New, and then choosing the Project option.

2. When the New Project dialog box appears, choose Visual Basic Projects (or Visual C# Projects) and Windows Applications. Name this project "ADO.NET24hoursDB." This creates a default form for you to start from.

Add the Data Connection, Data Adapter, and DataSet

We will be accessing the Customers table in SQL Server's Northwind database. So, first we will need to create a data connection and a data adapter to Microsoft SQL Server.

1. From the Data tab of the Toolbox, drag a SQLDataAdapter object into your form as shown in Figure 9.1 (or OleDBDataAdapter if you want).

    This will automatically invoke the Data Adapter Configuration Wizard. Both the data connection and the data adapter can be fully configured here.

    a. The wizard starts with the Choose Your Data Connection dialog box. If you already have a connection defined in your project, it will be placed in the dialog box. Otherwise, choose to create a new connection and specify the appropriate connection information (test the connection as well).

FIGURE 9.1

Visual Studio .NET Form with Data Toolbox SqlDataAdapter *object selected.*

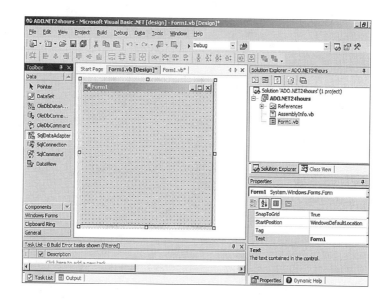

b. You will then have to decide to supply SQL statements, build a new stored procedure, or give the name of an existing stored procedure for the data access. In our example we will use the Use SQL Statements option.

c. You will be presented with a Generate the SQL Statements dialog box where you will simply type in a valid SQL statement, or you can use the Query Builder option to formulate the SQL query. For our example, just type in the following query:

```
SELECT * FROM Customers
```

d. The wizard will show you the tasks that it has done and indicate whether the SqlDataAdapter has been configured successfully.

2. After the SqlDataAdapter and DataConnection objects have been configured and added to the form, you must generate a DataSet and then add an instance of this DataSet to the form. We will be binding our TextBox properties to the columns in the DataSet.

a. Simply right-click on the SqlDataAdapter (SqlDataAdapter1) that is on your form and choose the Generate Dataset menu option as seen in Figure 9.2.

b. Now, just choose to create a *new* DataSet using the default name that it provides (DataSet1). Make sure you have checked the Customers table and checked the box for it to be added to the designer.

FIGURE 9.2

Generate a new
dataset for the form.

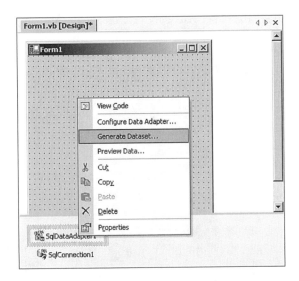

c. When the process finishes, a `DataSet` instance named `DataSet11` will be on
the form and a dataset schema will be in the Solutions Explorer (named
DataSet1.xsd).

Create Text Boxes, Labels, and Buttons

The next step is to complete the form example to include a few text boxes and a control
button. From the Windows Forms tab of the Toolbox, add the following (drag and drop
on the form):

- `Textbox`—With a name of `txtCustomerID` and `text` is blank.
- `Textbox`—With a name of `txtCompanyName` and `text` is blank.
- `Textbox`—With a name of `txtContactName` and `text` is blank.
- `Button`—With a name of `btnGetCustomer` and `text` of "Get Customer".

Go ahead and add labels in front of each text box so that it looks like the form in
Figure 9.3.

Add Code to Populate the `DataSet`

Now we are ready to complete the application by adding the code to fill the `DataSet`.

Just double-click on the Get Customer button to create a method for the `Click` event. You
will have to add code to make a call to the `DataSet`'s `Clear` method to clear the `DataSet`
out between iterations, and make a call to the data adapter's `Fill` method to get data
from the database (as you can see in Figure 9.4). The following code is added:

```
Customers1.Clear()
SqlDataAdapter1.Fill(Customers1)
```

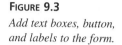

FIGURE 9.3

Add text boxes, button, and labels to the form.

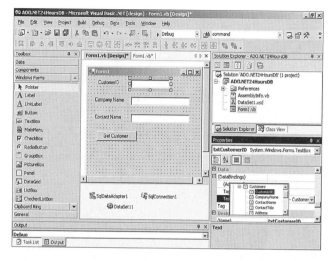

FIGURE 9.4

Adding code for the Button *method.*

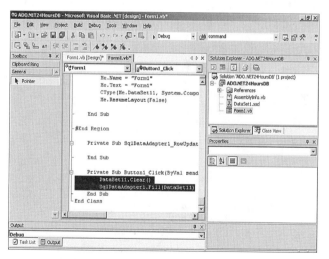

Bind the Text Boxes to the DataSet

Nothing is left to do other than bind (simple binding) the text boxes to the columns in the DataSet and run the application.

1. From the Forms Designer, select the txtCustomerID text box and press F4. This will position you to the properties window for this text box.

2. Expand the (DataBindings) node in the properties list and its text property.

3. Within the text property, expand DataSet1 and Customers nodes and select the CustomerID column from the list (look back at Figure 9.3 in the lower right corner to see the (DataBinding) property).

4. Now, from the Forms Designer, select the `txtCompanyName` text box and press F4.

5. Expand the `(DataBindings)` node in the properties list and its `text` property.

6. Within the `text` property, expand the `DataSet1` and `Customers` nodes and select the CompanyName column from the list.

7. Finally, from the Forms Designer, select the `txtContactName` text box and press F4.

8. Expand the `(DataBindings)` node in the properties list and its `text` property.

9. Within the `text` property, expand the `DataSet1` and `Customers` nodes and select the ContactName column from the list.

Test It!

That's it! Now just hit the F5 key and test your application by clicking on the Get Customer button. It will put the first customer's information (CustomerID, CompanyName, and ContactName) that it finds in the `DataSet` into the appropriate text boxes. In Figure 9.5, you can see the form displaying a customer's information successfully.

FIGURE 9.5

The Get Customer Forms application, showing simple binding.

The following snippet of code is from the forms1.vb program for this example and shows the explicit data binding for each text box. When you are using the Forms Designer, much of this code is generated for you (as you specify the data binding properties):

```
Me.txtCustomerID.DataBindings.Add(New System.Windows.Forms.Binding
("Text", Me.DataSet11, "Customers.CustomerID"))
Me.txtCompanyName.DataBindings.Add(New System.Windows.Forms.Binding
("Text", Me.DataSet11, "Customers.CompanyName"))
Me.txtContactName.DataBindings.Add(New System.Windows.Forms.Binding
("Text", Me.DataSet11, "Customers.ContactName"))
```

> **List Controls and** `DataGrid` **Controls**
>
> These are the key properties for list controls and `DataGrid` controls:
>
> - `DataSource`—An object that *must* implement the `Ilist` interface such as a `DataSet` or an array
>   - `IList` inherits from
>   - `Icollection`—A set of objects of similar type
>   - `Ienumerable`—Provides an enumerator, which allows you to traverse a collection one item at a time (via the `MoveNext()` method).
> - `DisplayMember/DataMember`—allows you to specify a table or elements within a table.
>
> **Note:** The classes and interfaces in the `System.Web.UI.WebControls` namespace are similar and equivalent.

Complex Data Binding in Windows Forms

In the next example, you will build a quick-and-dirty Windows Form that will display all customers in a bound `ListBox` and the customer's associated Orders in a bound `DataGrid`. A more complex `DataSet` will be needed that provides the relationship path to traverse from customers to orders using the primary key of Customers (CustomerID) to foreign key in Orders (CustomerID). You will have to do data bindings for both the `ListBox` control and the `DataGrid` control. This example is one of the classic data binding scenarios described earlier.

Create a New Project in VS .NET

1. Create a new project in VS .NET by choosing File, New, and then choosing the Project option. Or, you can just modify the "ADO.NET24hoursDB" that we just created for simple binding. If you choose to modify this one, delete all of the Forms objects, methods, and so on that we added so that you start from a clean slate. This will include deleting the `DataSet` schema that is shown in the Solution Explorer.

2. When the New Project dialog box appears, choose Visual Basic Projects (or Visual C# Projects) and Windows Applications. Name this project "ADO.NET24hoursE". This creates a default form for you to start from.

Add the Data Connection and Two Data Adapters

You will need to access both the Customers table and the Orders table, so two data adapters will be created, each populating different controls but using one database connection.

1. From the Data tab of the Toolbox, drag a `SQLDataAdapter` object into your form. This will automatically invoke the Data Adapter Configuration Wizard. Both the data connection and the data adapter can be fully configured here.

   a. The wizard starts with the Choose Your Data Connection dialog box. If you already have a connection defined in your project, it will be placed in the dialog box; otherwise, choose to create a new connection and specify the appropriate connection information (test the connection as well).

   b. Choose the Use SQL Statements option.

   c. You will be presented with a Generate the SQL Statements dialog box where you will simply type in a valid SQL statement, or you can use the Query Builder option to formulate the SQL query. For our example, just type in the following query:

   ```
   SELECT CustomerID, CompanyName FROM Customers
   ```

   d. Finally, the wizard will show you the tasks that it has done and indicate whether the `SqlDataAdapter` has been configured successfully (it should be named `SqlDataAdapter1` along with a `SqlConnection` name `SqlConnection1`.

2. Okay, we need one more data adapter for access to the Orders table. Drag another `SqlDataAdapter` object onto the form.

   a. Again, the wizard starts with the Choose Your Data Connection dialog box.

   b. Choose the Use SQL Statements option.

   c. You will be presented with a Generate the SQL Statements dialog box where you will type the following query:

   ```
   SELECT OrderID, CustomerID, OrderDate, ShipVia, Freight, ShipName
   FROM Orders
   ```

3. And lastly, the wizard will show you the tasks that it has done and indicate whether the `SqlDataAdapter` has been configured successfully (it should be named `SqlDataAdapter2`).

Generate a `DataSet`

Now that the `SqlDataAdapter` and `DataConnection` objects have been configured and added to the form, you must generate a `DataSet` and then add an instance of this `DataSet` to the form.

1. From the Data menu in Visual Studio, simply choose the Generate Dataset option. The resulting dialog box can be seen in Figure 9.6.

FIGURE 9.6

Generating a new dataset for the form.

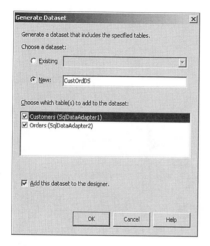

2. Now, just choose to create a new dataset using the name "CustOrdDS" (as also seen in Figure 9.6) that it provides (`DataSet1`). Make sure you have checked the Customers table, Orders table, and checked the Add Dataset to Designer box. Click OK.

3. When the process finishes, a `DataSet` instance named `CustOrdDS1` will be on the form and a dataset schema will be in the Solutions Explorer (named CustOrdDS.xsd).

4. You're not quite done yet. There must also be a way for the schema to know that there is a parent/child relationship between Customers and Orders. You do this by adding a `Relation` object onto the Orders table in the schema. First, double-click on the CustOrdDS.xsd schema file in the Solutions Explorer. This takes you immediately into the XML Schema editor. Figure 9.7 shows the two tables that are part of the CustOrdDS.xsd schema.

5. Next, drag a `Relation` object onto the Orders table (this is the child side of the parent/child relationship). You are immediately put into the Edit Relation dialog box.

6. Verify that the name of the `Relation` defaults to CustomersOrders, the Parent element is Customers, the Child element is Orders, and the Key Fields and Foreign

Key Fields both are CustomerID. Nothing else should be checked at this point.
Figure 9.8 shows the values in the Edit Relation dialog box. Click OK when you
are satisfied that all is correct.

FIGURE 9.7

XML Schema editor—
CustOrdDS.xsd
schema file.

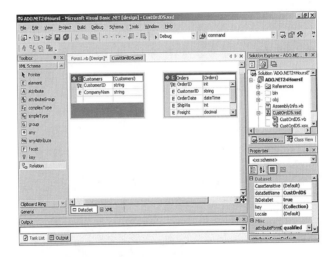

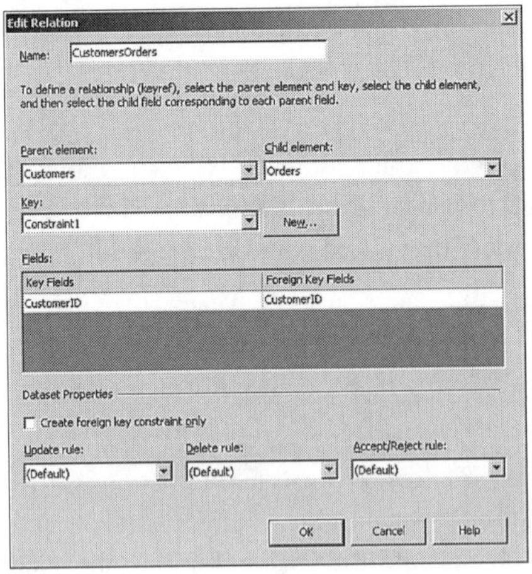

FIGURE 9.8

The Edit Relation dia-
log box for the
CustomersOrders rela-
tion.

7. The XML Schema editor should now show a one-to-many relationship line
   between the Customers and Orders table as seen in Figure 9.9. The following code
   is the content of the CustOrdDS.xsd XML Schema file that now reflects the new
   relationship:

```
<?xml version="1.0" standalone="yes" ?>
<xs:schema id="CustOrdDS" targetNamespace=
    "http://www.tempuri.org/CustOrdDS.xsd"
```

9

```
xmlns:mstns="http://www.tempuri.org/CustOrdDS.xsd" xmlns=
    "http://www.tempuri.org/CustOrdDS.xsd"
xmlns:xs="http://www.w3.org/2001/XMLSchema" xmlns:msdata=
    "urn:schemas-microsoft-com:xml-msdata"
attributeFormDefault="qualified" elementFormDefault="qualified">
  <xs:element name="CustOrdDS" msdata:IsDataSet="true">
    <xs:complexType>
    <xs:choice maxOccurs="unbounded">
    <xs:element name="Customers">
    <xs:complexType>
    <xs:sequence>
        <xs:element name="CustomerID" type="xs:string" />
        <xs:element name="CompanyName" type="xs:string" />
    </xs:sequence>
    </xs:complexType>
  </xs:element>
  <xs:element name="Orders">
    <xs:complexType>
    <xs:sequence>
     <xs:element name="OrderID" msdata:ReadOnly="true"
    msdata:AutoIncrement="true"
type="xs:int" />
    <xs:element name="CustomerID" type="xs:string" minOccurs="0" />
    <xs:element name="OrderDate" type="xs:dateTime" minOccurs="0" />
    <xs:element name="ShipVia" type="xs:int" minOccurs="0" />
    <xs:element name="Freight" type="xs:decimal" minOccurs="0" />
    <xs:element name="ShipName" type="xs:string" minOccurs="0" />
    </xs:sequence>
    </xs:complexType>
  </xs:element>
  </xs:choice>
  </xs:complexType>
<xs:unique name="Constraint1" msdata:PrimaryKey="true">
  <xs:selector xpath=".//mstns:Customers" />
  <xs:field xpath="mstns:CustomerID" />
</xs:unique>
<xs:unique name="Orders_Constraint1" msdata:ConstraintName="Constraint1"

msdata:PrimaryKey="true">
  <xs:selector xpath=".//mstns:Orders" />
  <xs:field xpath="mstns:OrderID" />
</xs:unique>
<xs:keyref name="CustomersOrders" refer="mstns:Constraint1">
  <xs:selector xpath=".//mstns:Orders" />
  <xs:field xpath="mstns:CustomerID" />
</xs:keyref>
</xs:element>
</xs :schema>
```

FIGURE 9.9

The XML Schema editor, showing the new relationship between Customers and Orders.

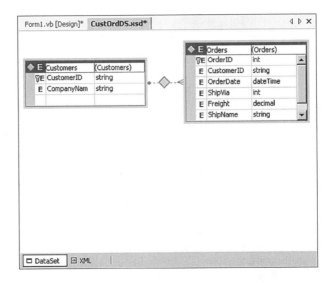

Adding the `ListBox` and `DataGrid` Controls

The next step is to add the `ListBox` control to display the Company Names and the `DataGrid` control to display the Order information associated with these companies.

1. First, let's create the `ListBox` to display all of the Company Names from the Customers table.

    a. Drag a `ListBox` object from the Windows Forms tab of the Toolbox onto the Form.

    b. Press F4 to go right to the properties of this `ListBox`.

    c. For the `DataSource` property, you will need to select the CustOrdDS1 data source.

    d. For the `DisplayMember` property, you will select Customers, expand this node, and select CustomerName. Figure 9.10 shows the complete `ListBox` property specifications for this example.

2. Now, let's create the `DataGrid` control to display all of the Orders that are associated with a particular Company that is selected. As the form is running, whenever you move from one CompanyName to another, the form's data binding framework queries the data relation object so it can provide the correct Orders (for that company).

    a. Drag a `DataGrid` object from the Windows Forms tab of the toolbox onto the Form.

    b. Press F4 to go right to the properties of this `DataGrid`.

FIGURE 9.10

ListBox *property specifications.*

c. For the `DataSource` property, you will need to select the CustOrdDS1 data source.

d. And, for the `DisplayMember` property, you will select and expand Customers, and then select CustomersOrders. This is actually the data relation (and the Orders table). So, we are binding to the data relation object! Figure 9.11 shows the `DataMember` property specifications.

3. Go ahead and add labels on the top of the `ListBox` and the `DataGrid` if you want. Figure 9.11 also shows this completed form with labels.

FIGURE 9.11

Completed ListBox, DataGrid, *and labels within VS .NET.*

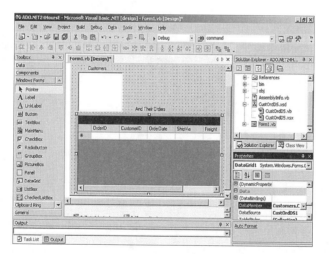

Properties or Methods Binding

For `ListBox` controls, you can bind the control to a `DataSet` class using the `DataSource` and `DisplayMember` properties as you have seen in our Windows Forms example:

```
Me.ListBox1.DataSource = Me.CustOrdDS1
Me.ListBox1.DisplayMember = "Customers.CompanyName"
```

Or, you can use the DataBinding method programmatically to achieve the same results.

```
Me.ListBox1.DataBindings.Add(New System.Windows.Forms.Binding
   ("SelectedItem", Me.CustOrdDS1, "Customers.CompanyName"))
```

For DataGrid controls, you bind the control to a DataSet class using the DataSource and DataMember properties:

```
Me.DataGrid1.DataMember = "Customers.CustomersOrders"
Me.DataGrid1.DataSource = Me.CustOrdDS1
```

Or, use the SetDataBinding method programmatically to achieve the same results:

```
Me.DataGrid1.SetDataBinding(CustOrdDS1,"Customers.CustomersOrders")
```

Add Code to Populate the DataSet

Now we are ready to complete the application by adding the code to fill the DataSet. We have determined that the best time to fill the DataSet is when the form is brought up (at form load time).

Just double-click on the form to create a handler for the form's Load event. You will need to clear the DataSet first, and then fill each data adapter that we defined.

```
CustOrdDS1.Clear()
SqlDataAdapter1.Fill(CustOrdDS1)
SqlDataAdapter2.Fill(CustOrdDS1)
```

Test It!

That's it! Now just hit the F5 key and test your application. When the form comes up, it should already display Company Names in the ListBox. When you select one of these (with orders), the DataGrid will display all related orders for that company.

In Figure 9.12, you can see the form displaying a valid customer's information successfully.

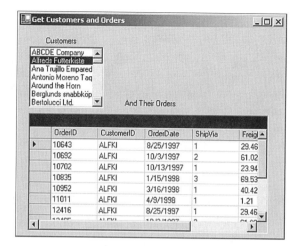

FIGURE 9.12

The Get Customer Forms application, showing complex DataGrid *binding.*

Summary

In this hour, you've been introduced to both simple data binding and complex data binding principles. Hopefully the brief discussion of different data binding scenarios has provided you with enough direction on what type to use based on the requirements that you are facing. Keep in mind that there are many subtleties between what you would code when developing Windows Forms control classes and what you would code for WEB.UI control classes. And, you have also seen the different properties and methods that must be used depending on whether you are doing TextBox controls, ListBox controls, or DataGrid controls. The good news is that they all follow nearly the same approach; just vary the method names or property names a bit. The two coding examples were chosen because they reflect typical coding problems that you will see over and over in the real world. There are many more things to discuss within the subject of data bindings related to some WEB.UI controls like Repeater classes and others, but they are a bit advanced for the one-hour lesson this chapter should provide.

Q&A

Q When using Visual Studio, must I use the properties approach to data binding for all my code?

A No; this chapter provided you with examples where either approach would work. All of the code contained in this chapter was also coded both ways.

Q Why don't you bind the Orders table in the `DataGrid` in the complex data binding example in this chapter?

A It was necessary to bind to the data relation in order to traverse the primary key to foreign key relationship within the `DataSet` (customer to orders). You want these to be coordinated in your display (the right orders for each customer). If you had bound to the Orders only, you would have a disconnected orders list. The code would run, but the results would be meaningless.

Workshop

These quiz questions are designed to test your knowledge of the material covered in this chapter. The answers to the quiz questions can be found in Appendix A, "Answers to Quizzes."

Quiz

1. What are the properties that are used to bind for list boxes and combo boxes?

    a. The `DataMember` and `DataSource` properties

    b. The `DataSet` and `DataSource` properties

    c. The `DisplayMember` and `DataSource` properties

2. True or false: A `CurrencyManager` object sits on top of all the `BindingContexts` for a form.

3. True or false: The Master/Detail single `DataSet` (with a relation) data-binding approach could have been coded using two separate bound `DataSets`.

4. For `TextBox` controls, which `(databinding)` property is set to bind a column to the control?

    a. `(databinding).(Advanced)`

    b. `(databinding).Tag`

    c. `(databinding).Text`

5. True or false: You can bind to both traditional data sources as well as almost any structure that contains data.

6. Windows Forms support binding data to:

    a. `DataSet` controls

    b. Array controls

    c. `ArrayLists` controls

Exercise

Go back to the complex data binding example and replace the data bindings properties code with explicit data binding methods code. You will have to undo the DataMember, DataSource, DisplayMember, and DataSource properties.

Remember, use the DataBinding method for ListBox controls and SetDataBinding method for DataGrid controls.

9

HOUR **10**

Working with XML

In recent years, XML has become one of the most well-known and important technologies for representing data. Regarded by many as the key to interoperability and flexibility across applications and platforms, XML is sure to become as prevalent as HTML some time in the not-so-distant future. It's fortunate, then, that XML support is embedded deeply into the Microsoft .NET Framework, and especially into ADO.NET.

In this hour, you will see how to:

- Read XML into a `DataSet`
- Write a `DataSet` to a file as XML
- Retrieve XML directly from SQL Server 2000

What Is XML?

Like HTML, XML is a markup language that can be used to represent complicated data in a hierarchical format. Because XML tags are user-defined, there's no limit to the kind of information you can embed into an XML document. Listing 10.1 shows a sample XML document.

LISTING 10.1   A Sample XML Document

```
<?xml version="1.0">
<customer type="web">
  <firstName>Ian</firstName>
  <lastName>Young</lastName>
  <address>555 Downtown Ln</address>
  <city>Cincinnati</city>
  <zip>45023</zip>
</customer>
```

In this case, the XML document in Listing 10.1 describes a customer of a fictitious Web site. The data and attributes were made up, yet if you were to run an XML parser on Listing 10.1, it would correctly identify each attribute and piece of data.

XML Parser

An *XML parser* is a program that reads an XML document and extracts the data and data descriptions from the XML data. An XML parser enables you to programmatically work with an XML document without having to manually parse the file.

XML is important because it lays the foundation for applications to share information, by providing an agreed-upon data transfer format.

Reading XML

Because XML is simply text, it can be read from a file, string, or stream using any data access method you're familiar with. To make life easier, the DataSet object can work with XML data directly, saving you the trouble of writing the code necessary to read from the XML text file or stream manually.

Creating a DataSet from an XML File

Internally, a DataSet is represented by XML. This enables a DataSet to accurately mirror data returned by any data source. In fact, this is one of the reasons the DataSet object in ADO.NET is so much more powerful than the recordset object in ADO 2.7. Not only does the DataSet store data, but it also stores data about the schema that was used to store the data. Because DataSets are essentially XML entities, moving data from a DataSet to XML and from XML into a DataSet is a painless and straightforward process.

The DataSet object has an overloaded method named ReadXml() that enables you to read XML data from a string, stream, or file. The example in Listing 10.2 demonstrates how to transfer the data and the data's schema from a file located in the root of the C drive.

LISTING 10.2   Creating a DataSet from an XML Document

```
<%@ Import Namespace="System.Data" %>

<HTML>
<HEAD>
    <LINK rel="stylesheet" type="text/css" href="Main.css">

    <script language="VB" runat="server" >
       Sub Page_Load(Source as Object, E as EventArgs)

           Dim dsCustomers as DataSet = new DataSet()
           dsCustomers.ReadXml("C:\Customers.xml", XmlReadMode.InferSchema)

           employees.DataSource = dsCustomers.Tables(0)
           employees.DataBind()

       End Sub
    </script>

</HEAD>
<BODY>

<h1>Creating a DataSet from an XML File</h1>
<hr>

<form runat="server" id=form1 name=form1>
    <asp:DataGrid id="employees" runat="server"></asp:DataGrid>
</form>
<hr>

</BODY>
</HTML>
```

In line 10 of Listing 10.2, a new DataSet is created. Then, in the next line, the ReadXml() method of the DataSet is used to load the data and schema present in an XML file on the hard disk. Lines 13–14 bind the DataSet to a DataGrid for display on the page. Incidentally, the Customers.xml file used to load the DataSet in Listing 10.2 was created using the WriteXml() method of the DataSet, covered in detail later in this hour in the section "Writing a DataSet to an XML File."

10

After the example in Listing 10.2 is run, you should see a screen much like the one in Figure 10.1. The customer data located in the XML document is loaded into the `DataSet` and then bound to a `DataGrid` Web control in order to display on a Web form.

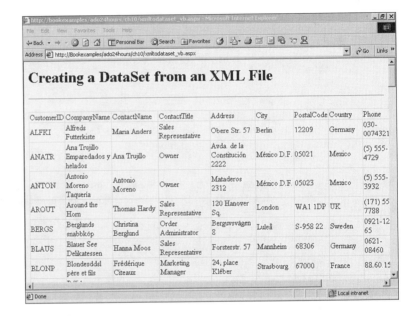

As mentioned, the `ReadXml()` method of the `DataSet` object performs the magic of locating and loading the XML file. It's a very robust method, with a few different ways to use it. Depending on what objects you pass `ReadXml()`, it will perform different actions:

- `ReadXml( XmlReader reader, XmlReadMode mode )`—By passing an `XmlReader` as the first argument, `ReadXml()` will read data from an `XmlReader` object. To learn more about the `XmlReader` object, see the last section of this hour.

- `ReadXml( Stream stream, XmlReadMode Mode )`—By passing a stream as the first argument, `ReadXml()` will read data from a stream.

- `ReadXml( String fileName, XmlReadMode Mode )`—As you saw in Listing 10.2, by passing a filename to `ReadXml()`, it will retrieve XML from a file.

Notice that the second argument of the `ReadXml()` method is of type `XmlReadMode`. This class exists in the `System.Data` namespace. The different values and explanations of those values can be found in Table 10.1. If the `XmlReadMode` argument is omitted from the `ReadXml()` method call, it automatically defaults to "Auto," as seen in the first entry in Table 10.1.

TABLE 10.1 `XmlReadMode` Options for Retrieving XML

Code	Symbol
Auto	ReadXml()automatically chooses `XmlReadMode` by examining the XML document.
ReadSchema	ReadXml()reads XML schema and loads both data and schema into `DataSet`.
IgnoreSchema	ReadXml()completely ignores XML schema and attempts to load data into `DataSet` using existing `DataSet` schema.
InferSchema	ReadXml()ignores explicit schema information in the XML using the structure of the XML data as the schema.
DiffGram	ReadXml()will read the XML as a `DiffGram`, appending and merging rows as needed.
Fragment	ReadXml()will read the document as partial XML and import the data matching the `DataSet` schema and ignore the rest.

Serialization

Serialization is defined as "a way of saving the state of an object." In Microsoft .NET, serialization usually refers to the conversion of an object's values into XML. Deserialization normally refers to the reverse process of building an object based on saved values in an XML document.

Serializing `DataSets` to XML

As mentioned in the preceding section, `DataSets` are represented internally by XML. Therefore, it is particularly easy to transfer a `DataSet` to an XML document and also to reverse the process.

Viewing the Contents of a `DataSet`

The example in Listing 10.3 uses the `GetXml()` method of the `DataSet` object to return the `DataSet`'s contents in XML form as a string. First, a table of information is retrieved from the Customers table in the Northwind database. Then it is placed into a label Web control in a Web form in order to display it.

LISTING 10.3 Viewing the Contents of a `DataSet`

```
<%@ Import Namespace="System.Data" %>
<%@ Import Namespace="System.Data.SqlClient" %>
```

LISTING **10.3** continued

```
<HTML>
<HEAD>
<script language="VB" runat="server" >
   Sub Page_Load(Source as Object, E as EventArgs)
      Dim conn as SqlConnection = new SqlConnection("Initial " + _
                   "Catalog=Northwind;Server=(local);UID=sa;PWD=;")
      Dim cmd as SqlCommand = new SqlCommand("SELECT * FROM Customers", conn)

      Dim adapt as SqlDataAdapter = new SqlDataAdapter(cmd)
      Dim dsCustomers as DataSet = new DataSet()

      conn.Open()
      adapt.Fill(dsCustomers, "Customers")
      conn.Close()

      lblOutput.Text = dsCustomers.GetXml()
   End Sub
</script>
</HEAD>

<body>
   <form runat="server">
      XML Output:<br>
      <asp:label id="lblOutput" runat="server"/>
   </form>
</body>

</html>
```

In the example in Listing 10.3, the XML representation of a `DataSet` is displayed on a Web form. To do this, lines 8–17 retrieve a `DataSet`, using methods you've already seen. Then, line 19 uses the `GetXml()` method of the `DataSet` object to create a new string containing the `DataSet`'s XML. This is then displayed in a label Web control in the Web form.

Writing a DataSet to an XML File

Though you could manually store the string returned from the `GetXml()` method in Listing 10.3 into a file, the `DataSet` object provides yet another method for working with XML: `WriteXml()`. Listing 10.4 fills a `DataSet` with customer information and then writes it to a file using this method.

LISTING 10.4 Serializing a `DataSet` to an XML File in Visual Basic .NET

```
<script language="VB" runat="server" >
   Sub Page_Load(Source as Object, E as EventArgs)
      Dim conn as SqlConnection = new SqlConnection("Initial " + _
                     "Catalog=Northwind;Server=(local);UID=sa;PWD=;")
      Dim cmd as SqlCommand = new SqlCommand("SELECT * FROM Customers", conn)

      Dim adapt as SqlDataAdapter = new SqlDataAdapter(cmd)
      Dim dsCustomers as DataSet = new DataSet()

      conn.Open()
      adapt.Fill(dsCustomers, "Customers")
      conn.Close()

      dsCustomers.WriteXml("c:\Customers.xml", XmlWriteMode.IgnoreSchema)
   End Sub
</script>
```

Much like the `ReadXml()` method of the `DataSet` object, the `WriteXml()` method uses the `XmlWriteMode` object to define exactly how the data is handled as it is placed in the file. Table 10.2 gives descriptions of the three modes.

TABLE 10.2 Three Different `XmlWriteModes`

Code	Symbol
IgnoreSchema	Writes the `DataSet` as XML without any additional schema information.
WriteSchema	Writes the `DataSet` as XML with additional schema information included as inline XSD schema.
DiffGram	Writes the `DataSet` as a `DiffGram`.

> **DiffGram**
>
> A `DiffGram` is an XML document that stores original and current values for the data in a `DataSet`. This is fairly important because, as you'll see in later hours, the `DataSet` can automatically apply changes back to the data source by keeping track of which values changed. By serializing a `DataSet` using this mode, you can ensure that those changes aren't lost.

Using `XmlReader`

In Hour 8, "Using the `DataReader` and `DataAdapter`," you learned how to use the `DataReader` object to handle a stream of data returned from Microsoft SQL Server. The

XmlReader object is a close cousin of the DataReader object and is used in much the same way, with XML. In the next few sections, you'll learn about some new features of Microsoft SQL Server 2000 and the XmlReader object.

Using XmlReader with SQL Server 2000

Microsoft SQL Server 2000 ships with numerous improvements and features not present in previous versions of SQL Server. One of my favorite new additions found in SQL Server 2000 is the ability to retrieve data in native XML format. If you add the keywords "FOR XML" to the end of your database query, the server will automatically send the results of your query in XML form. By being able to speak directly in XML, SQL Server 2000 is much better at cross-platform operations.

The example in Listing 10.5 demonstrates how to retrieve the results of a database query in XML form and then write that XML information to a file. However, as you've learned in this hour, that XML data could be bound to a Web control, saved to a file, or even transmitted to a remote client using Web Services.

There are three modes you can use to retrieve the XML information from SQL Server 2000:

- FOR XML AUTO—The query returns nested XML elements. The elements are organized based on the order of the fields and tables specified in your query.
- FOR XML EXPLICIT—The query enables you to shape the XML tree that is returned in detail. This is by far the most complex of the three modes.
- FOR XML RAW—The query returns XML elements surrounded by the "row" prefix. Table columns are represented as attributes.

LISTING 10.5   Retrieving XML Directly from a Microsoft SQL Server 2000 Database in C#

```
<%@ Import Namespace="System.Data" %>
<%@ Import Namespace="System.Data.SqlClient" %>

<HTML>
<HEAD>
    <LINK rel="stylesheet" type="text/css" href="Main.css">
    <!-- End Style Sheet -->

    <script language="C#" runat="server" >
      void Page_Load(Object Source, EventArgs E)
      {
          SqlConnection conn = new SqlConnection("Initial " +
                              "Catalog=Northwind;Server=(local);UID=sa;PWD=;");
```

LISTING 10.5   continued

```
        SqlCommand cmd = new SqlCommand("SELECT * FROM Customers " +
                                        "FOR XML AUTO", conn);

        DataSet dsCustomers = new DataSet();

        conn.Open();
        System.Xml.XmlReader xmlReader = cmd.ExecuteXmlReader();
        conn.Close();

        StringBuilder strBuilder = new StringBuilder();

        while( xmlReader.Read() )
        {
           while( xmlReader.MoveToNextAttribute() )
           {
               strBuilder.Append(xmlReader.ReadString() + "<br><br>");
           }
        }

        lblOutput.Text = strBuilder.ToString();
      }
    </script>
</HEAD>

<body>
    <form runat="server">
        XML Output:<br>
        <asp:label id="lblOutput" runat="server"/>
    </form>
</body>

</html>
```

10

The example in Listing 10.5 uses the FOR XML clause at the end of the database query to retrieve XML data instead of a standard resultset. The XML stream returned from SQL Server is placed into the XmlReader object using the ExecuteXmlReader() method of the Command object. Then, the XmlReader is used to return pieces of the XML data using its MoveToNextAttribute() and ReadString()methods.

Summary

In this hour, you've seen how to use ADO.NET to work with XML. You learned how the DataSet object easily serializes to XML and deserializes back, as well. You saw how to use ADO.NET to work with XML documents and Microsoft SQL Server 2000 and also how to use the XmlReader object.

Q&A

Q What else can I do with XML? Where can I learn more?

A XML is extremely versatile and the development world is only now cutting through the hype to realize solid benefits from using XML. The most up-to-date site on the status of XML along with technical specifications can be found at the World Wide Web consortium at `http://www.w3.org/XML/`. In addition, "XML for ASP.NET Developers" (Sams Publishing) is a great resource for learning to use XML using ASP.NET.

Workshop

These quiz questions are designed to test your knowledge of the material covered in this chapter. The answers to the quiz questions can be found in Appendix A, "Answers to Quizzes."

Quiz

1. Which method of the `DataSet` object can be used to view the `DataSet` in XML format?

2. What is a `DiffGram`?

Exercise

Create either a Web form or Windows form that loads only schema information from an XML file and display it on screen. Hint: An easy way to generate an XML file is to load a `DataSet` from a data source and then write it to disk.

Hour 11

Using the Built-In ASP.NET List Controls

ADO.NET, a revolutionary step forward in accessing and manipulating data, and its set of supporting display controls, called list controls, are both incredible. For those of you who ever used ADO in conjunction with ASP to dynamically create HTML, you will quickly realize the power and simplicity of list controls. However, don't worry if you've never used ADO; the concepts in this chapter do not require ADO as a prerequisite.

In Hour 9, you learned how to use data list controls with Windows forms in Visual Studio .NET. Throughout the book, you've seen data bound to the DataGrid control. In this hour, you'll see how to use the built-in ASP.NET list controls to display data retrieved from your data source. Specifically, in this hour you'll learn how to

- Use the Repeater Web control to display a simple menu
- Use the DataGrid to work with orders
- Use the DataList to work with products

Some General Notes About List Controls

List controls are standard Web controls that serve a single purpose: to display collections of data, such as the results of a database query, on a Windows form or Web form. In ASP, after filling a recordset (comparable to a `DataTable` object, roughly) with data, you would manually loop through each record in the resultset and build HTML dynamically. Although this is a very powerful and flexible way of building data-driven pages, often you ended up spending quite a bit of time tweaking the output. Rarely was the code reusable, so it had to be created by hand for each new page.

List controls solve these problems by wrapping up the aforementioned functionality into a single control that can be manipulated as one entity. This makes it much easier to work with and reuse list controls across various pages in your application.

Before looking at individual list controls, it makes sense to briefly discuss what they have in common:

1. List controls can bind to any object supporting the `IEnumerable` interface. For more information on interfaces, see the Coffee Break in this section.

2. Each list control is geared to display a particular type of data. `DataGrids` most easily display data that looks good when displayed horizontally in a table. A `DataList` best displays groupings of data either horizontally or vertically on the page. If you're confused, don't worry—each of these controls is covered in depth later in this chapter.

3. List controls can all be manipulated as a single entity server-side.

Interfaces? `IEnumerable`**?**

Typically in the Microsoft programming world, when you see a programming term with a capital "I" as the first character, it refers to an interface. A complete discussion of interfaces is beyond the scope of this book. However, list controls can be much more easily understood by knowing a few things about implementing interfaces.

An "interface" defines a set of properties and methods that an object must support in order to say it "implements" the interface. The `IEnumerable` interface defines the methods that an object must support in order for ASP.NET to generate the final HTML.

If you had built your own custom server control that contains data that you would like to use to bind directly to a list control, you would implement the `IEnumerable` interface. This amounts to implementing a single public method named GetEnumerator that returns an object that can iterate through the collection of items in your control.

When attempting to bind data, the list controls try to call the GetEnumerator method of the object they are attempting to bind. If successful, the list controls use the enumerator object returned to loop through all the items in the object getting the data. If the GetEnumerator method isn't present, an exception is returned.

Think of an interface as a set of rules an object must follow by implementing the interface. For more details on implementing IEnumerable or any of the thousands of other interfaces in the Microsoft .NET Framework or COM, please see the Microsoft documentation.

Working with the Repeater

The Repeater is the most basic of the built-in list control objects, yet offers a great deal of flexibility. To format the data it displays, the Repeater uses templates. Templates are blocks of HTML mixed with server logic that define how each row in the data collection will appear when sent to the client. Templates are defined within the body of the control instantiated within the Web form.

There are a number of different types of templates. The ItemTemplate, as seen in Listing 11.1, is responsible for formatting each record in the collection. The AlternatingItemTemplate lets you define a special appearance for every other item in the collection. A typical use of this would be to define a slightly different color for alternating items, to make the records displayed easier to read. The Repeater also supports templates that enable you to define a header and footer as well as a separator that is inserted between each item displayed.

Listing 11.1 shows how to use the Repeater list control to display a list of categories from the database. The server-side code should look familiar. ADO.NET calls a stored procedure named Categories_Get (seen in Listing 11.2), which returns a resultset containing the CategoryID and CategoryName for each item in the Categories table of the Northwind database. During data binding, the Repeater uses the ItemTemplate to format the data being returned from the database. In this case, the data returned is used to create a set of hyperlinks for the categories. Figure 11.1 shows how the example in Listing 11.1 appears when viewed in a Web browser.

Inside the ItemTemplate, notice that to insert fields from the resultset, you use the DataBinder.Eval() method. The template will insert the value of the field from the data source where this tag is placed.

The category links generated in Listing 11.1 reference a page named Products.aspx. Because this page does not exist in our application, the link will generate an error. However, it's rather easy to create a page that accepts the selected category ID and returns a list of products for that category.

LISTING 11.1   Generating a List of Categories Using the Repeater List Control

```
<% @Page Language="VB" %>
<%@ Import Namespace="System.Data" %>
<%@ Import Namespace="System.Data.SqlClient" %>

<HTML>
<HEAD>
    <LINK rel="stylesheet" type="text/css" href="Main.css">
    <!-- End Style Sheet -->

    <script language="VB" runat="server" >
        Sub Page_Load(Source as Object, E as EventArgs)

            LoadGridData( categories )

        End Sub

        Private Sub LoadGridData( _
                          myDataList as System.Web.UI.WebControls.Repeater )

            Dim conn as New SqlConnection("Initial Catalog=Northwind;" + _
                                     "Server=(local);UID=sa;PWD=;")
            Dim cmd as New SqlCommand("Exec Categories_Get ", conn)

            conn.Open()
            myDataList.DataSource = cmd.ExecuteReader()
            myDataList.DataBind()
            conn.Close()

        End Sub
    </script>

</HEAD>
<BODY>

<h1>Category Listing</h1>
<hr>

<form runat="server" id=form1 name=form1>
```

LISTING 11.1   continued

```
<asp:repeater id="categories" runat="server">
    <ItemTemplate>
        <a href='products.aspx?CategoryID=<%# DataBinder.Eval(Container.DataItem,
➥ "CategoryID") %>'>
            <%# DataBinder.Eval(Container.DataItem, "CategoryName") %>
        </a><br>
    </ItemTemplate>
</asp:repeater>

</form>
<hr>

</BODY>
</HTML>
```

As mentioned, Listing 11.1 generates a list of categories using the Repeater Web control. Lines 11–29 query the database, retreive a resultset, and then bind the data to the Repeater. In this example, the actual loading and binding of data has been moved into a separate method named LoadGridData(). This convention will be used more often for the remainder of the hours in this book, because many examples retrieve data from multiple sources, and this helps to make the code more readable. As you'll notice in line 24, we're using a stored procedure to generate the resultset. This resultset is no different than one you'd get by manually building the SELECT SQL query manually. For more information on using stored procedures, see Hour 15, "Working With Stored Procedures."

A Repeater is placed on the Web form in lines 40–47. Until now, you've only seen data displayed using a DataGrid or a label Web control. The Repeater is similar to the DataGrid, in that it is used to display and format data returned from the data source. Lines 4–46 define the ItemTemplate for the Repeater. The ItemTemplate contains the HTML that is generated for each row in the resultset returned from the data source. In this case, it builds a hyperlink for each category. The DataBinder.Eval() method is used to insert the value of the field from the resultset into the HTML output.

LISTING 11.2   The Stored Procedure Used to Return Data for the Example in Listing 11.1

```
CREATE PROCEDURE Categories_Get
AS

SELECT
    CategoryID,
```

LISTING 11.2   continued

```
        CategoryName
FROM
        Categories
```

Listing 11.2 contains the SQL query you can use to create the Categories_Get stored procedure used in Listing 11.1. You can think of this stored procedure as a method that exists in the database that is optimized for returning the data in this query. You can add the stored procedure in Listing 11.2 to your Northwind database by placing Listing 11.2 into the Query Analyzer and running the query against the Northwind database.

FIGURE 11.1

The appearance of the repeater control from Listing 11.1.

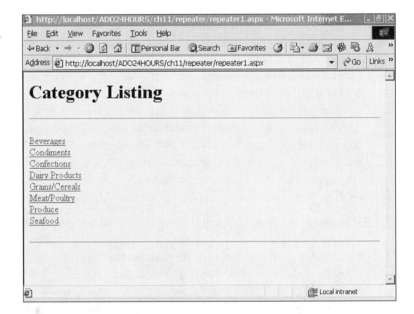

The Repeater is a generic list control best suited for generic uses. However, the DataGrid and the DataList are a bit more specialized, as you'll see in the next few sections.

Working with the **DataGrid**

The DataGrid Web control displays data in a grid, where each record is displayed horizontally. To see a DataGrid in action, see Figure 11.2 at the end of this section. The DataGrid generates an HTML table with the columns of data matching the columns of data returned from the data source.

> You've seen the DataGrid used quite a bit in this book thus far mainly because the DataGrid can automatically generate columns without configuration. This makes it invaluable when you'd like to display data quickly on a Web form for debug purposes or to display a database resultset without obscuring the data access code.

Because the DataGrid requires only a simple tag to display a potentially complicated DataTable, it's perfect for quick examples such as Listing 11.3. The example in Listing 11.3 returns a list of orders from the Northwind database and displays them on the page, as you can see in Figure 11.2.

LISTING 11.3   A Simple DataGrid Example

```
<% @Page Language="VB" %>
<%@ Import Namespace="System.Data" %>
<%@ Import Namespace="System.Data.SqlClient" %>

<HTML>
<HEAD>
    <LINK rel="stylesheet" type="text/css" href="Main.css">
    <!-- End Style Sheet -->

    <script language="VB" runat="server" >
        Sub Page_Load(Source as Object, E as EventArgs)

            LoadDataGrid(orders)

        End Sub

        Private Sub LoadDataGrid( _
                        myDataGrid as System.Web.UI.WebControls.DataGrid)

            Dim conn as New SqlConnection("Initial Catalog=Northwind;" + _
                                    "Server=(local);UID=sa;PWD=;")
            Dim cmd as New SqlCommand("SELECT OrderID, " + _
                                    "CustomerID, " + _
                                    "OrderDate, " + _
                                    "ShipName " + _
                                    "FROM Orders", conn)

            conn.Open()
            myDataGrid.DataSource = cmd.ExecuteReader()
            myDataGrid.DataBind()
            conn.Close()
```

LISTING 11.3   continued

```
        End Sub
    </script>

</HEAD>
<BODY>

<h1>A Simple DataGrid Example</h1>
<hr>

<form runat="server" id=form1 name=form1>
    <asp:DataGrid id="orders" runat="server"></asp:DataGrid>
</form>
<hr>

</BODY>
</HTML>
```

If you've been following along with the examples in this book thus far, Listing 11.3 should seem very familiar. The Page_Load() method in lines 11–15 passes the name of the DataGrid to the LoadDataGrid() method. The LoadDataGrid() method in lines 17–33 builds a SQL query, retrieves some orders from the Northwind database, and then binds them to the DataGrid Web control created on line 43, as you've seen many times before.

FIGURE 11.2

The appearance of the DataGrid *control from Listing 11.3.*

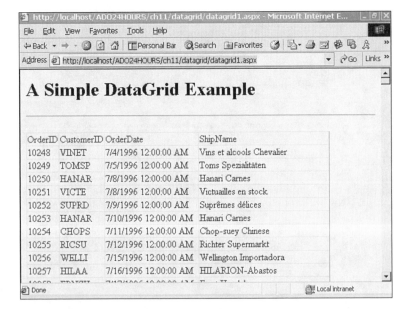

Though automatically generating columns is good for debugging/demonstration purposes, it is rarely useful for displaying data to a user in an application. Luckily, the
DataGrid has several options for formatting the appearance of individual columns.

You can define the appearance of individual columns in a DataGrid by using the
BoundColumn control. You can see an example of this in Listing 11.4. Note that most of
the code is the same as the example in Listing 11.3. However, the DataGrid tag on the
Web form itself has a new <columns> section. Within that section are several
BoundColumn controls. Intuitively enough, the HeaderText refers to the text displayed at
the top of that column. The DataField property refers to the name of the database field
being bound to that column.

A DataFormatString property can be specified for the column as well. This enables you
to format the appearance of the column data itself. The format codes here are the same
ones used by the String.Format() method. A complete listing of these codes can be
found in the Microsoft .NET Framework documentation. However, some very common
strings are "{0:d}", which formats the string as a date, and "{0:c}", which formats the
data as currency (using the user's localized monetary appearance).

LISTING 11.4 Showing a List of Database Orders Using the DataGrid

11

```
<% @Page Language="VB" %>
<%@ Import Namespace="System.Data" %>
<%@ Import Namespace="System.Data.SqlClient" %>

<HTML>
<HEAD>
    <LINK rel="stylesheet" type="text/css" href="Main.css">
    <!-- End Style Sheet -->

    <script language="VB" runat="server" >
        Sub Page_Load(Source as Object, E as EventArgs)

            LoadDataGrid(orders)

        End Sub

        Private Sub LoadDataGrid( _
                    myDataGrid as System.Web.UI.WebControls.DataGrid)

            Dim conn as New SqlConnection("Initial Catalog=Northwind;" + _
                                "Server=(local);UID=sa;PWD=;")
            Dim cmd as New SqlCommand("SELECT OrderID, " + _
                                "CustomerID, " + _
                                "OrderDate, " + _
                                "ShipName " + _
```

LISTING 11.4   continued

```
                                              "FROM Orders", conn)

            conn.Open()
            myDataGrid.DataSource = cmd.ExecuteReader()
            myDataGrid.DataBind()
            conn.Close()

        End Sub
    </script>

</HEAD>
<BODY>

<h1>Order Administration - List</h1>
<hr>

<form runat="server">
    <asp:DataGrid id="orders" width="90%"
                GridLines="Vertical" cellpadding="4" cellspacing="0"
                Font-Name="Verdana" Font-Size="8pt" ShowFooter="true"
                BorderColor="SaddleBrown" BackColor="PapayaWhip"
                AutoGenerateColumns="false" runat="server">
        <Columns>
            <asp:BoundColumn HeaderText="Order ID" DataField="OrderID" />
            <asp:BoundColumn HeaderText="Customer ID" DataField="CustomerID" />
            <asp:BoundColumn HeaderText="ShipTo Name" DataField="ShipName" />
            <asp:BoundColumn HeaderText="Order Date" DataField="OrderDate"
➡ DataFormatString="{0:d}" />
            <asp:HyperLinkColumn Text="Show Order Details"
                DataNavigateUrlField="OrderID"
                DataNavigateUrlFormatString="orderdetails.aspx?OrderID={0}" />
        </Columns>
    </asp:DataGrid>
</form>
<hr>

</BODY>
</HTML>
```

Notice the last of the bound columns in Listing 11.4. It's a special type of bound column called a HyperLinkColumn. As you might guess, this generates a column of hyperlinks. This is used primarily to wire up a list screen to a detail screen. For instance, Listing 11.4 displays a list of orders, as you can see from Figure 11.3. Each order can consist of several items purchased. Notice how each item in the HyperLinkColumn specifies a URL that links to a Web form called orderdetails.aspx, and passes the OrderID. This gives the next screen all the information it needs to display details for the order.

FIGURE **11.3**

The appearance of the DataGrid *control from Listing 11.3.*

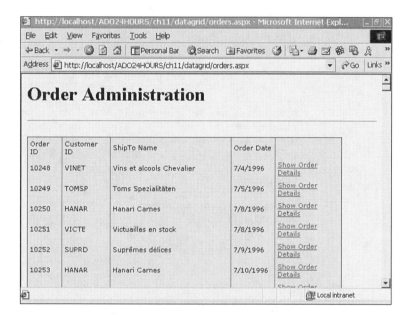

Listing 11.5 displays the code necessary to display the details of each order. At the beginning of the Page_Load event, the OrderID is accepted and then passed to a method that calls a stored procedure that returns all details for a particular OrderID. The stored procedure is provided for you in Listing 11.6.

LISTING 11.5   Showing Order Details Using the DataGrid Control

```
<% @Page Language="VB" %>
<%@ Import Namespace="System.Data" %>
<%@ Import Namespace="System.Data.SqlClient" %>

<HTML>
<HEAD>
    <LINK rel="stylesheet" type="text/css" href="Main.css">
    <!-- End Style Sheet -->

    <script language="VB" runat="server" >
        Sub Page_Load(Source as Object, E as EventArgs)
```

LISTING 11.5   continued

```
                'Get OrderID
                Dim OrderID As Integer = Int32.Parse(Request.Params("OrderID"))

                LoadGridData( OrderID, orderdetails )

        End Sub

        Private Sub LoadGridData( orderID as Int32, _
                            myDataGrid as System.Web.UI.WebControls.DataGrid )

            Dim conn as New SqlConnection("Initial Catalog=Northwind;" + _
                                    "Server=(local);UID=sa;PWD=;")
            Dim cmd as New SqlCommand("Exec Order_GetDetails " + _
                                    orderID.ToString(), conn)

            conn.Open()
            myDataGrid.DataSource = cmd.ExecuteReader()
            myDataGrid.DataBind()
            conn.Close()

        End Sub
    </script>

</HEAD>
<BODY>

<h1>Order Administration - Details</h1>
<hr>

<form runat="server">

    <asp:DataGrid id="orderdetails" width="90%" BorderColor="SaddleBrown"
                BackColor="PapayaWhip" GridLines="Vertical" cellpadding="4"
                cellspacing="0" Font-Name="Verdana" Font-Size="8pt"
                ShowFooter="true" AutoGenerateColumns="false"
                runat="server">
      <Columns>
        <asp:BoundColumn HeaderText="Order ID" DataField="OrderID" />
        <asp:BoundColumn HeaderText="Product Name" DataField="ProductName" />
        <asp:BoundColumn HeaderText="Unit Price" DataField="UnitPrice"
                DataFormatString="{0:c}" />
        <asp:BoundColumn HeaderText="Quantity" DataField="Quantity" />
        <asp:BoundColumn HeaderText="Discount Received" DataField="Discount" />
        </Columns>
    </asp:DataGrid>
```

LISTING 11.5   continued

```
</form>
<hr>

</BODY>
</HTML>
```

LISTING 11.6   Stored Procedure for Showing Order Details

```
CREATE PROCEDURE Order_GetDetails
(
    @OrderID int
)
AS

SELECT
    OrderID,
    Products.ProductName,
    [Order Details].UnitPrice,
    Quantity,
    Discount
FROM
    [Order Details]
    INNER JOIN Products on
    [Order Details].ProductID = Products.ProductID
WHERE
    OrderID = @OrderID
```

 The query in Listing 11.5 uses an INNER JOIN. As you recall from Hour 4, this is necessary because only the ProductID is stored in the Order Details table. To get the product name, we have to join the Products table and then access the ProductName field.

When run, the Web form in Listing 11.5 will look much like the one in Figure 11.4. Notice that the Order Details table stores each product ordered as a different record. Therefore, by using the stored procedure from Listing 11.6, we can easily create an itemized list of all products in a particular order.

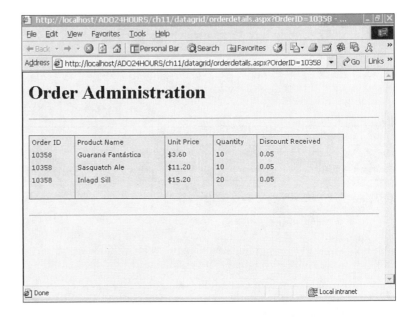

FIGURE **11.4**

Listing order details using the DataGrid *control from Listing 11.5.*

Working with the **DataList**

Much like the DataGrid, the DataList is geared toward displaying data in a particular format. Whereas the DataGrid is best at organizing data into horizontal rows in a table, the DataList is best at grouping data into chunks, as you can see in Figure 11.5. Notice how the information about each product is closely grouped in its own section. Though it can be used to display data horizontally, the DataList is primarily used to display a set of information grouped together.

Unlike the DataGrid, however, the DataList will not automatically generate a default appearance for your data. You must define a template, just as you did earlier for the repeater. To implement a screen like the one in Figure 11.5, you must define an ItemTemplate. In the ItemTemplate, you place the code necessary to display a single product. Then, for each product returned from the data source, an instance of the ItemTemplate is placed on the page.

An implementation of a product list screen is shown in Listing 11.6. Much like the other examples in this hour, product information is retrieved from the data source and then bound to the DataList control. The DataList control has an ItemTemplate defined that builds a separate HTML table for each record. When run, the Web form looks much like the one in Figure 11.6.

FIGURE 11.5

The IBuySpy Product List page.

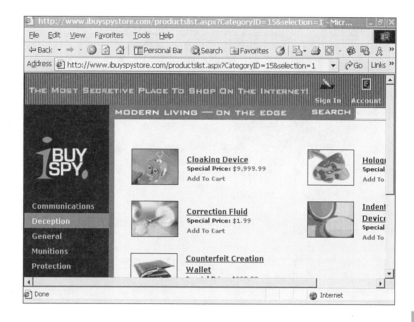

LISTING 11.6   Showing Order Details Using the DataGrid Control

```vb
<% @Page Language="VB" %>
<%@ Import Namespace="System.Data" %>
<%@ Import Namespace="System.Data.SqlClient" %>

<HTML>
<HEAD>
    <LINK rel="stylesheet" type="text/css" href="Main.css">
    <!-- End Style Sheet -->

    <script language="VB" runat="server" >
        Sub Page_Load(Source as Object, E as EventArgs)

            LoadGridData( products )

        End Sub

        Private Sub LoadGridData( _
                        myDataList as System.Web.UI.WebControls.DataList )

        Dim conn as New SqlConnection("Initial Catalog=Northwind;" + _
                                "Server=(local);UID=sa;PWD=;")
        Dim cmd as New SqlCommand("Exec Products_GetAll ", conn)
```

11

LISTING 11.6   continuedl

```
                conn.Open()
                myDataList.DataSource = cmd.ExecuteReader()
                myDataList.DataBind()
                conn.Close()

        End Sub
    </script>

</HEAD>
<BODY>

<h1>Product List</h1>
<hr>

<form runat="server" id=form1 name=form1>

<asp:DataList id="products" RepeatColumns="2" runat="server">
    <ItemTemplate>
        <table border="0" width="300">
          <tr>
              <td width="25">
                   
              </td>
              <td width="100" valign="middle" align="right">
                <a href='productdetails.aspx?productID=
➡<%# DataBinder.Eval(Container.DataItem, "ProductID") %>'>
                    <img src='/ADO24HOURS<%# DataBinder.Eval
➡ (Container.DataItem, "ImagePath") %>' width="72" height="72" border="0">
                </a>
              </td>
              <td width="200" valign="middle">
                <a href='ProductDetails.aspx?productID=
➡<%# trim(DataBinder.Eval(Container.DataItem, "ProductID")) %>'>
                    <%# DataBinder.Eval(Container.DataItem,
➡ "ProductName") %></a><br>
                <b>Price: </b>
                    <%# DataBinder.Eval(Container.DataItem,
➡"UnitPrice", "{0:c}") %>
                <b>Units In Stock: </b>
                    <%# DataBinder.Eval(Container.DataItem,
➡"UnitsInStock") %>
                <br>
                </a>
              </td>
          </tr>
        </table>
    </ItemTemplate>
</asp:DataList>
```

LISTING 11.6   continuedl

```
    </form>
    <hr>

    </BODY>
    </HTML>
```

FIGURE 11.6

The Product List page implemented in Listing 11.6.

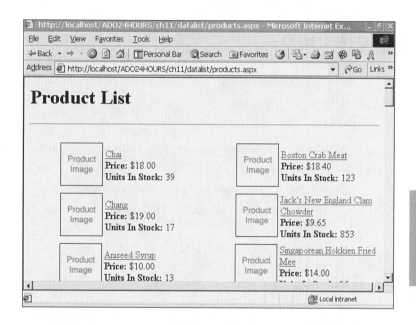

Note that the product hyperlinks generated in Listing 11.6 reference a page named pro-ductdetails.aspx, and pass to it the ProductID of the selected item. The code for that screen is not provided in this hour. However, it can be downloaded online at http://www.sams.com.

Summary

In this hour, you've seen quite a bit of information on list controls. You saw how to use the Repeater to display a set of product category hyperlinks. Then you saw how to use a DataGrid to work with order list and order detail screens. Then you saw how to use the DataList to display a list of products. However, this only scratches the surface of possi-ble uses for these controls. Indeed, there are many more ways to configure and use these controls than are provided here. In the next chapter, you'll see some of the various ways to format the appearances of these controls.

Q&A

Q Where can I find more information on using list controls?

A *Pure ASP.NET*, also from Sams Publishing, provides an excellent reference on list controls including much more information on using templates, bound columns, and formatting techniques.

Workshop

These quiz questions are designed to test your knowledge of the material covered in this chapter. The answers to the quiz questions can be found in Appendix A, "Answers to Quizzes."

Quiz

1. Which list control is primarily used to display content horizontally, in a single table?

2. Which list control is used to group information about a single entity?

3. True or false: List controls can bind to any object implementing the IEnumerable interface.

4. True or false: List controls are Web controls.

Exercise

Using the examples in this hour as a guide, create a Web form that displays a list of employees from the Employees table of the Northwind database. Make sure to include a column (or field if you choose to use a DataList) that will enable a user to link to more information about the selected employee.

Hour **12**

Formatting ASP.NET List Controls

In the preceding hour, you saw some of the numerous presentation techniques made possible through the use of list controls in ASP.NET. In this hour, you'll learn much more about formatting the appearance of list controls and their data. You'll see the basics of working with CSS (Cascading Style Sheets). You'll also learn some additional formatting techniques, including:

- Using CSS to control the appearance of list controls
- Additional formatting and layout options for the `Repeater`, `DataList`, and `DataGrid`
- Data paging with the `DataGrid`

A Quick Overview of CSS

A cascading style sheet (referred to as just a style sheet from now on) enables you to control formatting options for a limitless number of HTML elements in a single place. The style sheet exists as a file in your Web project that typically has a .css extension. In this file, you place formatting information for HTML tags, as well as any custom types (called classes) that you want. If you include this file into any of your existing Web forms, the Web forms will automatically pick up the formatting from the CSS file. These concepts are best grasped by looking at some examples. Consider the simple DataGrid example from the preceding hour shown again in Listing 12.1. There are only a few differences between this listing and the one in the preceding hour. First, inside the <head></head> tags, there is the following entry:

```
<LINK rel="stylesheet" type="text/css" href="ADO24HRS.css">
```

This includes an external style sheet into the existing Web form. By modifying the contents of the ADO24HRS.css file in the same directory, you can control the appearance of almost any element in the DataGrid example in Listing 12.1. Most of the examples in this book so far have used the Main.css style sheet. This hour uses a style sheet named ADO24HRS.css with some additional formatting.

LISTING 12.1 A Simple DataGrid Example

```
<% @Page Language="VB" %>
<%@ Import Namespace="System.Data" %>
<%@ Import Namespace="System.Data.SqlClient" %>

<HTML>
<HEAD>
    <LINK rel="stylesheet" type="text/css" href="ADO24HRS.css">
    <!-- End Style Sheet -->

    <script language="VB" runat="server" >
        Sub Page_Load(Source as Object, E as EventArgs)

            LoadDataGrid(orders)

        End Sub

        Private Sub LoadDataGrid( _
                        myDataGrid as System.Web.UI.WebControls.DataGrid)

            Dim conn as New SqlConnection("Initial Catalog=Northwind;" + _
                                "Server=(local);UID=sa;PWD=;")
            Dim cmd as New SqlCommand("SELECT OrderID, " + _
                                "CustomerID, " + _
                                "OrderDate, " + _
                                "ShipName " + _
                                "FROM Orders", conn)
```

LISTING 12.1   continued

```
            conn.Open()
            myDataGrid.DataSource = cmd.ExecuteReader()
            myDataGrid.DataBind()
            conn.Close()

        End Sub
    </script>

</HEAD>
<BODY>

<h1 class="MainHeader">A Simple DataGrid Example</h1>
<hr>

<form runat="server" id=form1 name=form1>
    <asp:DataGrid id="orders" runat="server"></asp:DataGrid>
</form>
<hr>

</BODY>
</HTML>
```

Before you make any modifications, take a look at the Web form as it currently exists. Figure 12.1 shows the appearance of the Web form with no modifications made through the style sheet. It's bland, which makes the data difficult to read. Luckily, we can easily spice things up a bit.

FIGURE 12.1

The default appearance of the Web form in Listing 12.1 before any CSS modifications are made.

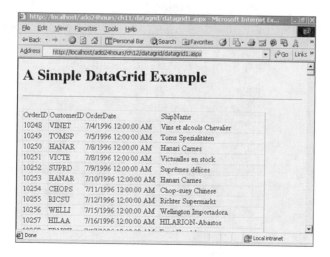

By just adding the lines in Listing 12.2 to the ADO24HRS.css file, you can drastically change the appearance of the Web form in Listing 12.1 without directly editing that file. Examining the code in Listing 12.2, you can see that we're modifying the appearance of the <TD> and <TABLE> HTML tags. Specifically, we're adding a border, changing the font, padding the content inside the table cells, and changing the background color of the table. Figure 12.2 shows the appearance of the example in Listing 12.1 with the new style sheet applied.

LISTING 12.2 A Simple Stylesheet

```
TD
{
    border-color: black;
    font-family: sans-serif;
    border-width: thin
    border-bottom: black;
    border-left-width: 0;
    border-right-width: 0;
    padding: 5px;
}

TABLE
{
    background-color: gold;
    border-color: black;
}
```

FIGURE 12.2

The appearance of the Web form in Listing 12.1 with a basic style sheet applied.

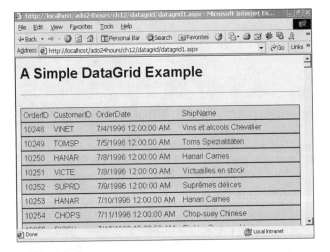

Certain style sheet properties are not supported by all browsers. For instance, version 4 of Netscape does not support the border-left and border-right properties used in Listing 12.2. A quick search of the World Wide Web turns up a number of reference guides to developing cross-platform style sheets. One particularly good reference is located at `http://www.webreview.com/style/index.shtml`.

Any Web form that includes this style sheet will have its tables modified in the same way, however. This might sound desirable, but because tables are an extremely popular HTML formatting device, you probably wouldn't want this appearance given to standard text tables. You could include multiple style sheets based on the type of page, but this introduces a lot of overhead and opportunity for error. The easiest solution is to use a CSS class.

Listing 12.3 contains a new class to add to the ADO24HRS.css file. It contains a class called `MainHeader` that is applied to the `H1` HTML tag only. By omitting the `H1.` before the `MainHeader` class name, you can apply the class to any HTML element that supports the properties.

LISTING 12.3 Adding a CSS Class

```
H1.MainHeader
{
    font-size: 30px;
    font-weight: bold;
    font-family: sans-serif;
    text-decoration: overline;
}
```

12

This changes the appearance of the header, as you can see in Figure 12.3.

This section on style sheets has covered the bare minimum necessary to explain how to use these concepts to format list controls. The sheer number of changes you can make to the user interface using style sheets is staggering. For a terrific list of tutorials, references, and online books on the subject of CSS, visit the official home page at `http://www.w3.org/Style/CSS/`.

By using the same style sheet for all of the pages in your application, you can control the appearance of all pages from a single location. This is an

extremely powerful tool that lets you customize the appearance of your
entire application by making changes in one place.

FIGURE **12.3**

*The appearance of the
header in Listing 12.1
with a CSS class
applied.*

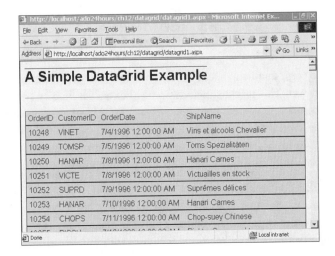

Formatting the Repeater

Most of the formatting that can be performed by the Repeater list control is done within
the various templates supported by the control. In other words, the formatted output of the
the Repeater is only as good as your skills in HTML, because you design and implement these templates yourself. Nonetheless, by using the provided template types along
with some smart CSS, you can achieve some good-looking results easily.

In the preceding hour, we took a look at formatting the Repeater output using the
ItemTemplate. As you recall, this enabled us to insert data fields returned from our data
source into some static HTML content. In addition to the ItemTemplate, the Repeater
also supports a HeaderTemplate, FooterTemplate, AlternatingItemTemplate, and a
SeparatorTemplate. Most of these template types are self-explanatory.

Listing 12.4 shows an example using all the provided templates. The
AlternatingItemTemplate applies a grey background to every other item bound. The
HeaderTemplate and FooterTemplate add headers and footers to the control, and the
SeparatorTemplate ensures that there is a new line after each item is bound. Figure 12.4
shows how the Repeater example in Listing 12.4 appears when run.

LISTING 12.4 Using the Various Repeater Templates

```
<% @Page Language="VB" %>
<%@ Import Namespace="System.Data" %>
<%@ Import Namespace="System.Data.SqlClient" %>

<HTML>
<HEAD>
    <LINK rel="stylesheet" type="text/css" href="Main.css">
    <!-- End Style Sheet -->

    <script language="VB" runat="server" >
        Sub Page_Load(Source as Object, E as EventArgs)

            LoadGridData( categories )

        End Sub

        Private Sub LoadGridData( _
                        myDataList as System.Web.UI.WebControls.Repeater )

            Dim conn as New SqlConnection("Initial Catalog=Northwind;" + _
                                    "Server=(local);UID=sa;PWD=;")
            Dim cmd as New SqlCommand("Exec Categories_Get ", conn)

            conn.Open()
            myDataList.DataSource = cmd.ExecuteReader()
            myDataList.DataBind()
            conn.Close()

        End Sub
    </script>

</HEAD>
<BODY>

<form runat="server">

<asp:repeater id="categories" runat="server">
    <HeaderTemplate>
        <h1>Product Categories!</h1>
    </HeaderTemplate>
    <ItemTemplate>
        <span>
        <a href='products.aspx?CategoryID=
➡<%# DataBinder.Eval(Container.DataItem, "CategoryID") %>'>
            <%# DataBinder.Eval(Container.DataItem, "CategoryName") %>
        </a>
        </span>
    </ItemTemplate>
</asp:repeater>
```

12

LISTING 12.4   continued

```
        <SeparatorTemplate>
            <br>
        </SeparatorTemplate>
        <AlternatingItemTemplate>
            <span style="background-color: #CCCCCC;">
            <a href='products.aspx?CategoryID=
➥<%# DataBinder.Eval(Container.DataItem, "CategoryID") %>'>
                <%# DataBinder.Eval(Container.DataItem, "CategoryName") %>
            </a>
            </span>
        </AlternatingItemTemplate>
        <FooterTemplate>
            <br><font size="-2">
            Copyright 2002 Your Company</font>
        </FooterTemplate>
    </asp:repeater>

    </form>
    <hr>

    </BODY>
    </HTML>
```

FIGURE 12.4

The appearance of the example in Listing 12.4.

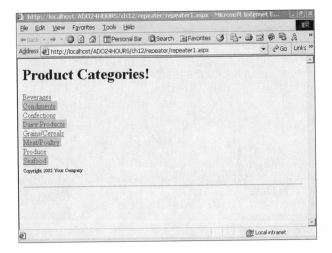

Formatting the DataList

Each of the list controls can be formatted easily using a set of built-in style properties. A complete list of these properties can be found in the documentation for the Microsoft .NET Framework. Additionally, you can see these properties by looking up the list control in the Microsoft Classbrowser sample application provided with the .NET Framework SDK (list controls are located in the `System.Web.UI.WebControls` namespace). However, Listing 12.5 shows a few of the properties available.

LISTING 12.5 Formatting the `DataList` Control

```
<% @Page Language="VB" %>
<%@ Import Namespace="System.Data" %>
<%@ Import Namespace="System.Data.SqlClient" %>

<HTML>
<HEAD>
    <LINK rel="stylesheet" type="text/css" href="Main.css">
    <!-- End Style Sheet -->

    <script language="VB" runat="server" >
        Sub Page_Load(Source as Object, E as EventArgs)

            LoadGridData( products )

        End Sub

        Private Sub LoadGridData( _
                        myDataList as System.Web.UI.WebControls.DataList )

            Dim conn as New SqlConnection("Initial Catalog=Northwind;" + _
                                "Server=(local);UID=sa;PWD=;")
            Dim cmd as New SqlCommand("Exec Products_GetAll ", conn)

            conn.Open()
            myDataList.DataSource = cmd.ExecuteReader()
            myDataList.DataBind()
            conn.Close()

        End Sub
    </script>

</HEAD>
<BODY>

<h1>Product List</h1>
<hr>

<form runat="server" id=form1 name=form1>

<asp:DataList id="products" RepeatColumns="3"
        AlternatingItemStyle-backcolor="#DDDDDD"
        runat="server">
    <ItemTemplate>
```

12

LISTING 12.5   continued

```
                <table border="0" width="300">
                 <tr>
                     <td width="25">
                          
                     </td>
                     <td width="72" valign="middle" align="right">
                       <a href='productdetails.aspx?productID=
➥<%# DataBinder.Eval(Container.DataItem, "ProductID") %>'>
                          <img src='/ADO24HOURS<%# DataBinder.Eval(
➥Container.DataItem, "ImagePath") %>' width="72" height="72" border="0">
                       </a>
                     </td>
                     <td width="150" valign="middle">
                       <a href='ProductDetails.aspx?productID=
➥<%# trim(DataBinder.Eval(Container.DataItem, "ProductID")) %>'>
                          <%# DataBinder.Eval(Container.DataItem,
➥"ProductName") %></a><br>
                       <b>Price: </b>
                          <%# DataBinder.Eval(Container.DataItem,
➥"UnitPrice", "{0:c}") %><br>
                       <b>Units In Stock: </b>
                          <%# DataBinder.Eval(Container.DataItem,
➥"UnitsInStock") %>
                       <br>
                       </a>
                     </td>
                  </tr>
               </table>
            </ItemTemplate>
      </asp:DataList>

   </form>
   <hr>

</BODY>
</HTML>
```

Generally speaking, the property names are built from the template name and then the actual property you are specifying. From Listing 12.5, you can see that AlternatingItemStyle-backcolor is set to grey. For every other row in the DataList, the background color will be set to grey, improving the readability of your content in many cases. This is a very useful way to make changes to alternate rows without having to specify an entirely new AlternatingItemTemplate that only differs from the ItemTemplate by the background color.

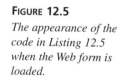

FIGURE 12.5

The appearance of the code in Listing 12.5 when the Web form is loaded.

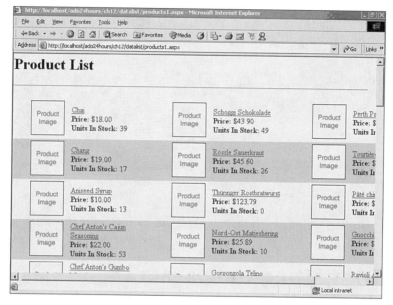

The DataList control also has a property called RepeatColumns. This value determines the number of columns the DataList will output to the page. As you can see in Figure 12.4, the number of RepeatColumns has been set to 3 in the code in Listing 12.5.

The DataList control provides all templates provided by the Repeater control plus one additional one: the SelectedItemTemplate. It's possible to set a particular look and feel for a selected item within the DataList. You can create a brand new template for the selected item, giving you complete control over its appearance, or you can just use the aforementioned style properties.

Only two additional changes are necessary to the code in Listing 12.5 to change the appearance of the selected item. Within the DataList control, specify the SelectedIndex property to whichever item should be selected (as determined by a user click or programmatically). Then, specify a style for the selected item. In the case in Figure 12.6, the background color has been set to blue as follows:

```
SelectedItemStyle-backcolor="cadetblue"
```

In Figure 12.4, you can see that this has changed the background of the Aniseed Syrup product listing.

12

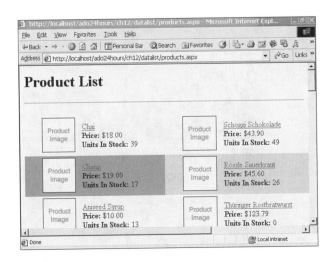

Formatting the DataGrid

The DataGrid control can be formatted using many of the techniques mentioned already in this hour. All of the built-in style properties discussed for the DataList are still accessible with the DataGrid with one addition: Because it is possible to edit content directly in the DataGrid, the DataGrid also has a style named EditItemStyle. You can use this to change the appearance of the row currently being modified by a user.

In addition to this type of formatting, you can also tell the DataGrid control to not generate columns automatically and work with the columns directly. This is normally a wise choice; though the automatically generated columns are handy, they will rarely, if ever, be a good choice for a production application. Simply set the AutoGenerateColumns property of the DataGrid to false to turn off automatic generation of columns.

After that is done, you'll need to set up the columns manually using any of the different column types present. Several different kinds of columns are available for different purposes. You saw the BoundColumn at the end of the preceding hour. This is primarily used to add a typical data column to the DataGrid.

However, there's also a TemplateColumn that provides complete control over the appearance of a column in the same way that the ItemTemplate provides complete customization for a DataList. Data fields are added to the HTML in the template through the use of the DataBinder.Eval() method, covered in the preceding hour. One additional column type you can use is the HyperLinkColumn, which enables you to create a hyperlink column, which is normally used to link to a detail screen for the record selected. There is also a ButtonColumn that is very similar to the HyperLinkColumn, except that it generates a button instead of a hyperlink, as you might have guessed.

In addition to these formatting methods, the `DataGrid` enables you to set up paging for large sources of data. Rather than display 300 items on the screen at once, overwhelming the user, you can display 20 at a time. The code in Listing 12.6 shows how to set up paging for the `DataGrid`.

> You can't use `DataGrid` paging when binding to a `DataReader` object. If you need to page through a set of records from a database, use the `DataAdapter` object instead.

LISTING 12.6   Paging with the `DataGrid`

```
<% @Page Language="VB" %>
<%@ Import Namespace="System.Data" %>
<%@ Import Namespace="System.Data.SqlClient" %>

<HTML>
<HEAD>
    <LINK rel="stylesheet" type="text/css" href="Main.css">
    <!-- End Style Sheet -->

    <script language="VB" runat="server" >
        Sub Page_Load(Source as Object, E as EventArgs)

            LoadDataGrid(orders)

        End Sub

        Private Sub LoadDataGrid( _
                        myDataGrid as System.Web.UI.WebControls.DataGrid)

            Dim conn as New SqlConnection("Initial Catalog=Northwind;" + _
                                    "Server=(local);UID=sa;PWD=;")
            Dim cmd as New SqlCommand("SELECT OrderID, " + _
                                    "CustomerID, " + _
                                    "OrderDate, " + _
                                    "ShipName " + _
                                    "FROM Orders", conn)

            Dim adapter as New SqlDataAdapter(cmd)
            dim dsOrders as New DataSet()

            adapter.Fill(dsOrders)

            conn.Open()
            myDataGrid.DataSource = dsOrders
```

12

LISTING 12.6   continued

```
                myDataGrid.DataBind()
                conn.Close()

            End Sub

            Private Sub GetPage(src as Object, e as DataGridPageChangedEventArgs)

                src.CurrentPageIndex = e.NewPageIndex
                LoadDataGrid(src)

            End Sub
        </script>

    </HEAD>
    <BODY>

    <h1>Paging With the DataGrid</h1>
    <hr>

    <form runat="server" id=form1 name=form1>
        <asp:DataGrid id="orders" width="90%"
                    BorderColor="SaddleBrown" BackColor="PapayaWhip"
                    GridLines="Vertical" cellpadding="4" cellspacing="0"
                    Font-Name="Verdana" Font-Size="8pt" ShowFooter="true"
                    AutoGenerateColumns="false"
                    AllowPaging="true"
                    PagerStyle-Mode="NextPrev"
                    PagerStyle-PrevPageText="::Previous Page"
                    PagerStyle-NextPageText="Next Page::"
                    PagerStyle-Visible="true"
                    PageSize="10"
                    OnPageIndexChanged="GetPage"
                    runat="server">
            <Columns>
                <asp:BoundColumn HeaderText="Order ID" DataField="OrderID" />
                <asp:BoundColumn HeaderText="Customer ID" DataField="CustomerID" />
                <asp:BoundColumn HeaderText="ShipTo Name" DataField="ShipName" />
                <asp:BoundColumn HeaderText="Order Date"
                        DataField="OrderDate" DataFormatString="{0:d}" />
                <asp:HyperLinkColumn Text="Show Order Details"
                        DataNavigateUrlField="OrderID"
                        DataNavigateUrlFormatString="orderdetails.aspx?OrderID={0}" />
            </Columns>
        </asp:DataGrid>
    </form>
    <hr>

    </BODY>
    </HTML>
```

As you can see in Listing 12.6, to set up paging for the DataGrid, you first need to specify AllowPaging="true". Then you can set a number of configurable properties controlling the appearance and location of the paging hyperlinks. Lastly, you must define a method to handle the work of grabbing the next page of data. In this example, a method named GetPage was created to handle this. The new page number is sent to the method through the DataGridPageChangedEventArgs object. Figure 12.7 shows the appearance of a DataGrid when in paging mode.

FIGURE 12.7

Paging through a DataTable with the DataGrid.

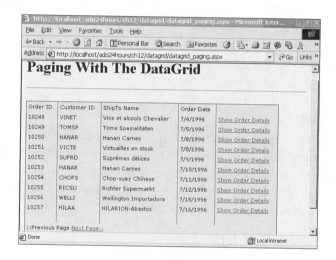

Summary

In this hour, you've seen several different ways of formatting the appearance of data and the built-in ASP.NET list controls, including the Repeater, DataList, and DataGrid controls. A short section was provided on how to use cascading style sheets. Then those style sheets were applied to each of the list controls. You then saw how to use some additional templates and columns for the DataList and DataGrid controls. Lastly, you saw how to page through the results of a database query automatically using the DataGrid.

Q&A

Q **Where can I find more information about style sheets?**

A The Cascading Style Sheet home page is located at http://www.w3.org/Style/CSS/. There, you'll find links to CSS tutorials, user communities, and software designed to make style sheet creation easier.

Workshop

These quiz questions are designed to test your knowledge of the material covered in this chapter. The answers to the quiz questions can be found in Appendix A, "Answers to Quizzes."

Quiz

1. True or false: You can use templates to format the content of the Repeater control.

2. Name the property of the DataList that is used to specify the number of columns generated.

3. True or false: You can use the Repeater object to automatically page through a large quantity of data.

Exercise

Create a Web form that creates the main page for a storefront of a fictitious company. Make sure that the page contains a category menu on the left side that can be used for navigation. You can utilize the examples in this chapter and the last as the basis for this exercise. If you like, feel free to create your own database structure as you see fit, or just use the schema provided for you in the Northwind database.

Hour **13**

Handling ADO.NET Errors

The Microsoft .NET Framework provides a rich set of approaches, mechanisms, and events to handle the myriad of runtime code error situations that are possible for any type of application you will be writing—whether it is Web or Windows forms. One significant addition for .NET involves being able to add error messages to each row of data in a DataSet. This enables you to zoom in on issues on a row-by-row basis. In addition, these row errors persist with the DataSet even when being transferred using XML or XML Web services. This chapter deals with the errors that directly relate to ADO.NET and identifies the typical error scenarios you need to be aware of along with presenting several basic principles of how to handle ADO.NET-related errors. We will not cover them all, just the ones you need to survive with.

In this hour, you will learn about the following topics:

- Formal error handling for ADO.NET
- The most common errors that you must deal with
- A sample application with many of the basics

Using Formal Error Handling (Ready, "Catch"!)

An exception occurs when an error condition is encountered. Whether you want to handle it depends on the requirements that you are trying to meet. Certain error conditions might be tolerable but others are not. Typical error conditions would be things like database connection denied or lost, unsuccessful update operations, or even divide-by-zero errors. .NET refers to these conditions as "exceptions" and provides several features to the developer to devise the appropriate response (or lack of response). The primary error-handling constructs we will be using are either the `Try/Catch/Finally` structure or the `On Error` construct. But, before discussing these constructs, let's look at an overall error-handling strategy.

Design Considerations

When designing an application, the developer needs to consider the possible exceptions and to design an overall strategy on how to handle them. If this analysis and design are postponed until the end of the development cycle, a steeper price will be paid in code reconstruction and testing delays. Among the issues that the developer needs to consider are which errors to report and how to report them to the different audiences of the application. For instance, a user needs to get feedback about whether an operation was successful, and if not successful, what the next step might be. If the condition is a serious error, a log might need to be generated for the system administrator that describes the issue along with where and when it happened so that the problem can be traced and then possibly fixed by other means. Errors such as database corruption and other data resource integrity issues are good candidates for formal error handling as well. If the application doesn't handle an exception, it bubbles up the stack until the application crashes and system messages are displayed to the user. In most scenarios, this is not a desirable outcome.

If an application handles every possible error scenario, the application is said to be "robust." However, being robust is just a relative term—most applications and operating systems are more or less robust. But, having too much error handling comes at a price in terms of extra code that needs to be written, tested, and later maintained.

The moral of the story is that the application developer should consider the general processing requirements from the beginning so that he or she can strike a balance between costs and benefits for the specific application. So, on the one hand, an Internet stock brokerage application needs to be extremely robust; it must account for all different types of error conditions, handle them nicely, and provide automatic recovery. An in-house small intranet application can probably get by with general error trapping and a request for the user to retry things, or even settle for a system-generated error (unhandled error).

How the Exception Mechanism Works

At runtime, applications use a stack of method calls. Normally, at the bottom of the stack is the `Main` method, which then calls other methods, which then call other methods. The system uses the program stack to keep track of where to return after a method finishes. A stack might look like this:

```
HowTo.ADONET24.Samples.TryCatch.Run()
    HowTo.ADONET24.Samples.TryCatch.Main()
```

When an error occurs, the system checks whether the code was executed within a `Try/Catch/Finally` structure or an `On Error` handler has been enabled. Control is changed to the appropriate place and the current stack location is part of the error information.

If an exception occurs, and the developer didn't include a `Try/Block/Finally` structure or enable an `On Error` handler, the system stops executing at the current stack level. The system then removes the current level from the stack, and transfers controls to the previous stack level, where the system continues to move back up the stack. The system repeats the process of stopping, removing, and transferring to the previous stack level, until a `Try/Catch/Finally` structure is found or until the last level is reached, at which time the system aborts execution. This is called crashing an application, and should be avoided. In other words, catch it somewhere before it hits the end user.

As an alternative to the `Try/Catch/Finally` structure, .NET provides an `On Error` handler structure as well. Either structure can be used for error handling.

The `Try/Catch/Finally` Structure

The .NET Common Language Runtime (or CLR) provides the `Try/Catch/Finally` structure from which areas of code that encounter exceptions can be handled. When an exception does occur to code that is part of the `Try` block, the .NET CLR stops the normal logic flow and transfers control from the `Try` block to the `Catch` block where the developer can take a course of action (such as notifying the user or some recovery action). Regardless of whether an exception occurred, the `Finally` block will be executed (if one is provided).

If errors occur that the developer has not handled, the VS .NET application simply provides its normal error messages to the user. This isn't always handled very gracefully, so we encourage you to handle the errors and provide the appropriate correction or recovery logic.

13

> **The** `Try/Catch/Finally` **Statement**
>
> The `Try` block contains the code where an error can occur. The `Catch` block contains the code to handle the error when it occurs. When an error does occur, program control is passed to the appropriate catch statement for evaluation. The `exception` argument is an instance of the `Exception` class and contains information about the error, the error number, and the error message. The `When` expression can be used when looking for a specific error and should evaluate to true. After the normal execution or after the `Catch` block, the system executes the `Finally` block, which is typically used for clean-up operations. The following pseudocode shows the structure of the `Try/Catch/Finally` block:
>
> ```
> Try
>    [ try statements ]
> [ Catch [ exception [ As type ] [When expression]
>    [ catch statements ]  ]
> [ Exit Try ]
> [ additional Catch blocks, if desired ... ]
> [ Finally
>    [ Finally statements ] ]
> End Try
> ```

The short piece of code in Listing 13.1 illustrates the `Try/Catch/Finally` error-handling structure. The program has two sections of code. The first section will use the `Try/Catch/Finally` structure and handle a simple error (divide by zero), and the second code section will create the same error but without any type of error-handling structure. Note the differences when you execute the code.

LISTING 13.1   The `Try/Catch/Finally` Structure (13TryCatch.vb)

```
Imports System
namespace HowTo.ADONET24.Samples
public class TryCatch
  public shared sub Main()
    Dim myTryCatch as TryCatch
    myTryCatch = new TryCatch()
    myTryCatch.Run()
  end sub
  public sub Run()
    Dim a As Integer = 100
    Dim b As Integer = 0
    try
      Console.WriteLine("*** TRY BLOCK - WE WILL DO A DIVISION BY ZERO ***")
      a /= b     ' Divide by zero... arithmetic error
    Catch e As Exception When b = 0
      Console.WriteLine("*** CATCH BLOCK - ERROR - WE
        WILL HANDLE THIS OURSELVES ***")
```

LISTING 13.1   continued

```
    Console.WriteLine(e.ToString())
  Finally
    Console.WriteLine("*** FINALLY BLOCK - ALWAYS EXECUTED ***")
  end try
  Console.WriteLine()
  Console.WriteLine("*** NOW, DO A DIVISION BY ZERO
    AGAIN WITHOUT HANDLING IT ***")
  a /= b    ' Divide by zero... arithmetic error
  end sub
end class
```

Let's compile and execute this to show the logic flow of this `Try/Catch/Finally` structure as follows:

```
C:\ADOSAMPLES>  vbc.exe 13TryCatch.vb  /r:System.dll
```

You should see the following .NET VB compiler messages:

```
Microsoft (R) Visual Basic .NET Compiler version 7.00.9447
for Microsoft (R) .NET Framework version 1.00.3617
Copyright (C) Microsoft Corporation 1987-2001. All rights reserved.
```

This message is followed by the DOS command prompt again (if it is a successful compile). Otherwise, you will be getting compile errors of one kind or another. Now, to execute, just specify the sample name at the DOS command prompt and press Enter.

```
C:\ADOSAMPLES> 13TryCatch.exe <press enter>
*** TRY BLOCK - WE WILL DO A DIVISION BY ZERO ***
*** CATCH BLOCK - ERROR - WE WILL HANDLE THIS OURSELVES ***
System.OverflowException: Arithmetic operation resulted in an overflow.
   at HowTo.ADONET24.Samples.TryCatch.Run()
*** FINALLY BLOCK - ALWAYS EXECUTED ***
*** NOW, DO A DIVISION BY ZERO AGAIN WITHOUT HANDLING IT ***
Unhandled Exception: System.OverflowException: Arithmetic operation resulted in
an overflow.
   at HowTo.ADONET24.Samples.TryCatch.Run()
   at HowTo.ADONET24.Samples.TryCatch.Main()
```

13

The `On Error` Construct

As an alternative to `Try/Catch/Finally`, you can use the `On Error` construct. This
approach enables an error-handling routine and specifies the location of the routine
within a procedure. The `On Error` routine takes the following form:

```
On Error { GoTo [ line | 0 | -1 ] | Resume Next }
```

You first have to enable the On Error handler before it can be utilized. The GoTo provides the branch to an enabled handler. The Resume Next directs the control of flow to go to the statement immediately following the statement where the error occurred, and execution continues from that point. The code example in Listing 13.2 illustrates the On Error construct.

LISTING 13.2   The On Error Construct (13OnError.vb)

```
Imports System
Imports Microsoft.VisualBasic
namespace HowTo.ADONET24.Samples
public class OnErrorT
  public shared sub Main()
    Dim myOnErrorT as OnErrorT
    myOnErrorT = new OnErrorT()
    myOnErrorT.Run()
  end sub
  public sub Run()
    Dim a As Integer = 100
    Dim b As Integer = 0
    Console.WriteLine(">>> Enable the error handler <<<")
    On Error Goto EHandler
    Err.Clear
    Console.WriteLine("*** WE WILL DO A DIVISION BY ZERO ***")
    a /= b     ' Divide by zero... arithmetic error
    Console.WriteLine("*** Recovered from error, ending ***")
    Exit Sub
    EHandler:
            Console.WriteLine("     *** ERROR HANDLER ***")
            Select Case Err.Number
              Case 6
                 Console.Writeline("     *** you have divided by zero ***")
              Case Else
                 Console.Writeline("     *** other error encountered ***")
            End Select
            Resume Next
  end sub
end class
end namespace
```

Let's compile and execute this one as well to show the logic flow of the On Error construct:

```
C:\ADOSAMPLES>  vbc.exe 13OnError.vb  /r:System.dll
```

This is followed by the DOS command prompt again (if it is a successful compile). Otherwise, you will be getting compile errors of one kind or another. Now, to execute, just specify the sample name at the DOS command prompt and press Enter.

```
C:\ADOSAMPLES> 13OnError.exe <press enter>
>>> Enable the error handler <<<
*** WE WILL DO A DIVISION BY ZERO ***
    *** ERROR HANDLER ***
    *** you have divided by zero ***
*** Recovered from error, ending ***
```

Throw It If You Know It

You can also utilize the Throw statement in either Try/Catch/Finally or On Error constructs. The Throw statement raises an exception that is represented by an instance of a type derived from the System.Exception class.

Here's a Throw statement with the On Error construct:

```
On Error Goto Ehandler
Throw New DivideByZeroException()
Ehandler:
    If (typeof Err.GetException() Is DivideByZeroException) Then
        Console.writeline("using throw exception setting")
    End If
```

Or, with the Try/Catch/Finally construct:

```
Try
   a /= b      ' Divide by zero... arithmetic error
Catch e As Exception When b = 0
   Throw New DivideByZeroException()
```

Typical Errors to Handle

When using the ADO.NET capabilities, much of what you will encounter centers on getting to data sources, pulling data out of data sources and into datasets, manipulation of the data within your datasets, and pushing that data back out to the data sources. The errors that you will see the most can be categorized as:

- Connection errors—Failure to connect, stay connected, disconnect, or other connection-related failures

- Data retrieval errors—Failure to get data, fill errors, and so on

- Dataset manipulation errors—Update, delete, or insert issues in your cached dataset

- Data source manipulation errors—Failures of deletes, inserts, or updates such as optimistic concurrency violations or primary key constraint violations, and so on

13

We will now build up a quick Windows Forms application that will use a
Try/Catch/Finally structure as part of its data refresh operation to handle errors when
connecting to the data source (in this case, the SQL Server Northwind database).

1. Create a new project in VS .NET by choosing File, New, and then choosing the
   Project option.

2. When the New Project dialog box appears, choose Visual Basic Projects (or Visual
   C# Projects) and Windows Applications. Name this project ADO.NET24hoursERROR.
   This creates a default form for you to start from.

3. You will need to access the Customers table. From the Data tab of the Toolbox,
   drag a SQLDataAdapter object into your form. This will automatically invoke the
   Data Adapter Configuration Wizard. Both the data connection and the data adapter
   can be fully configured here.

   a. The wizard starts with the Choose Your Data Connection dialog box. If you
      already have a connection defined in your project, it will be placed in the
      dialog box; otherwise, choose to create a new connection and specify the
      appropriate connection information (test the connection as well).

   b. Choose the Use SQL Statements option.

   c. You will be presented with a Generate the SQL Statements dialog box where
      you will simply type in a valid SQL statement, or you can use the Query
      Builder option to formulate the SQL query. For this example, just type in the
      following query:

      ```
      SELECT CustomerID, CompanyName, ContactName, ContactTitle, phone
      FROM Customers
      ```

   d. Last, the wizard will show you the tasks that it has done and indicate whether
      the SqlDataAdapter has been configured successfully (it should be named
      SqlDataAdapter1 along with a SqlConnection named SqlConnection1).

4. Now that the SqlDataAdapter and DataConnection objects have been configured
   and added to the form, you must generate a dataset and then add an instance of this
   dataset to the form.

   a. From the Data menu in Visual Studio, simply choose the Generate Dataset
      option. Figure 13.1 shows this option.

   b. Now, just choose to create a new dataset using the name CustomerDS. Make
      sure you have checked the Customers table and have indicated that the
      dataset is to be added to the Designer. Click OK.

   c. When this process finishes, a DataSet instance named CustomerDS1 will be
      on the form and a DataSet schema will be in the Solutions Explorer (named
      CustomerDS.xsd).

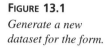

FIGURE 13.1

Generate a new dataset for the form.

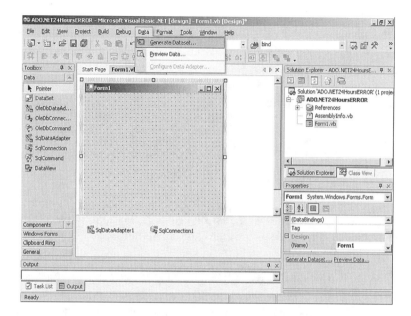

5. The next step is to add the `DataGrid` control to display the Customer information.

   a. Drag a `DataGrid` object from the Windows Forms tab of the Toolbox onto the form.

   b. Press F4 to go right to the properties of this `DataGrid`.

   c. For the `DataSource` property, you will need to select the `CustomerDS1` data source.

   c. And, for the `DisplayMember` property, you will select Customers.

   d. Go ahead and add a label to the top of the `DataGrid` entitled "Customer Inquiry". And change the form name (text property) if you want.

6. Now we are ready to complete the application by adding the code to fill the `DataSet` and refresh the data with a button. We have determined that the best time to fill the dataset is when the form is brought up (at form load time).

   a. Just double-click on the form to create a handler for the form's `Load` event. You will need to clear the dataset first, and then fill the dataset using the `DataAdapter` that we defined.

   ```
   Me.CustOrdDS1.Clear()
   Me.SqlDataAdapter1.Fill(Me.CustomerDS1)
   ```

   b. Next we add a button so that we can refresh the dataset's data anytime we want to. Start by dragging a `Button` object from the Windows Forms Toolbox onto the form.

   c. Press F4 to take you directly to the properties of this button. Change the name of the button to `btnRefresh` and the text of the button to `Refresh`.

13

d. Now, double-click the Button object on the form so that you can add the Try/Catch structure logic. Then you add the following to first clear the dataset, refill the dataset (which used the SqlDataAdapter and the SqlConnection), and make sure that no connection error has occurred. If an error has occurred, display a message box to the user:

```
Try
        Me.CustomerDS1.Clear()
        Me.SqlDataAdapter1.Fill(Me.CustomerDS1)
    Catch ee As System.Data.SqlClient.SqlException
        MessageBox.Show("Refresh Failed. Check With DBA.")
    End Try
```

Test It!

That's it. Now just hit the F5 key and test your application. When the form comes up, it should already display all the Customer information in the DataGrid. Now, do the following:

1. Click on the Refresh button to make sure it works properly.
2. Bring up the Microsoft SQL Server Service Manager and "pause" the SQL Server you are using (assuming that no one else is using it right now). What you are doing is creating an error situation for the Try/Catch in the Refresh button logic.
3. Now, click on the Refresh button again. You should see the message box appear indicating that an exception has occurred.

In Figure 13.2 you can see the original form displaying a valid DataGrid of Customer information, the SQL Server Service Manager and the Pause option, and the form encountering the "Refresh Failed" error that we coded for.

FIGURE 13.2

Customer Inquiry form successful execution, SQL Server Service Manager, and Customer Inquiry form with Refresh Failed exception displayed.

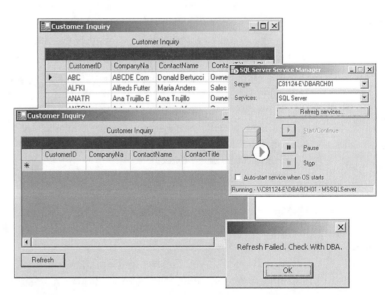

Now, let's change the `Try/Catch` logic to provide the exact error message number and description that is being returned by the `SqlDataAdapter`. From the Windows Form designer, double-click on the Refresh button object we built, and change the logic as follows:

```
Try
        Me.CustomerDS1.Clear()
        Me.SqlDataAdapter1.Fill(Me.CustomerDS1)
    Catch ee As System.Data.SqlClient.SqlException
        Dim j As Integer
        For j = 0 To ee.Errors.Count - 1
            MessageBox.Show("Error # " & j & ControlChars.Cr & _
                            "Error: " & ee.Errors(j).ToString() & 
                            ControlChars.Cr)
        Next j
    End Try
```

Now, once again, hit F5 and test your application as follows:

1. Click on the Refresh button to make sure it works properly.

2. Bring up the Microsoft SQL Server Service Manager and "pause" the SQL Server you are using (assuming that no one else is using it right now). What you are doing is creating an error situation for the `Try/Catch` in the Refresh button logic.

3. Now, click on the Refresh button again. You should now see the message box appear indicating that an exception has occurred.

In Figure 13.3 you can see the original form displaying a valid `DataGrid` of Customer information and the form encountering the Refresh error. This time, we see the full SQL error information in the message box.

FIGURE 13.3

Customer Inquiry form successful execution and Customer Inquiry form with SQL error message displayed.

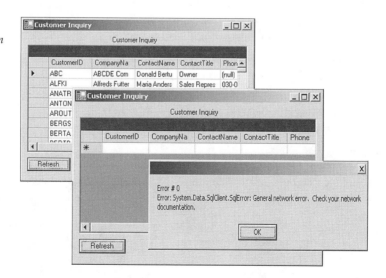

13

Using `RowError` of the `DataSet`

To be much more efficient in responding to individual row error conditions, you can add error information to the row itself (even at the column level). The `DataRow` object allows you to do this by providing a `RowError` property for each row in the `DataSet`. As data rows are processed (for example, when updating them), you can set the `RowError` property for a row to indicate that it has an error. Then, simply use the `HasErrors` property to determine whether any error information has been added to any of the rows in the dataset. You can use the `GetErrors` method to return and examine only the rows with errors. It's all very slick.

Listing 13.3 is a short piece of code that adds a `RowError` condition to a particular row in the Customers `DataSet` (the first row), testing to see if any rows in the `DataSet` have errors, and then displaying the company name and error text of any row with an error.

LISTING 13.3   Adding a `RowError` condition to a Row (13ADOErrors.vb)

```
. . .
CustomerDS.Tables("Customers").Rows(0).RowError = "Invalid Customer row - Error"
if CustomerDS.Tables("Customers").HasErrors then
   Dim ErrDataRows as DataRow()
   ErrDataRows = CustomerDS.Tables("Customers").GetErrors()
   Console.WriteLine("DataTable {0} has {1} Error(s)",
CustomerDS.Tables("Customers").TableName, ErrDataRows.Length.ToString())
   Dim i as integer
   for i = 0 to ErrDataRows.Length -1
     Console.WriteLine("Row Error for {0} **
{1}",ErrDataRows(i)("CompanyName").ToString(),ErrDataRows(i).RowError)
      next
else
   Console.WriteLine("DataTable {0} Has no errors",
CustomerDS.Tables("Customers").TableName)
end if
```

When executed, the preceding code yields:

```
C:\ADOSAMPLES> 13ADOErrors.exe <press enter>
DataTable Customers has 1 Error(s)
Row Error for ABCDE Company ** Invalid Customer row - Error
```

And lastly, we can go back and enhance our Customer Inquiry form application to include a significant validation error-handling improvement that we invoke with a new Validate button.

1. From the Windows Forms Designer, drag another `Button` object from the Windows Forms Toolbox onto the form.

2. Press F4 to take you directly to the properties of this button. Change the name of the button to btnValidate and the text of the button to Validate.

3. Now, double-click the Validate button object on the form so that you can add the following For Each row logic. The logic will check each row to see if the ContactTitle is "Owner", and if it finds one, it sets an error for that row and also sets a specific error for the column of the row. This will have a dramatic effect on what is displayed in the DataGrid for any data row that has this error condition.

```
Dim CustomersTable As DataTable
CustomersTable = Me.CustomerDS1.Tables("Customers")
Dim row As DataRow
For Each row In CustomersTable.Rows
    If (row("ContactTitle") = "Owner") Then
        row.RowError = "No Owners Please"
        row.SetColumnError("ContactTitle",
                "Contact cannot be Owners")
    End If
Next row
```

Now, once again, hit F5 and test your application by just clicking on the Validate button. You should now see red error indications for each row that has this validate error, and the ContactTitle column should also have this indication. To clear this validation indication, just click the Refresh button. Figure 13.4 shows the initial form with all customers and then the same form after the validation button was clicked.

FIGURE 13.4

Customer Inquiry form successful execution and Customer Inquiry form with validate exceptions displayed.

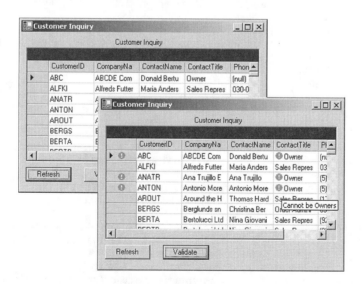

DataAdapter Events

The ADO.NET DataAdapter exposes three events that you can use to respond to changes made to data at the data source. These are the RowUpdating event, RowUpated event, and FillError event. You will typically use the status property to

determine what to do about any error that has occurred during the execution of the
DataAdapter.

- RowUpdating event—This event is raised before any update, insert, or delete on a
  row has been pushed to the data source. It has only been done at the dataset.

- RowUpdated event—This event is raised after any update, insert, or delete has been
  completed to the data source.

- FillError event—This event is raised when an error occurs during a Fill operation.

By far, the RowUpdated event yields the most value, especially because most coding you
will do must support the optimistic concurrency model and using the RowUpdated method
to handle this condition is very straightforward. The following piece of code implements
the optimistic concurrency approach for an update that utilizes the RowUpdated method
for its handler.

You first have to set up a shared subroutine that will look at whether the UPDATE
statement returned any rows. If it returns a row, the update was successful. If
recordsaffected is 0, the WHERE comparison in the UPDATE statement failed, and this is
an optimistic concurrency violation.

```
Private Shared Sub OnRowUpdated(sender As Object, updevent
        As SqlRowUpdatedEventArgs)
    If updevent.RecordsAffected = 0
        updevent.Row.RowError = "Optimistic Concurrency Violation"
        updevent.Status = UpdateStatus.SkipCurrentRow
    End If
End Sub
```

Then in the main code, you add the handler, fill the dataset, make your updates, and issue
the update back to the data source. The handler will do the rest.

```
AddHandler CustomerAdapter.RowUpdated, New SqlRowUpdatedEventHandler
                        (AddressOf OnRowUpdated)
Dim CustomerDataSet As DataSet = New DataSet()
CustomerAdapter.Fill(CustomerDataSet, "Customers")
CustomerAdapter.Update(CustomerDataSet, "Customers")
Dim CustRow As DataRow
For Each CustRow In CustomerDataSet.Tables("Customers").Rows
  If CustRow.HasErrors Then Console.WriteLine(CustRow(0) &
      vbCrLf & CustRow.RowError)
  if not CustRow.HasErrors then Console.Writeline
                    ("No optimistic concurrency error found")
Next
```

XML Persisted Row Errors

As mentioned earlier, row errors can also be persisted in the XML structure that is to be passed to other consumers of XML. The following illustrates the additional XML structure as provided by the `DiffGram` XML option. `DiffGram` is great for dealing with issues such as optimistic concurrency violations.

Basically, a `DiffGram` is divided into three sections (blocks). The first one contains the current data (the current `DataSet` values block), the second is the original data block (`<diffgr:before>` the data as it was read in from the data source before it was modified), and the third is the error block (`<diffgr:errors>`) for noting whether any errors (like optimistic concurrency) have occurred as you processed (updated) the data.

For a more complete explanation, take a look at Hour 14, "Managing ADO.NET Concurrency." A full example is described in that hour.

Summary

In this hour, you've seen the two major error-handling constructs of `Try/Catch/Finally` and `On Error` in action. These constructs along with the general design considerations should help you in your error-handling code. The general rule of thumb is to overhandle errors during development and trim back the excess when you near implementation. In addition, you've had a chance to build up a Windows Forms application that utilized a few of the typical error-handling situations that you will face day in and day out. These techniques, coupled with the data updating error conditions, will cover most of what you need for ADO.NET.

Q&A

Q What is the best construct for handling errors?

A The `Try/Catch/Finally` structure is becoming the most common error-handling construct. It has significant advantages over `On Error`.

Q How will I know what errors to test for?

A You test for error conditions that are right for the application you are building. See the earlier discussion on design considerations.

13

Workshop

These quiz questions are designed to test your knowledge of the material covered in this chapter. The answers to the quiz questions can be found in Appendix A, "Answers to Quizzes."

Quiz

1. What is the `Catch` block used for?

    a. Processing error conditions

    b. `Else` processing

    c. Common processing

2. True or false: ADO.NET cannot tell you if you have any errors indicated in a `DataSet`.

3. True or false: Always close a connection in the `Finally` block.

4. You can set errors in a `DataSet` at what level?

    a. `DataTable` level

    b. `DataRow` level

    c. Column level

    d. Data type level

5. True or false: There is no way to pass `DataRow` error indications to other XML consumers or Web services.

6. What is the most commonly used `DataAdapter` event?

    a. `FillError` event

    b. `DataUpdated` event

    c. `RowUpdated` event

    d. `RowUpdating` event

Exercise

For the Windows Forms application that we developed in this chapter, add a new button to the form that will perform a validation for any NULL phone number columns. Name the button "NO PHONE". It's best to go back and follow the same type of addition that we did for the Validate button with ContactTitles.

HOUR **14**

Managing ADO.NET Concurrency

Concurrency is critical in any multiuser environment where data is to be updated. Concurrency, as you can see in Figure 14.1, is best thought of as "multiple users vying to update data without affecting each other as they update it." In this illustration, each client application (Client A, Web Client B, and Web Client C) has read the same Customer data values at approximately the same time. They all see the same Customer data, and some will choose to update this data and expect their updates to be successful. The type of concurrency model you utilize will directly determine how these data resources are treated (held/locked/enqueued), what type of performance to expect, and how scalable your application will be.

In the classic client/server architectures, most programming languages and database servers support multiple types of concurrency models such as optimistic, pessimistic, and everything in between (different isolation levels). In the multitiered .NET architecture, the focus is on utilizing a "disconnected" mode of data retrieval to minimize data concurrency issues and to increase scalability. This correlates well with using the optimistic concurrency approach.

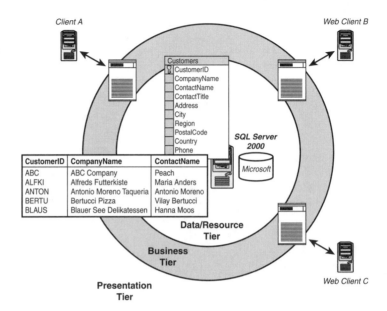

FIGURE 14.1
A typical multiuser data access in a .NET architecture of Customer data stored in Microsoft SQL Server 2000.

In this hour, you will learn about the following topics:

- An overview of optimistic versus pessimistic concurrency
- What's happening at the data provider level
- How to use data in the DataSet to compare against what's in the database before updates are done
- Utilizing a timestamp approach if available
- Using the DataAdapter.RowUpdated event in conjunction with some of these approaches
- How DiffGrams and XML handle optimistic concurrency

Optimistic Versus Pessimistic Concurrency

An old adage says: "If I can get something but it is tainted, it does me no good to get it in the first place."

Well, that's what managing concurrency is all about—making sure you can update data along with the guarantee that what you are updating hasn't changed because someone else came along and updated it right out from under you. Let's first look at optimistic concurrency because it is the preferred approach in most .NET programming.

Optimistic concurrency allows for multiple users to read the same data row at the same time without having to lock it (for update). Then any one of the users can change (update) the data values at this point. An optimistic concurrency violation will occur when a user tries to update the previously read data, but another user has already updated it since the last time the first user read it. That can really be a disaster if not understood well or not handled properly.

What is so significant here is that by *not* locking the data resource (the data row) for update, the whole level of performance of your system is improved due to the major reduction of additional server resources needed to lock data. And, for an application to hold a lock on a data resource, it must also maintain a persistent connection to the database server that houses the data. Because this is not happening in optimistic concurrency (no persistent connection is needed and no data lock is being used), connections to the database server are available to handle many more clients in less time. This directly achieves the scalability and performance goals we mentioned earlier.

Looking back at Figure 14.1, let's describe optimistic concurrency in a multiuser situation with Client A and Web Client B:

1. Client A reads the Customer data row for customerID = 'ABC' at 9:14:32 AM. The data values are as follows:

CustomerID	CompanyName	ContactName
ABC	ABC Company	Peach

2. Web Client B reads the same Customer data row at 9:14:34 AM. The data values are as follows:

CustomerID	CompanyName	ContactName
ABC	ABC Company	Peach

3. Web Client B updates the ContactName value from "Peach" to "Donald Renato" at 9:14:40 AM. These updates are committed to the database in a single short transaction and Web Client B is finished. This update succeeds because the values in the database at the time of the update match the originally read values exactly. The data values in the database are now as follows:

CustomerID	CompanyName	ContactName
ABC	ABC Company	Donald Renato

4. Meanwhile, Client A updates the ContactName value from "Peach" (as they see it in their locally cached `DataSet`) to the value of "Peter Johnson" at 9:14:42 AM. They then try to commit this change back to the database but have now

14

encountered an optimistic concurrency violation. In other words, the values in the database no longer match the original values that Client A was expecting (or was working with). Client A must now decide whether they should make their update (overriding what Web Client B did) or cancel their current update.

In general, the optimistic concurrency approach is highly successful when the application's data has minimal contention situations (when the application's users rarely work on the same data at the same time) and when there are many, many users.

In contrast, pessimistic concurrency must lock rows at the data source to prevent other users from updating that data from under them. The lock must be held for the duration of their update intent time and will be released when they either (1) update the data and commit the changes or (2) just release the update intent. The issues here are enlisting the data source's lock manager to hold a lock on the intended data, keeping a persistent connection maintained during the entire intent and update time, and the extra coding that must establish explicit transactions and commit points. If we look at the same sequence of events described earlier, but utilizing a pessimistic concurrency approach, our example now changes:

1. Client A reads the Customer data row for customerID = 'ABC' at 9:14:32 AM. Must also "lock" this data for the length of time of their update intent. In addition, a persistent connection must be maintained with the data source in order to hold the lock for this user. The data values are as follows:

CustomerID	CompanyName	ContactName
ABC	ABC Company	Peach

2. Web Client B reads the same Customer data row at 9:14:34 AM. The data can be read by others but not updated because of the lock being held on it. The data values are as follows:

CustomerID	CompanyName	ContactName
ABC	ABC Company	Peach

3. Web Client B updates the ContactName value from "Peach" to "Donald Renato" at 9:14:40 AM. This update fails because the data is being locked by Client A. No changes are made to the data source. The data values in the database are still

CustomerID	CompanyName	ContactName
ABC	ABC Company	Peach

4. Meanwhile, Client A updates the ContactName value from "Peach" to the value of "Peter Johnson" at 9:14:42 AM. They then try to commit this change back to the

database and succeed (and their locks are released). The data values in the database are now

CustomerID	CompanyName	ContactName
ABC	ABC Company	Peter Johnson

Very different results from that of optimistic concurrency!

For the pessimistic concurrency approach, the cost of holding those locks, maintaining the persistent connections, and doing the extra coding needed is huge. The results may be what was desired, but at what price to scalability and performance? Using the pessimistic concurrency approach is much better suited for systems that have heavy contention for data, fewer users, and where the cost of protecting that data with locks is less than the cost of rolling back transactions if concurrency conflicts occur.

> Remember, you are always at the mercy of the underlying database management system's locking granularity (row-level, page-level, table-level, key-range, and so forth). If the DBMS is using page-level (default) locking and if there are many data rows in a single page of a table that you are updating, you may be holding up others from updating their data even though you are not updating the same data. Their update will eventually succeed, but you have inadvertently slowed up that process. Good database design along with using the optimistic concurrency approach will usually minimize this situation.

Coding for Optimistic Concurrency

In general, there are two basic coding techniques you can use to implement the optimistic concurrency approach within ADO.NET. The default approach is to compare each column of data in the database (or other data provider data source) table to the original data values you read into your DataSet (cached copy) as part of your UPDATE statement (WHERE clause). This will detect any optimistic concurrency violations. If any of the database data values have changed since you last read the data row, your UPDATE statement will fail (as you would probably want it to). At a minimum, this would force you to reread the data values from the database, see what they are, and see if you wanted to again update some data value further.

Another, quicker technique of doing the same thing is to utilize a timestamp column that may be available in the data table you are working with (as is available in MS SQL Server tables that have defined one). This technique allows you to read a timestamp value that is part of the database data row and then compare timestamps at the time you want to update the data back to the database. If the timestamp value has changed since the last time you read the data values, your UPDATE statement will fail (again, as you would want it to do).

Comparing DataSet Values Against the Database for Optimistic Concurrency

To do optimistic concurrency correctly (with 100% data integrity), you really should compare all the original data column's data values against what is in the database for your update to be considered valid (not violating optimistic concurrency). Perhaps another user has updated another column's data values for a particular data row (like the ContactName column's data value) and, at the same time, you have updated some other column's data values (like the ContactTitle column's data value). The resulting data row (after both of the updates) will have potentially mismatched data values for this particular data row (the ContactName data value doesn't correspond to the ContactTitle data value any longer). This can potentially cause a difficult data integrity anomaly. It would look like this:

1. Client A reads the ContactName value from the database for CustomerID = 'ABC' at 9:14:42 AM. The data values in the database are now:

CustomerID	ContactName	ContactTitle
ABC	Peach	Owner

2. Client B reads the ContactTitle value from the database for the same CustomerID = 'ABC' at 9:14:43 AM. The data values in the database are still:

CustomerID	ContactName	ContactTitle
ABC	Peach	Owner

3. Client A updates the ContactName value from "Peach" to the value of "Peter Johnson" at 9:14:55 AM. Client A's application only compared the original ContactName value (that they read into cache) with what is on the database at the time of their update. These matched, so they committed their update. The data values in the database are now:

CustomerID	ContactName	ContactTitle
ABC	Peter Johnson	Owner

4. Client B updates the ContactTitle value from "Owner" to the value of "Assistant buyer" at 9:15:05 AM. Client B's application only compared the original ContactTitle value (that they read into cache) with what is on the database at the time of their update. These matched, so they committed their update. The data values in the database are now:

CustomerID	ContactName	ContactTitle
ABC	Peter Johnson	Assistant buyer

Unfortunately, the data for CustomerID = 'ABC' is now all messed up. Peter Johnson is the owner, not the assistant buyer of the ABC company. The application just wasn't completely implementing optimistic concurrency correctly.

Listing 14.1 is a short piece of Visual Basic code that you can execute as practice for learning more on this subject. This example uses the ADO.NET `DataSet` fill and update approach from the Customers table in the Northwind database (that comes with Microsoft SQL Server).

```
CustomerAdapter.Fill(CustomerDataSet, "Customers")
CustomerAdapter.Update(CustomerDataSet, "Customers")
```

It will also save the original data row values as they were originally read from the database.

```
OldParms = CustomerAdapter.UpdateCommand.Parameters.Add("@oldCustomerID",
        SqlDbType.NChar, 5, "CustomerID")
 OldParms.SourceVersion = DataRowVersion.Original
```

These will be used in a comparison (`WHERE` clause) that will be part of the `UPDATE` statement.

```
CustomerAdapter.UpdateCommand = New SqlCommand(
"UPDATE Customers (CustomerID, CompanyName, ContactName) " &
"VALUES(@CustomerID, @CompanyName, @ContactName) " & _
"WHERE CustomerID = @oldCustomerID AND CompanyName = @oldCompanyName " &
" AND ContactName = @oldContactName", nwindConn)
```

By doing this comparison of the original data values read from the database with what's in the database at the time the update is issued, you will be guaranteeing yourself that no other user has slipped in and updated something before you. This is optimistic concurrency.

LISTING 14.1 Comparing Original Data Values to Current Data Values (File 14OptCon.vb)

```
Imports System
Imports System.Data
```

14

LISTING 14.1   continued)

```
Imports System.Data.SqlClient
Imports Microsoft.VisualBasic
namespace HowTo.ADONET24.Samples
Public Class OptConSample
  Public Shared Sub Main()
    Dim nwindConn As SqlConnection = New SqlConnection
        ("Data Source=localhost;Integrated Security=SSPI;Initial
➥Catalog=northwind")
    Dim CustomerAdapter As SqlDataAdapter = New SqlDataAdapter
        ("SELECT CustomerID, CompanyName, ContactName " &
        " FROM Customers ORDER BY CustomerID", nwindConn)
  CustomerAdapter.UpdateCommand = New SqlCommand
        ("UPDATE Customers (CustomerID, CompanyName, ContactName) " &
        "VALUES(@CustomerID, @CompanyName, @ContactName) " & _
        "WHERE CustomerID = @oldCustomerID AND CompanyName = @oldCompanyName " &
        " AND ContactName = @oldContactName", nwindConn)
  CustomerAdapter.UpdateCommand.Parameters.Add
        ("@CustomerID", SqlDbType.NChar, 5, "CustomerID")
  CustomerAdapter.UpdateCommand.Parameters.Add
        ("@CompanyName", SqlDbType.NVarChar, 40, "CompanyName")
  CustomerAdapter.UpdateCommand.Parameters.Add
        ("@ContactName", SqlDbType.NVarChar, 30, "ContactName")
  'Set up OldParms to hold the rows original values
  'These are then used in the WHERE clause for the
  'optimistic concurrency comparison
  Dim OldParms As SqlParameter
  OldParms = CustomerAdapter.UpdateCommand.Parameters.Add
        ("@oldCustomerID", SqlDbType.NChar, 5, "CustomerID")
  OldParms.SourceVersion = DataRowVersion.Original
  OldParms = CustomerAdapter.UpdateCommand.Parameters.Add
        ("@oldCompanyName", SqlDbType.NVarChar, 40, "CompanyName")
  OldParms.SourceVersion = DataRowVersion.Original
  OldParms = CustomerAdapter.UpdateCommand.Parameters.Add
        ("@oldContactName", SqlDbType.NVarChar, 30, "ContactName")
  OldParms.SourceVersion = DataRowVersion.Original
  Dim CustomerDataSet As DataSet = New DataSet()
  Console.Writeline ("Go get some customer data - Fill")
  CustomerAdapter.Fill(CustomerDataSet, "Customers")
  Console.Writeline ("Update the rows")
  CustomerAdapter.Update(CustomerDataSet, "Customers")
  Dim CustRow As DataRow
  Console.Writeline ("Look for optimistic concurrency violations")
  For Each CustRow In CustomerDataSet.Tables("Customers").Rows
    Console.Writeline ("Looking for errors for row with CustomerID of " &
        CustRow(0) )
    If CustRow.HasErrors Then Console.WriteLine(CustRow(0) &
        vbCrLf & CustRow.RowError)
    if not CustRow.HasErrors then Console.Writeline
        ("No optimistic concurrency error found")
```

LISTING 14.1   continued)

```
  Next
  Console.Writeline ("Show contents of DataSet")
  For each CustRow in CustomerDataSet.Tables("Customers").Rows
      Console.Writeline("Customer Contacts Selected: "
      + CustRow("ContactName").ToString())
  Next
 End Sub
End Class
End namespace
```

To execute this code, you must first quickly compile it from a DOS command prompt.
Change directories to the location of the VB source code that contains this example
(14optcon.vb). You might need to change the data source statement in the
SQLConnection string (Data Source=localhost) to point to a specific MS SQL Server
instance if it can't resolve "localhost". Then just compile the code as follows:

```
C:\ADOSAMPLES>  vbc.exe 14optcon.vb  /r:System.dll  /r:System.Data.dll
          /r:System.Xml.dll
```

You should see the following .NET VB compiler messages:

```
Microsoft (R) Visual Basic .NET Compiler version 7.00.9447
for Microsoft (R) .NET Framework version 1.00.3617
Copyright (C) Microsoft Corporation 1987-2001. All rights reserved.
```

This will be followed by the DOS command prompt again (if it is a successful compile).
Otherwise, you will be getting compile errors of one kind or another.

After the code has compiled successfully, you will need to make sure that you have
Microsoft SQL Server up and running and the Northwind database has been installed
(usually by default). To execute this sample, just specify the sample name at the DOS
command prompt and press Enter.

```
C:\ADOSAMPLES> 14OptCon.exe <press enter>
Go get some customer data - Fill
Update the rows
Look for optimistic concurrency violations
Looking for errors for row with CustomerID of ABC
No optimistic concurrency error found
Looking for errors for row with CustomerID of ALFKI
No optimistic concurrency error found
. . .
Looking for errors for row with CustomerID of WOLZA
No optimistic concurrency error found
Show contents of DataSet
Customer Contacts Selected: Peach
```

14

```
Customer Contacts Selected: Maria Anders
Customer Contacts Selected: Ana Trujillo
. . .
Customer Contacts Selected: Zbyszek Piestrzeniewicz
```

Great! To make things a bit more robust, you can add in an `OnRowUpdated` subroutine as follows:

```
Private Shared Sub OnRowUpdated(sender As Object, updevent As
     SqlRowUpdatedEventArgs)
  If updevent.RecordsAffected = 0
     updevent.Row.RowError = "Optimistic Concurrency Violation"
     updevent.Status = UpdateStatus.SkipCurrentRow
  End If
End Sub
```

The test for ZERO records affected will be true if the `UPDATE` statement comparisons fail (indicating that some original data did not match what is now in the database—thus an optimistic concurrency violation).

Then you add the `SqlRowUpdatedEventHandler` handler to the main subroutine as follows:

```
AddHandler CustomerAdapter.RowUpdated,
           New SqlRowUpdatedEventHandler(AddressOf OnRowUpdated)
```

Now each row that violates optimistic concurrency will be marked as having this error. This also makes it much easier to narrow in on the rows that have only this error. Then you can decide what you want to do with this update situation.

Timestamps in ANSI SQL-92 and Higher

In ANSI-SQL 92 and higher, the timestamp column is just a datetime column. In SQL Server 2000, you can also use a `rowversion` data type that is equivalent to the old SQL Server timestamp column. If you specify the timestamp column in SQL Server 2000, it will behave as it always has. The real trick comes when you are looking at other data providers' interpretations of timestamp. Don't get these mixed up! SQL storage is Varbinary 8 (null), or binary 8 (not null) for the timestamp column.

Using a Timestamp for Optimistic Concurrency

If you are using a data source (table) on a DBMS such as Microsoft SQL Server 2000 that allows for a timestamp column to be defined in a table, the coding for optimistic concurrency can be made much simpler. You must remember, though, that the code you write for DBMS-specific nuances (like that of timestamp) must only be used with that DBMS.

The timestamp column, if present in a table, will be updated automatically each time the data row is changed. This provides a single table column that can be used for comparison in the UPDATE statement rather than having to compare all the data columns. However, you must first have a timestamp column in the table that you are using.

Listing 14.2 is the Customers table (renamed CustomersTS for TimeStamp) with a time-stamp column (as supported by MS SQL Server 2000).

LISTING 14.2 The Customer Table with a Timestamp Column (File 14OptConTS.sql)

```
CREATE TABLE [dbo].[CustomersTS] (
    [CustomerID] [nchar] (5) NOT NULL ,
    [CompanyName] [nvarchar] (40) NOT NULL ,
    [ContactName] [nvarchar] (30) NULL ,
    [ContactTitle] [nvarchar] (30) NULL ,
    [Address] [nvarchar] (60) NULL ,
    [City] [nvarchar] (15) NULL ,
    [Region] [nvarchar] (15) NULL ,
    [PostalCode] [nvarchar] (10) NULL ,
    [Country] [nvarchar] (15) NULL ,
    [Phone] [nvarchar] (24) NULL ,
    [Fax] [nvarchar] (24) NULL ,
    timestamp
)
```

Taking advantage of the timestamp column is very similar to what we did before except that we only need to save this one column for comparison: the timestamp column (other than the column(s) that are needed to locate the row itself—such as CustomerID).

This time, we will read the rows and the timestamp column.

```
Dim CustomerAdapter As SqlDataAdapter = New SqlDataAdapter
        ("SELECT CustomerID, ContactName, timestamp " &
        "FROM CustomersTS ORDER BY CustomerID", nwindConn)
```

We then must save the original timestamp values for use in our comparison later.

```
OldParms = CustomerAdapter.UpdateCommand.Parameters.Add
        ("@oldTimestamp", SqlDbType.Varbinary, 8, "timestamp")
  OldParms.SourceVersion = DataRowVersion.Original
```

14

And then we will only need to supply this additional one column in the UPDATE statement.

```
CustomerAdapter.UpdateCommand = New SqlCommand
        ("UPDATE CustomersTS (CustomerID, ContactName, timestamp) " &
         "VALUES(@CustomerID, @ContactName, null) " & _
"WHERE CustomerID = @oldCustomerID AND timestamp = @oldTimestamp", nwindConn)
```

Again, if any other user has updated the data row before your update is executed, the timestamp value would have changed and your update will fail (optimistic concurrency violation).

There is also another comparison syntax for issuing an update in Microsoft SQL Server (up through SQL Server 2000) when using timestamp. It is called the TSEQUAL update syntax. When you use this syntax, it yields a true or false result when the TSEQUAL portion is executed. It is as follows:

```
CustomerAdapter.UpdateCommand = New SqlCommand
        ("UPDATE CustomersTS (CustomerID, ContactName, timestamp) " &
         "VALUES(@CustomerID, @ContactName, null) " & _
         "WHERE CustomerID = @oldCustomerID AND TSEQUAL " &
         "(timestamp, @oldTimestamp) ", nwindConn)
```

This is basically the same thing as before, but just specified slightly differently. The data row is located by using the CustomerID comparison, and TSEQUAL yields true or false depending on the results of the timestamp comparison.

XML and Optimistic Concurrency

An XML format can also be used to identify the current and original data values (data elements) along with row error information and row order. This is referred to as the DiffGram XML format. The DiffGram XML format is what is usually used in the .NET Framework to send and receive information by the applications. It is what is serialized for transport across a network connection to other applications or services and is the persistent DataSet representation. You load up the contents of the DataSet from XML with the ReadXml method and write the contents of this DataSet to XML using the WriteXml method. One of the options you have is to specify that the contents be read or written in a DiffGram XML format. This is mentioned here because you can use the DiffGram XML format to update data in tables in a Microsoft SQL Server 2000 database environment. Also, the DiffGram format is pretty much already set up to handle your optimistic concurrency needs.

Basically, a DiffGram is divided into three sections (blocks). The first one contains the current data (the current DataSet values block), the second is the original data block

(`<diffgr:before>` the data as it was read in from the data source before it was modified), and the third is the error block (`<diffgr:errors>`) for noting whether any errors
(such as optimistic concurrency) have occurred as you processed (updated) the data.

As you can see from the following `DiffGram` example, the data row with `DiffGram` ID of
"Customers1" has been modified (`diffgr:hasChanges="modified"`), and there is a corresponding `<diffgr:before>` entry that contains the original values as they were read
from the database. These will be used in checking for optimistic concurrency violations.

In addition, the data row `DiffGram` ID of "Customers2" shows that an error was encountered when it was updated (`diffgr:hasErrors="true"`). Also, there is a corresponding
entry in the `diffgr:errors` block that shows that the error is an "Optimistic
Concurrency Violation."

```
<diffgr:diffgram xmlns:msdata="urn:schemas-microsoft-com:xml-msdata"
        xmlns:diffgr="urn:schemas-microsoft-com:xml-diffgram-v1">
<CustomerDataSet>
<Customers diffgr:id="Customers1" msdata:rowOrder="0"
                         diffgr:hasChanges="modified">
<CustomerID>ABC  </CustomerID>
<ContactName>Peter Johnson</ContactName>
</Customers>
<Customers diffgr:id="Customers2" msdata:rowOrder="1" diffgr:hasErrors="true">
    <CustomerID>ALFKI</CustomerID>
    <ContactName>Maria Anders</ContactName>
</Customers>
<diffgr:before>
<Customers diffgr:id="Customers1" msdata:rowOrder="0">
    <CustomerID>ABC  </CustomerID>
    <ContactName>Peach</ContactName>
</Customers>
</diffgr:before>
<diffgr:errors>
    <Customers diffgr:id="Customers2"
        diffgr:Error="Optimistic Concurrency Violation."/>
</diffgr:errors>
</CustomerDataSet>
</diffgr:diffgram>
```

Summary

In this hour, you became familiar with the differences between pessimistic and optimistic
concurrency models along with a few techniques of implementing optimistic concurrency
for .NET. The XML format of the `DiffGram` was also described so that you can easily
consume XML into any type of .NET application and still be able to implement

14

optimistic concurrency from what it contains. If you use this approach, your applications are positioned to be high-performing and scalable from the start.

Q&A

Q Is it wrong to create an explicit transaction (Begin Trans/Commit Trans) in .NET?

A No, not at all. This is pessimistic concurrency and it just won't scale as well as optimistic concurrency. However, it might be what your .NET application requires.

Q What type of applications should I be using optimistic concurrency with?

A Using an optimistic concurrency approach is highly successful when the application's data has minimal contention situations (when the application's users rarely work on the same data at the same time) and when there is a high volume of users—very optimal for Web applications.

Workshop

These quiz questions are designed to test your knowledge of the material covered in this chapter. The answers to the quiz questions can be found in Appendix A, "Answers to Quizzes."

Quiz

1. What must be maintained when using the pessimistic concurrency approach?

    a. Locks on data resources

    b. Database connections

    c. Events

2. In general, how is optimistic concurrency implemented?

    a. Compare original values to current values in the data source

    b. Identify key changes, then commit updates

    c. Delete old values, then insert new values

3. True or false: Pessimistic concurrency is designed for fast, scalable applications in .NET.

4. What should be used when using the optimistic concurrency approach and XML?

    a. Blocks

    b. Tags

    c. DiffGrams

Exercise

From the optimistic concurrency code samples, modify 14optcon.vb to utilize the `DataAdapter.RowUpdated` handler. When completed, this can serve as a template for all of your coding.

14

HOUR **15**

Working with Stored Procedures

In the preceding hour, you saw various techniques for managing concurrency issues and eliminating points of contention for data in your application. In this hour, you'll learn how to work with stored procedures, which offer a superior way to access and modify the data in a database. Although stored procedures are offered on several different platforms, including Oracle, this hour concentrates on using stored procedures with Microsoft SQL Server.

In this hour, you'll learn how to

- Use SQL Server Enterprise Manager to create and edit stored procedures
- Use SQL Query Analyzer to test your stored procedures
- Call a stored procedure from ADO.NET and retrieve the results of a query
- Call a stored procedure and pass arguments to achieve dynamic functionality

What Are Stored Procedures?

In the Microsoft SQL Server documentation, a stored procedure is defined as "a precompiled collection of SQL statements and optional control-of-flow statements stored under a name and processed as a unit." Put more simply, a stored procedure is like a method or function—it performs a set of actions on the data in your database. They normally encapsulate an area of functionality, such as adding a new record to a table, or returning a specific set of information.

Stored procedures offer a number of benefits. First, because they are precompiled, they generally perform better than a straight SQL call directly from your application. Additionally, by channeling all data access in your application through a set of stored procedures, you can more easily debug and manage your code. Also, keep in mind that changes made in a stored procedure do not directly require you to recompile your application.

To add a new stored procedure to the Northwind Microsoft SQL database, perform these steps:

1. Load SQL Server Enterprise Manager, found in the Microsoft SQL Server program group.

2. Expand the tree "Microsoft SQL Servers," "SQL Server Group," and locate your database server. With SQL installed locally, the default server will be (LOCAL) as seen in Figure 15.1.

3. Locate and expand the Northwind database. Select Stored Procedures. On the right side of the screen, you'll see any default stored procedures included with the Northwind database.

4. Right-click anywhere on the right pane of the Enterprise Manager and select New Stored Procedure. As shown in Figure 15.2, this brings up a very basic text editor that will enable you to input your stored procedure.

5. Erase the default text in the stored procedure window and input the code from Listing 15.1. After you select OK, a very simple stored procedure is created that will perform a query and return the resultset.

LISTING 15.1 A Simple Stored Procedure

```
CREATE PROCEDURE [Customers_Get] AS

SELECT
    CustomerID,
    CompanyName,
```

LISTING 15.1   continued

```
        ContactName,
        Address,
        City,
        Phone
FROM
        Customers
```

FIGURE 15.1

The Northwind data-base seen in the Microsoft SQL Enterprise Manager.

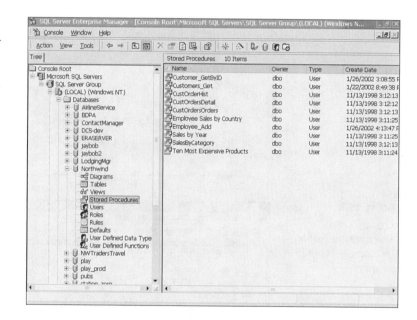

There are several ways to test the stored procedure. Probably the simplest way to test is to load up another of SQL Server's management tools called the Query Analyzer. It can be found in the same program group as the Enterprise Manager. After loading the Query Analyzer, enter (**local**) as your servername if SQL Server is running locally. Otherwise, enter the name of your server. After the Query Analyzer is loaded, your screen will look like Figure 15.3.

Before you can test the stored procedure, you first must select the Northwind database from the database drop-down list. Now, the Query Analyzer is ready to process SQL statements against Northwind. You can run any type of SQL statement against the data-base from this window. To run a stored procedure, you can simply type the following:

```
exec stored_procedure_name
```

FIGURE 15.2

Creating a new stored procedure using Microsoft SQL Enterprise Manager.

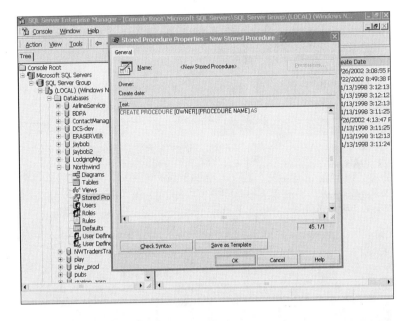

FIGURE 15.3

The SQL Query Analyzer also enables you to create stored procedures.

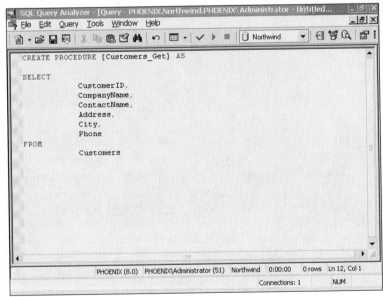

If your stored procedure accepts any arguments, you can add them after the stored procedure's name, separated by commas. If the stored procedure returns results, they will be displayed in the bottom half of the screen of the Query Analyzer, as seen in Figure 15.4.

FIGURE 15.4

The SQL Query Analyzer displays the results of a query.

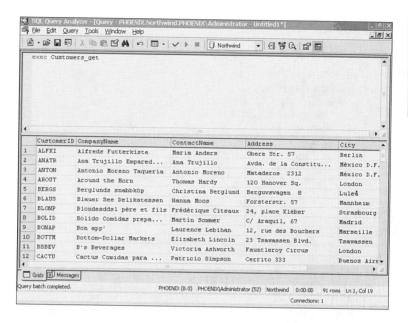

15

 This section only scratches the surface of what the Query Analyzer is capable of. You can actually use the Query Analyzer to optimize table indexes and to display SQL Server's execution plan for your query, along with the time it takes to perform each step. This is an invaluable tool in optimizing your queries. For more information, consult Microsoft SQL Server Books Online, found in the Microsoft SQL Server program group.

In addition to returning a resultset, it's possible to pass specific values into and out of the stored procedure, just like method arguments. Stored procedure arguments, called parameters, are defined just after the stored procedure name, as you can see in Listing 15.2. Stored procedure variables always have the "@" symbol prepended to their name. Following the parameter declaration, the data type and length of the parameter is declared, as well. The stored procedure in Listing 15.2 takes a CustomerID as a parameter. The parameter is used in the WHERE portion of the query. Only customers with the CustomerID you pass in will be returned by the query.

LISTING 15.2 A Stored Procedure with an Input Parameter

```
CREATE PROCEDURE Customer_GetByID
(
    @CustomerID nchar(5)
```

LISTING 15.2   continued

```
)
AS
SELECT
    ContactTitle,
    ContactName,
    CompanyName,
    Address,
    City,
    Region,
    PostalCode,
    Phone
FROM
    Customers
WHERE
    CustomerID = @CustomerID
```

It's also possible to create a parameter used to return extra information. These are called output parameters. By simply placing the OUTPUT keyword after the parameters' type declaration, you can use the parameter to store specific information to return.

Now that you've seen how to create and test stored procedures, it's time to see how to work with stored procedures using ADO.NET.

Executing a Stored Procedure

There are a few different ways to execute stored procedures within ADO.NET. The first section following uses methods you've already seen. Then, you'll see the generally accepted standard way of executing the stored procedure.

Using Exec()

In Hour 6, "Retrieving Data from the Data Source," you saw how to create Connection, Command, and DataReader objects and use them to retrieve data from your database. As you recall, the ExecuteReader() method of the DataReader object returns a forward-only, read-only resultset, which you can then use to bind to a list control, or step through manually.

Almost precisely the same code can be reused to call a stored procedure. Rather than placing a query into the Command object, you can call the stored procedure directly, as you did with the Query Analyzer. Listing 15.3 shows a Web form that calls the Customers_Get stored procedure using this method.

LISTING 15.3   A Simple Stored Procedure

```
<%@ Import Namespace="System.Data" %>
<%@ Import Namespace="System.Data.SqlClient" %>

<HTML>
<HEAD>
    <LINK rel="stylesheet" type="text/css" href="Main.css">
    <!-- End Style Sheet -->

    <script language="VB" runat="server" >
        Sub Page_Load(Source as Object, E as EventArgs)
            'Create and Open Connection
            Dim conn as SqlConnection = new SqlConnection("Data Source=" + _
                          "localhost;Initial Catalog=northwind;UID=sa;PWD=;")
            conn.Open()

            'Create Command object
            Dim cmd as SqlCommand = new SqlCommand("Exec Customers_Get", conn)

            Dim nwReader as SqlDataReader = cmd.ExecuteReader()

            customers.DataSource = nwReader
            customers.DataBind()
        End Sub
    </script>

</HEAD>
<BODY>

<h1>Creating a DataSet</h1>
<hr>

<form runat="server" id=form1 name=form1>
    <asp:DataGrid id="customers" runat="server"></asp:DataGrid>
</form>
<hr>

</BODY>
</HTML>
```

This method works quite well for stored procedures that only return data. However, calling stored procedures using this method makes it impossible to access any output parameters that the stored procedure may have. In the next section, you'll see another way to call a stored procedure that gives you full access to these values.

15

Specifying `CommandType`

The `Command` object has a property named `CommandType`. Normally, you do not need to worry about this property because, by default, ADO.NET assumes you will be sending a query directly to the database, instead of calling a stored procedure. To tell ADO.NET that you're calling a stored procedure, you set the `CommandType` property as in the following line of code:

```
cmd.CommandType = CommandType.StoredProcedure
```

Then you only need to place the name of the stored procedure in the `Command` object. The ADO.NET code in Listing 15.4 can be placed into the preceding example in Listing 15.3, and will function identically.

LISTING 15.4   Another Way to Call a Stored Procedure

```vb
<script language="VB" runat="server" >
    Sub Page_Load(Source as Object, E as EventArgs)
        'Create and Open Connection
        Dim conn as SqlConnection = new SqlConnection( _
                "Data Source=localhost;" + _
                "Initial Catalog=northwind;UID=sa;PWD=;")

        'Create Command
        Dim cmd as SqlCommand = new SqlCommand("Customers_Get", conn)
        cmd.CommandType = CommandType.StoredProcedure

        conn.Open()
        Dim nwReader as SqlDataReader = cmd.ExecuteReader()

        customers.DataSource = nwReader
        customers.DataBind()

        conn.Close()
        nwReader.Close()
    End Sub
</script>
```

Now that you've seen how to call simple stored procedures from ADO.NET, it's time to see how to call some stored procedures that have input and output parameters.

Using Parameters

The `Command` object contains a collection of stored procedure parameters named, aptly enough, Parameters. If your stored procedure requires input parameters or returns values using one or more output parameters, you will need to add each parameter to the Parameters collection.

For example, consider the `Customer_GetByID` stored procedure you created at the beginning of this hour. To set up the parameter object, the first step is to declare the parameter, as follows:

```
Dim parameterCustomerID As SqlParameter = New SqlParameter("@CustomerID", _
                                            SqlDbType.NChar, 4)
```

Note that the name of the parameter must match the name of the parameter declared inside the stored procedure. Additionally, the type must match, as well. After the parameter is declared, you must specify its value.

Specifying Parameter Value

Specifying a parameter's value is simple. You just set the `Value` property of the parameter object to whatever value you choose. Typically, the value is not hard-coded, as it is in the following example, but provided by user input or other means. The following code specifies the value for the `@CustomerID` parameter:

```
parameterCustomerID.Value = "ALFKI"
```

Setting Parameter Direction

Specifying the parameter direction is also straightforward. There are only two types of parameters in ADO.NET for stored procedures: input and output. By default, when a parameter is created, it is an input parameter by default. If you're creating an output parameter, you'll need to change the `Direction` property to the output value, as in the following code:

```
parameterCustomerID.Direction = ParameterDirection.Output
```

After you've specified all the parameter's properties and values, you can add it to the Parameters collection of the `Command` object:

```
cmd.Parameters.Add(parameterCustomerID)
```

Putting It All Together

The example in this section uses the concepts from this hour to create a Web form that adds a new employee to the Employees table of the Northwind database. Before creating the Web form, you need to create a stored procedure. By looking at the schema of the Employees table shown in Figure 15.5, you can see that most of the fields in the table allow null values. Therefore, we can ignore most of the fields and only add the ones we need, plus a few extra to make it interesting.

Listing 15.5 contains the stored procedure that will be called to perform the insert into the database. As you can see, the stored procedure has nine parameters, the last of which is an output parameter used to return the EmployeeID of the recently added employee record.

LISTING 15.5   Another Way to Call a Stored Procedure

```
/*
  This stored procedure adds a new record
  to the employees table
*/

CREATE PROCEDURE Employee_Add
(
    @LastName nvarchar(20),
    @FirstName nvarchar(10),
    @Title nvarchar(30),
    @BirthDate datetime,
    @HireDate datetime,
    @Address nvarchar(60),
    @City nvarchar(15),
    @PostalCode nvarchar(10),
    @retval int OUTPUT
)

AS

INSERT INTO Employees
(
    LastName,
    FirstName,
    Title,
    BirthDate,
    HireDate,
    Address,
    City,
    PostalCode
)
VALUES
(
    @LastName,
    @FirstName,
    @Title,
    @BirthDate,
    @HireDate,
    @Address,
    @City,
    @PostalCode
```

LISTING 15.5   continued

```
)

SELECT @retval = @@IDENTITY
```

 The @@IDENTITY variable always stores the ID of the most recently added record.

Listing 15.6 contains a Web form that accepts information about a new employee record and then saves it to the database using the stored procedure in Listing 15.5. Notice that after the stored procedure has been run, you can access the return value simply by calling the Value property of the output parameter.

LISTING 15.6   Another Way to Call a Stored Procedure

```
<%@ Import Namespace="System.Data" %>
<%@ Import Namespace="System.Data.SqlClient" %>

<HTML>
<HEAD>
    <LINK rel="stylesheet" type="text/css" href="Main.css">
    <!-- End Style Sheet -->

    <script language="VB" runat="server" >
        Sub Page_Load(Source as Object, E as EventArgs)

          If IsPostBack then
            'Create and Open Connection
            Dim conn as SqlConnection = new SqlConnection("Data Source=" + _
                      "localhost;Initial Catalog=northwind;UID=sa;PWD=;")

            'Create Command
            Dim cmd as SqlCommand = new SqlCommand("Employee_Add", conn)
            cmd.CommandType = CommandType.StoredProcedure

            Dim pLastName As SqlParameter = New SqlParameter("@LastName", _
                                                SqlDbType.NVarChar, 20)
            pLastName.Value = Request("txtLastName")
            cmd.Parameters.Add(pLastName)

            Dim pFirstName As SqlParameter = New SqlParameter("@FirstName", _
                                                SqlDbType.NVarChar, 10)
            pFirstName.Value = Request("txtFirstName")
            cmd.Parameters.Add(pFirstName)
```

LISTING 15.6   continued

```
        Dim pTitle As SqlParameter = New SqlParameter("@Title", _
                                            SqlDbType.NVarChar, 30)
        pTitle.Value = Request("txtTitle")
        cmd.Parameters.Add(pTitle)

        Dim pBirthDate As SqlParameter = New SqlParameter("@BirthDate", _
                                            SqlDbType.DateTime, 8)
        pBirthDate.Value = Request("txtBirthDate")
        cmd.Parameters.Add(pBirthDate)

        Dim pHireDate As SqlParameter = New SqlParameter("@HireDate", _
                                            SqlDbType.DateTime, 8)
        pHireDate.Value = Request("txtHireDate")
        cmd.Parameters.Add(pHireDate)

        Dim pAddress As SqlParameter = New SqlParameter("@Address", _
                                            SqlDbType.NVarChar, 60)
        pAddress.Value = Request("txtAddress")
        cmd.Parameters.Add(pAddress)

        Dim pCity As SqlParameter = New SqlParameter("@City", _
                                            SqlDbType.NVarChar, 15)
        pCity.Value = Request("txtCity")
        cmd.Parameters.Add(pCity)

        Dim pPostalCode As SqlParameter = New SqlParameter("@PostalCode", _
                                            SqlDbType.NVarChar, 10)
        pPostalCode.Value = Request("txtPostalCode")
        cmd.Parameters.Add(pPostalCode)

        Dim pRetval As SqlParameter = New SqlParameter("@retval", _
                                            SqlDbType.Int, 4)
        pRetval.Direction = ParameterDirection.Output
        cmd.Parameters.Add(pRetval)

        conn.Open()
        cmd.ExecuteNonQuery()
        conn.Close()

        lblStatus.Text = "Employee added with EmployeeID # " + _
                        pRetval.Value.ToString()
      End If

    End Sub

  </script>

</HEAD>
<BODY>
```

LISTING 15.6   continued

```html
<h1>Add a New Employee to the Northwind Database</h1>
<hr>

<form runat="server" id=form1 name=form1>
  <asp:label id=lblStatus runat="server" />
  <table>
    <tr>
        <td>First Name:</td>
        <td><asp:textbox id="txtFirstName" runat="server" /></td>
    </tr>
    <tr>
        <td>Last Name:</td>
        <td><asp:textbox id="txtLastName" runat="server" /></td>
    </tr>
    <tr>
        <td>Title:</td>
        <td><asp:textbox id="txtTitle" runat="server" /></td>
    </tr>
    <tr>
        <td>Birth Date:</td>
        <td><asp:textbox id="txtBirthDate" runat="server" /></td>
    </tr>
    <tr>
        <td>Hire Date:</td>
        <td><asp:textbox id="txtHireDate" runat="server" /></td>
    </tr>
    <tr>
        <td>Address:</td>
        <td><asp:textbox id="txtAddress" runat="server" /></td>
    </tr>
    <tr>
        <td>City:</td>
        <td><asp:textbox id="txtCity" runat="server" /></td>
    </tr>
    <tr>
        <td>Postal Code:</td>
        <td><asp:textbox id="txtPostalCode" runat="server" /></td>
    </tr>
  </table>

  <input type="submit" value="add new employee">

</form>
<hr>

</BODY>
</HTML>
```

The code in Listing 15.6 might appear a bit intimidating at first. However, keep in mind that much of the code is repetitive. Lines 10–19 create and configure the `Connection` and `Command` objects. Then, lines 20–67 set up a series of parameters that are required by the `Employee_Add` stored procedure. After all the parameters are created, the `ExecuteNonQuery()` method of the `Command` object executes the stored procedure. The remainder of the example in Listing 15.6 is display logic, necessary to present a form to the user so they can submit a new record.

Summary

In this hour, you've seen how to work with stored procedures in a Microsoft SQL Server database. You saw how to use the SQL Enterprise Manager to create and edit stored procedures. Then you used the Query Analyzer to test a stored procedure and verify that it was returning data as expected. Finally, you saw how to call the stored procedure within ADO.NET and send and retrieve parameters.

Q&A

Q Where can I find more information about building stored procedures?

A As is usually the case, Microsoft SQL Server Books Online contains a great deal of information on creating and using stored procedures. Additionally, "Writing Stored Procedures for Microsoft SQL Server" by Matt Shepker is an excellent resource.

Workshop

These quiz questions are designed to test your knowledge of the material covered in this chapter. The answers to the quiz questions can be found in Appendix A, "Answers to Quizzes."

Quiz

1. True or false: You can execute any valid SQL statement in a stored procedure.

2. What is the purpose of parameters in the context of a stored procedure?

Exercise

Choose a few examples from previous hours such as Hour 9, "Binding Data to List Controls," or Hour 6, "Retrieving Data from the Data Source," where the SQL query is built dynamically. Modify the examples to use stored procedures instead.

Hour **16**

ADO Upgrade Concerns

Even developers critical of Microsoft technologies have to agree that ADO.NET is a giant leap forward in data access when compared with ADO. However, this does not invalidate the millions of lines of existing Visual Basic and C++ code in applications that make use of ADO. For many companies, it would simply be impossible to convert all existing data-access COM objects to .NET assemblies, just as it would be impossible to convert all Visual Basic 6.0 applications to Visual Basic .NET Windows forms.

Luckily, these companies have the option of converting their codebase to .NET piecemeal. Several options are available that enable you to work directly with your legacy code and objects. In this hour, you'll see some practical methods for accessing your Visual Basic 6.0 data access objects.

Specifically, in this hour, you'll learn

- How to deal with general upgrade issues when upgrading to ADO.NET
- How to access an ADO recordset within ADO.NET
- How to convert an ADO recordset into an ADO.NET `DataSet`

General Upgrade Issues from ADO to ADO.NET

You have a number of architectural issues to consider when converting your codebase to work within the managed code of the Microsoft .NET Framework. ADO.NET walks a fine line: The ADO.NET object model is similar enough to ADO as to be instantly familiar to an ADO developer, yet your ADO code will not work without modifications in a .NET Windows form or Web form application. If you've worked with ADO, you're going to feel at home with ADO.NET, but you're going to have to spend a significant amount of time upgrading your codebase.

The next few sections discuss some of the major architectural changes you'll face upgrading from ADO to ADO.NET.

ADO.NET Completely Disconnected

ADO.NET is a completely disconnected set of data access objects. This means that, unlike ADO, it is impossible to bind a table directly to a control, like the `DataGrid`. ADO.NET objects connect to the data source, retrieve the data (and related schema), thus creating a snapshot, which you can use as you please.

A number of benefits are associated with a disconnected set of data access objects, the most important of which is scalability. Creating and maintaining an open connection to a database is a very costly procedure, in terms of memory and licensing. For a single-user standalone Visual Basic 6.0 application using a Microsoft Access database, this is not an issue. However, when you consider a Visual Basic 6.0 application supporting multiple users or a Web application with thousands of potential simultaneous users, the disconnected view of data makes more sense.

Therefore, any legacy code that makes use of a server-side cursor to navigate records or any objects that bind directly to database objects will have to be examined closely and in most cases re-engineered.

ADO.NET Is Strongly Typed

All database results in ADO are returned as a `Variant` data type, and then converted. The `Variant` data type is roughly analogous to the `Object` type in the Microsoft .NET Framework. The `Variant` data type carries a large amount of associated overhead by default. Conversely, in ADO.NET, you can access columns returned from the database using their native data types. As you might have guessed, the ADO types and their corresponding ADO.NET types do not match up exactly. Table 16.1 shows a list of ADO

types and their corresponding ADO.NET data types, which you can use in your code
conversions.

TABLE 16.1   ADO Versus ADO.NET Data Types

Code	Symbol
adEmpty	null
adBoolean	Int16
adTinyInt	SByte
adSmallInt	Int16
adInteger	Int32
adBigInt	Int64
adUnsignedTinyInt	promoted to Int16
adUnsignedSmallInt	promoted to Int32
adUnsignedInt	promoted to Int64
adUnsignedBigInt	promoted to Decimal
adSingle	Single
adDouble	Double
adCurrency	Decimal
adDecimal	Decimal
adNumeric	Decimal
adDate	DateTime
adDBDate	DateTime
adDBTime	DateTime
adDBTimeStamp	DateTime
adFileTime	DateTime
adGUID	Guid
adError	ExternalException
adIUnknown	object
adIDispatch	object
adVariant	object
adPropVariant	object
adBinary	byte[]
adChar	string
adWChar	string

16

TABLE 16.1 continued

Code	Symbol
adBSTR	string
adChapter	not supported
adUserDefined	not supported
adVarNumeric	not supported

Accessing an ADO Recordset from ADO.NET

Even if you aren't ready to convert your existing codebase to work within the managed Microsoft .NET Framework, you still have a few options for reusing your old components. It's possible to use COM interoperability to work directly with your old methods and objects. A complete discussion of COM interoperability is out of the scope of this book. However, in this section and the next few sections following, you'll see how to access a Visual Basic 6.0 COM object method that returns a recordset object.

The function in Listing 16.1 is written in Visual Basic 6.0. It's fairly simple; it connects to a data source and retrieves some employee information from the Northwind database, places the results in a recordset object, and then returns that object. If you have Visual Basic 6.0, and would like to follow along, create a new ActiveX DLL project in Visual Basic and place the code in Listing 16.1 into a class called DataAccess. Name your project "Northwind." You'll also need to add a reference to the ADO 2.6 type library (by clicking on the Project menu and selecting References). After you have performed these steps, click on the File menu and select Make Northwind.dll. Your screen should look like Figure 16.1. Click OK to compile the project. After you compile the project, a new class named Northwind.DataAccess will be registered on your system.

LISTING 16.1 A Legacy Visual Basic 6.0 Northwind Data Access Component

```
Public Function GetAllEmployees() As ADODB.Recordset

    Dim conn As ADODB.Connection
    Dim cmd As ADODB.Command
    Dim rs As ADODB.Recordset

    Set conn = New ADODB.Connection
    Set cmd = New ADODB.Command
    Set rs = New ADODB.Recordset

    sSQL = "SELECT FirstName, " + _
```

LISTING 16.1 continued

```
            "LastName, " + _
            "Address, " + _
            "City, " + _
            "PostalCode, " + _
            "HomePhone " + _
            "FROM Employees"

    conn.Open "DSN=NorthwindSQL;Initial Catalog=Northwind;" & _
            "Server=(local);UID=sa;PWD=;"
    rs.ActiveConnection = conn

    rs.Open sSQL

    Set GetAllEmployees = rs

End Function
```

The examples in this chapter require the use of a DSN. Make sure you have a system DSN named Northwind that points to your Northwind database.

FIGURE 16.1

Compiling a Visual Basic 6.0 component.

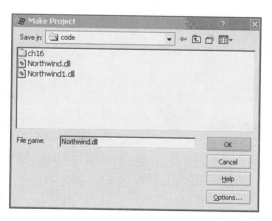

In ASP 3.0, this newly created ActiveX object would typically be used to pass some employee information to another Visual Basic application or to an ASP page, as is the case in Listing 16.2. As you can see from the code at the top of the page, the Northwind.DataAccess object is created, and then the GetAllEmployees() method is called to fill a recordset. The recordset object is then looped through on the page to display information about each employee in the database. Figure 16.2 shows how the code in Listing 16.2 appears when run in a browser.

LISTING 16.2   Legacy Usage of the `Northwind.DataAccess` ActiveX DLL

```
<%@ Language=VBScript %>

<%
dim rsEmployees
dim oNorthwind

set oNorthwind = Server.CreateObject("Northwind.DataAccess")

set rsEmployees = oNorthwind.GetAllEmployees

set oNorthwind = nothing
%>
<HTML>
<HEAD>
</HEAD>
<BODY>
<h1>Northwind Employees</h1>
<table>
  <tr>
    <th>
      First Name
    </th>
    <th>
      Last Name
    </th>
    <th>
      Address
    </th>
    <th>
      City
    </th>
    <th>
      Postal Code
    </th>
    <th>
      Home Phone
    </th>
  </tr>
<%
do while not rsEmployees.EOF
  'Add a single table row for each record
%>
  <tr>
    <td>
      <%=rsEmployees("FirstName")%>
    </td>
    <td>
      <%=rsEmployees("LastName")%>
```

LISTING 16.2   continued

```
      </td>
      <td>
        <%=rsEmployees("Address")%>
      </td>
      <td>
        <%=rsEmployees("City")%>
      </td>
      <td>
        <%=rsEmployees("PostalCode")%>
      </td>
      <td>
        <%=rsEmployees("HomePhone")%>
      </td>
    </tr>
<%
  'Advance to the next record
  rsEmployees.MoveNext
loop
%>

</BODY>
</HTML>
```

In ASP 3.0, the code in Listing 16.2 is one standard way of displaying database data. Lines 3–13 create an instance of the COM object created from Listing 16.1. The GetAllEmployees() method is then invoked, returning an ADO recordset of data. The remainder of the listing is display logic; the inline ASP code iterates through the rows in the recordset, manually building a table. Note that in ADO.NET, this has been replaced by the DataGrid control.

The next few sections demonstrate how to use this legacy codebase to build a similar screen using ADO.NET and an ASP.NET Web form.

COM Interoperability

COM interoperability is the bit of magic that enables you to use legacy COM objects inside the Microsoft .NET Framework. There are two different ways to access legacy objects: by using early binding or late binding. Binding, in this instance, refers to when the object's type information is available.

When you use early binding, the correct type is compiled into your application, improving performance and readability. You need not worry about the correct type not being present at runtime.

FIGURE **16.2**

The output of Listing 16.2.

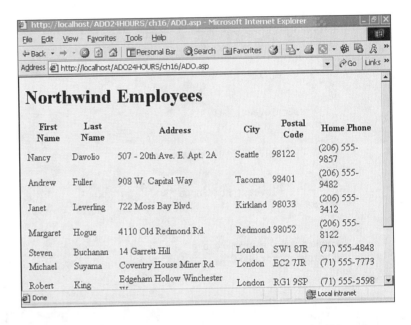

However, the `Server.CreateObject()` method is still available for use. If you pass it a valid Programmatic Identifier (ProgID), it will attempt to create the object and return it as type `Object`. You will get a runtime error in your application if the ProgID cannot be located.

Both of these methods for COM interoperability are covered in detail in the next few sections.

Importing Type Libraries

As mentioned earlier, one method of accessing your legacy COM objects is to import their type libraries into your existing applications and then work with them as you would any other .NET object. The application used to import the type library is called tblimp.exe. For the current example, you're going to need to import two libraries. Because you will need to create an instance of the recordset object, you must import its type library. If ADO is installed in the default path, you can run the following line of code from a command prompt:

```
tlbimp "c:\program files\common files\system\ado\msado15.dll" /out:adodb.dll
```

This generates a new DLL containing the type information for the recordset object. Place this DLL in the /bin directory of your ASP.NET application. Likewise, you'll need to compile the type library for the `Northwind.DataAccess` object you created at the beginning of this hour:

```
tlbimp Northwind.dll /out:NorthwindDOTNET.dll
```

Place this DLL in your /bin directory as well.

Server.CreateObject

The other method you can use to access legacy ActiveX objects is to create them at runtime using the following line of code:

```
Server.CreateObject("Northwind.DataAccess")
```

This returns `Northwind.DataAccess` as type `Object`. After the object is created, you can use its public methods and properties.

Filling a DataSet with ADO Recordset Data

To use early binding, as you saw in the section "Importing Type Libraries," you would need to import the two DLLs you created and placed into your bin directory using the following code:

```
<%@ Import Namespace="NorthwindDOTNET" %>
<%@ Import Namespace="adodb" %>
```

However, this is not necessary for the following example, because it uses the second method, or late binding, in order to access the object.

The `Fill()` method of the `OleDbAdapter` object is overloaded to accept a recordset object directly. It converts the recordset object into a `DataTable` inside a `DataSet`. You can see this in the example in Listing 16.3. In the `LoadDataGrid()` method, an instance of the legacy `Northwind.DataAccess` COM object is created. Then a legacy recordset object is created. Then the `GetAllEmployees()` method from Listing 16.1 is called, which, as you'll recall, returns a recordset of employee information.

Then, the recordset object is passed to the `Fill()` method of the `OleDbDataAdapter`, along with a `DataSet` and a table name. The `Fill()` method imports the recordset into the `DataSet`. The `DataSet` can then be manipulated any way you like. In this instance, it was bound to a `DataGrid` object to display it on a Web form. You can see the results in Figure 16.3.

LISTING 16.3   A Legacy Visual Basic 6.0 Northwind Data Access Component

```
<% @Page Debug="true" Language="VB" aspcompat="true" %>
<%@ Import Namespace="System.Data" %>
<%@ Import Namespace="System.Data.OleDb" %>
```

LISTING 16.3   continued

```
<HTML>
<HEAD>
    <LINK rel="stylesheet" type="text/css" href="ADO24HRS.css">
    <!-- End Style Sheet -->

    <script language="VB" runat="server" >
        Sub Page_Load(Source as Object, E as EventArgs)

            LoadDataGrid(orders)

        End Sub

        Private Sub LoadDataGrid( _
                        myDataGrid as System.Web.UI.WebControls.DataGrid)

            'Create Instance of Legacy Object
            Dim adoComponent as Object = _
                                Server.CreateObject("Northwind.DataAccess")

            'Create Instance of Legacy Recordset
            Dim adoRS As ADODB.Recordset

            'Access Legacy Method that returns recordset
            adoRS = adoComponent.GetAllEmployees()

            'Create ADO.NET objects
            Dim adapter As OleDbDataAdapter = New OleDbDataAdapter
            Dim dsEmployees As DataSet = New DataSet

            'Use overloaded Fill() method to place recordset contents into
            'a DataTable in the dsEmployees Dataset
            adapter.Fill(dsEmployees, adoRS, "Employees")

            'Bind!
            orders.DataSource = dsEmployees
            orders.DataBind()

        End Sub
    </script>

</HEAD>
<BODY>

<h1 class="MainHeader">Northwind Employees</h1>
<hr>

<form runat="server" id=form1 name=form1>
```

LISTING 16.3   continued

```
        <asp:DataGrid id="orders" runat="server"></asp:DataGrid>
    </form>
    <hr>

    </BODY>
    </HTML>
```

16

The example in Listing 16.3 is like many that you have seen before, with a few differences. First, notice that the `System.Data.OleDb` namespace is imported instead of the `System.Data.SqlClient` namespace. OLE DB provides access to the legacy ADO objects. Also, the `Page` attribute `aspcompat` is set to true. This makes the Web form run in a mode compatible with legacy single-threaded COM objects.

The `LoadDataGrid()` method encapsulates the data access for the Web form. First, it creates an instance of the COM object compiled from Listing 16.1 using `Server.CreateObject()` in lines 21–22. On line 28, the `GetAllEmployees()` method is called, just as in Listing 16.2, to retrieve an ADO recordset of data from the database. Then, on line 36, the recordset is passed as the second argument to the `OleDbDataAdapter`'s `Fill()` method. This imports the ADO recordset directly into a `DataSet`.

FIGURE 16.3

A recordset object fills a `DataSet` *and displayed in a* `DataGrid`.

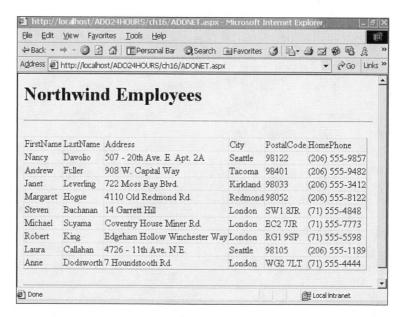

Summary

In this hour, you have seen some techniques for making use of your legacy ActiveX objects without converting them to managed .NET Framework objects. First we analyzed some possible rough spots you might see when upgrading from ADO to ADO.NET. Then you saw how to directly access legacy objects from within a Web form. In the next hour, you'll see how to use connection pooling with ADO.NET.

Workshop

These quiz questions are designed to test your knowledge of the material covered in this chapter. The answers to the quiz questions can be found in Appendix A, "Answers to Quizzes."

Quiz

1. What is the name of the application that imports type libraries?
2. Name two differences between ADO and ADO.NET.

Exercise

If the option is available to you, practice retrieving data from recordset objects created by either Visual Basic 6.0 or C++.

Hour **17**

Using Connection Pooling

Many design considerations must be addressed when building Web-based applications, especially Web applications that need to handle a large number of users and promise great scalability. Deciding how to use a technical design feature such as "connection pooling" can make the difference between a slow and clunky Web app or a fast and sleek Web app. Connection pooling deals with how the database connections are utilized (used and reused) to enhance the overall efficiency of the whole system. In fact, this one little feature translates directly into being able to support a much larger number of users with minimum performance impact. Ah, the promise is fulfilled.

Basically, the Microsoft .NET Framework has taken the approach (the commitment) of using connection pooling as the default. In other words, connection pooling will always be "true" unless you specifically disable it. This allows you to utilize the internal connection-pooling capabilities of the .NET data providers, such as the SQL Server .NET data provider and the OLE DB data provider, to achieve much more efficient and scalable applications without lifting a finger.

In this hour, you will learn about the following topics:

- An overview of connection pooling
- How to create connection pools in ADO.NET
- Connection pools and transaction enlisting
- Controlling connection pools with the connection string

What Is Connection Pooling?

In brief, connection pooling allows applications to reuse an existing database connection from a pool of already established connections, instead of having to repeatedly re-establish new connections to that same database. Establishing database connections is fairly expensive if you compare that aspect to the overall work that will be handled with a database connection in the first place. It is expensive because when a user establishes a connection to a database, the user must be identified and pass authentication (security) before the connection is even allowed. Repeating this over and over puts a huge burden on the database management system and the server, not to mention the overall network traffic that results. This, in turn, directly affects the overall performance of your system and can limit its scalability significantly.

A simple breakdown of the time spent with connection establishment versus actual database work being done with a short query to the Customers table of the Northwind database supplied with Microsoft SQL Server 2000 yielded 84% of the time in the connection/authentication part, and 16% in the actual retrieval and display of a single row from this table. Wow, that's expensive when compared to the overall transaction. It is also ripe for some type of improvement; hence, connection pooling.

So, once again, the overall design approach is to avoid repeatedly establishing these database connections if you can!

Connection pooling is handled at the .NET data provider level. In other words, each .NET data provider, such as the SQL Server .NET data provider and the OLE DB .NET data provider, has a connection-pooling capability embedded in it. Figure 17.1 depicts this aspect.

There are slight differences in how connection pooling works with the different .NET data providers. But, in general, this is fairly transparent from the .NET programmer's point of view.

FIGURE 17.1
Microsoft ADO.NET data provider connection-pooling architecture.

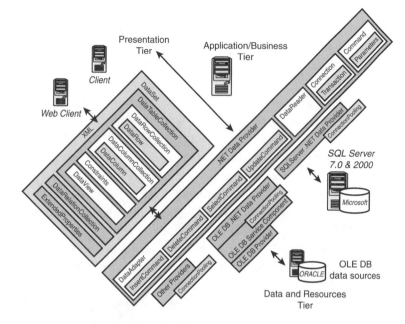

What will actually happen is that when a connection is opened to a database, a connection pool entry, based on the connection string, will be automatically created in the connection pool (on a per-process basis). These pools are not destroyed until the process ends.

A connection pool entry would be created when the following connection string is used in a SqlConnection open:

```
"server=localhost;Trusted_Connection=yes;database=northwind;"
```

All subsequent connections are pooled (utilized) through an exact match algorithm on the connection string. If even one character is different in another connection string that is connecting to the same server and database (that is conceptually the same connection string), a new connection pool will be created and any others that might have been present will not be used. The following connection string, although almost exactly the same as the earlier one, will be considered different because it is not an exact match.

```
"server=localhost;Trusted_Connection=yes ;database=northwind;"
```

In addition, several connection-string keywords in the connection string change or adjust the behavior of the connection pool. These are as follows:

- Connection Lifetime—When a connection is returned to the pool, its creation time is compared with the current time, and the connection is destroyed if that time span (in seconds) exceeds this value. A value of zero (0) will cause pooled connections to have the maximum timeout. Zero is also the default. The only time you would vary this value is when you are in a load-balancing situation where you want connection pools to expire fairly quickly so that work can be spread out to other servers.

- `Connection Reset`—Determines whether the database connection is reset when being removed from the pool. In all cases, the connection state (such as the database context) is not being reset. The default value is "true".

- `Enlist`—When this is set to "true", the pooler automatically enlists the connection in the current transaction context of the creation thread (if a transaction context exists). If no transaction context exists, it is ignored. The default value is "true".

- `Max Pool Size`—Indicates the maximum number of connections allowed in this specific connection pool. The correct setting depends on your needs here. If the application has an opportunity to take advantage of the connection pool in a big way, a large value will be specified. Otherwise, smaller values will suffice. The default value is 100.

- `Min Pool Size`—Indicates the minimum number of connections that will be present (maintained) in this specific connection pool. So, if you know that the application will be making frequent usage of the connection pool, set this up to be enough to make a difference quickly. What will actually happen is when the first open connection occurs, more connection pool entries will be created up to the `Min Pool Size` you specified. The default value is 0.

- `Pooling`—Indicates that a connection should be drawn from the appropriate connection pool, or if necessary, created and added to the appropriate connection pool. The default value here is "true". In other words, you are, by default, using connection pooling.

The following Visual Basic code is a typical example of defining a connection string with a few of the connection-string keywords that control connection-pooling behavior. In addition, this code opens the connection and, transparently to us, an entry will be created in the connection pool based on this connection string.

```
Dim connString1 as String
connString1 = "server=localhost;Trusted_Connection=yes;database=northwind;" & _
            "connection reset=true;" & _
                "connection lifetime=0;" & _
                "enlist=true;" & _
                "min pool size=1;" & _
                "max pool size=50"
Dim myConnection1 as SqlConnection = new SqlConnection(connString1)
Dim CustomerAdapter1 As SqlDataAdapter = New SqlDataAdapter
```

```
          ("SELECT CustomerID, CompanyName, ContactName " &
           "FROM Customers WHERE CustomerID like 'B%' " &
           "ORDER BY CustomerID", myconnection1)
myConnection1.Open()
```

Perhaps the most important thing to remember is to *close* the connection. This releases
the connection back to the pool for possible reuse. If you don't close the connection
explicitly, it will not be released back to the pool (thus defeating the whole purpose of
establishing connection pools to begin with).

```
myConnection1.Close()
```

It is also interesting to see that the connection pool is actually divided up into multiple
transaction-specific pools and one pool for connections not currently enlisted in a transaction. This makes it easier to work with enlisted transaction connections.

OLE DB .NET Data Provider

The OLE DB .NET data provider pools connections by using the underlying services of
OLE DB resource pooling. This is essentially the same thing, just worded differently.
You will be able to use the connection string to configure, enable, or disable resource
pooling (connection pooling), use the registry to configure OLE DB resource pooling
(not recommended), and programmatically configure resource pooling. OK, so if you
want to disable OLE DB .NET connection pooling and use the COM+ object pooling,
you will have to supply a connection string keyword that turns it off (OLE DB
Services=-4) because it is "on" as the default. The connection would look like this:

```
Dim nwindConn As OleDbConnection = New OleDBConnection
        ("Provider=SQLOLEDB;OLE DB Services=-4;Data Source=localhost;
         Integrated Security=SSPI;")
NwindConn.Open()
```

When a connection is opened and a pool created, multiple connections are
added to the pool to bring the connection count to the configured minimum level (as specified with the Min Pool Size keyword). To establish a
minimum pool size, there will be a small amount of overhead when the
pool is initially created. These additional entries are serialized and will not
bog down your server.

Connections can be subsequently added to the pool up to the configured
maximum pool count (as specified with the Max Pool Size keyword). When
the maximum count is reached, new requests to open a connection are
queued.

17

Keep an eye on connection-pooling usage by using either Profiler or Performance Monitor. As you can see from Figure 17.2, you can monitor the User Connections entry of the General Statistics performance counters for SQL Server to see the level of connections established by all applications for a particular SQL Server instance. With the .NET Framework, you will also get many other performance counters. For monitoring connection pooling, you can focus in on the .NET CLR Data performance object.

In addition, you can also use the trace properties of Profiler for basically the same type of information by selecting the Security Audit event classes. We will see more on this later in this hour.

FIGURE 17.2

The Microsoft Performance Monitor counters and profiler event classes for monitoring connection-pooling results.

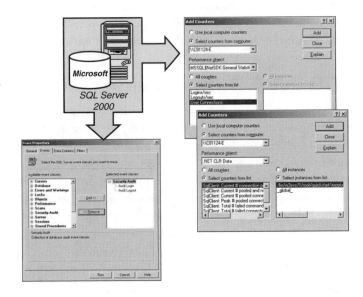

Managing Security?

When you get into the connection-pooling business, you will no longer be able to use security at the individual user and database level. It just isn't feasible any longer. Connection pooling relies on exact matches of connection strings, and if users' IDs are substituted into the connection strings, the resulting connection strings would not match any existing entries in the connection pool.

All of the examples shown in this chapter rely on Windows authentication and trusted connections.

The .NET Beta 2 performance results showed that it took longer to open a pooled database connection when using Windows authentication, compared to using SQL Server authentication. However, in general, it is better to use Windows authentication rather than SQL Server authentication for many other reasons.

In the following Visual Basic code sample (17conpool.vb), a series of connection strings are defined and used to establish connection pools for subsequent processing (Pool A and Pool B). In addition, several separate SQLConnections will be made that will take advantage of the connection pools being established. This code was designed to require input from the console at certain points of its execution so that you can see the results of the performance counters along the way. Listing 17.1 provides the code.

LISTING 17.1 Visual Basic Connection Pooling Code Sample (from file 17conpool.vb)

```
. . .
public class conpool
  public shared sub Main()
    Dim myconpool as conpool = new conpool()
    myconpool.Run()
  end sub
  public sub Run()
    try
      Dim connString1 as String
      connString1 = "server=localhost;Trusted_Connection=yes;
            database=northwind;" & _
                "connection reset=true;" & _
                "connection lifetime=0;" & _
                "enlist=true;" & _
                "min pool size=1;" & _
                "max pool size=50"
      Dim connString3 as String
      connString3 = "server=localhost;Trusted_Connection=yes;database=pubs;" & _
                "connection reset=true;" & _
                "connection lifetime=0;" & _
                "enlist=true;" & _
                "min pool size=10;" & _
                "max pool size=50"
      Dim myConnection1 as SqlConnection = new SqlConnection(connString1)
      Dim myConnection2 as SqlConnection = new SqlConnection(connString1)
      Dim myConnection3 as SqlConnection = new SqlConnection(connString1)
      Dim myConnection5 as SqlConnection = new SqlConnection(connString3)
. . .
'********************* establish first connection pool *********************
      Console.WriteLine ("Opening two connections in pool A")
```

17

LISTING 17.1 continued

```
      myConnection1.Open()
      myConnection2.Open()
. . .
      Console.WriteLine ("Now Returning both of the connections to pool A")
      myConnection1.Close()
      myConnection2.Close()
      Console.WriteLine ("Open another connection from the same pool A")
      myConnection3.Open()
. . .
      Console.WriteLine ("Returning this connection to pool A")
      myConnection1.Close()
'*************** establish a separate connection pool ***************
      Console.WriteLine ("Opening a new connection in pool B")
      myConnection5.Open()
. . .
      Console.WriteLine ("Returning this connection to pool B")
      myConnection5.Close()
    catch e as Exception
      ' Display the error.
      Console.WriteLine(e.ToString())
    end try
  end sub
end class
end namespace
```

To execute this code, you must first compile it from a DOS command prompt. Change directories to the location of the VB source code that contains this example (17conpool.vb). Then just compile the code as follows:

```
C:\ADOSAMPLES>  vbc.exe 17conpool.vb  /r:System.dll  /r:System.Data.dll
                /r:System.Xml.dll
```

After the code has compiled successfully, you will need to make sure that you have Microsoft SQL Server up and running and the Northwind database has been installed (usually by default). To execute this sample, just specify the sample name at the DOS command prompt and press Enter. Again, this VB program will be prompting you to press Enter at certain points so that you can go look at the performance and user connection information as it is executing. Figure 17.3 shows the actual execution of this sample VB program. You should be able to get the same results.

After you have executed this sample once, open the Performance Monitor console and choose to add (Plus +) the following counters to the monitor console:

- ".NET CLR Data" performance object → "SqlClient:Current # connection Pools" counter

FIGURE **17.3**

The Connection Pooling sample VB program executing at the DOS prompt.

- ".NET CLR Data" performance object → "SqlClient:Current # pooled connections" counter

- ".NET CLR Data" performance object → "SqlClient:Peak # of Pooled connections" counter

- "MSSQL$NetSDK:General Statistics" performance object → "User connections" counter

For the ".NET CLR Data" performance objects, be sure to indicate the instance selection when adding these (the "17conpool" instance entry). These are all the connection pools being generated by this process.

Then run the sample VB program again and monitor the connection pool levels and user connections during execution. User connections will remain low, but the connection pools will grow and hopefully be utilized in the future.

In Figure 17.4, you can see the different connection counter levels during this execution. The top line in the monitor shows a stepped increase in the pooled connections ("SQLClient:Peak # pooled connections") counter. The first step was the open of the first connection string for Pool A processing. In that connection string, we had indicated a minimum pool size value of 1. The second, much larger, step is the second connection string open. In that connection string, we had indicated a minimum pool size value of 10. As the program ends (when the top line reaches a plateau), you can also see the user connections drop off to zero (the monitor line that looks like a mountain).

FIGURE 17.4

Performance Monitor showing connection pooling behavior.

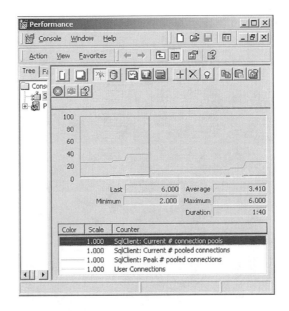

Summary

In this hour, you've seen how connection pools are orchestrated and that they are embedded in the individual .NET data providers themselves. This maximizes the strengths and individual characteristics of each data provider's implementation. In addition, you have learned about the connection keywords that are directly related to connection pooling and control its behavior. Because connection pooling is such a critical aspect of large applications and scalability, it is always a good idea to monitor how effectively the values you choose are being utilized over time. Adjust these as needed. You can use Performance Monitor to regularly get a good feel for how things are going.

The really good news to this whole story is that Microsoft has decided to make connection pooling the default approach from the start. You will find that most applications you will ever code will take full advantage of this decision.

Q&A

Q How will I know if connection pooling is being used?

A Remember, connection pooling is the default (`pooling = "true"`)! You will have to specifically disable this setting if you don't want to use it. In addition, you can always flip on the Performance Monitor for your process (as we did for 17conpool) and see the connection pool's usage.

Q Which security model should you use with connection pooling?

A Windows authentication should be your default security model approach. It is much more oriented to allowing you to construct and use general connection strings that will be easily matched in the connection pool entries.

Workshop

These quiz questions are designed to test your knowledge of the material covered in this chapter. The answers to the quiz questions can be found in Appendix A, "Answers to Quizzes."

Quiz

1. When is a connection pool entry established?

    a. When you open a connection to the database

    b. When you fill a `DataSet`

    c. When you close a connection to the database

    d. When you read the rows from the `DataSet`

2. True or false: Connection pooling is automatically turned off for .NET.

3. What must you do every time in coding to make sure that you and others can take advantage of the connection pool in subsequent processing?

    a. Store it in cache

    b. Record the time it was used in a local variable

    c. Close the connection to the database

    d. Open a new connection to a different database

4. What must match exactly for the application to draw on an already established connection pool entry?

    a. The entire connection string

    b. The database portion of the connection string

    c. The `DataSet` name

    d. The minimum pool size

5. What performance object can you use to monitor usage of connection pooling?

    a. MSSQL$NetSDK:Buffers

    b. .NET CLR Security—performance object

    c. ASP.NET—performance object

    d. .NET CLR Data—performance object

17

Exercise

Part I: Modify the 17conpool.vb code to request a minimum pool size of 20 and a maximum pool size of 200 for both connection strings. Monitor the behavior of these changes using Performance Monitor.

Part II: The 17conpool.vb code uses the .NET SQL Server data provider. Recode this program to use the OLE DB data provider instead.

HOUR 18

Working with Transactions

In the preceding hour, you saw how to use SQL and OLE DB connection pooling in your applications to increase your application's responsiveness and decrease the amount of system resources used. In this hour, you're going to see how database transactions can help maintain the integrity of your database. A transaction is a set of actions that are executed as a group, with all actions succeeding or all actions failing.

In this hour, you'll see how to

- Initiate a database transaction using ADO.NET
- Roll back changes made to a database
- Save changes made while using a transaction
- Perform a database transaction in a stored procedure

What Is a Transaction?

Consider this classic transaction example: A bank needs to transfer a million dollars from bank account A to bank account B. First, the money in A needs to be placed in B. Then, after the transfer has been verified, the money needs to be removed from account A. Obviously, if there is any sort of problem placing the money in account B, you do not want to remove it from account A. Likewise, if the money is placed successfully in account B, you want to ensure that it is removed from account A. All actions need to fail or all actions need to succeed.

If you were coding an application to perform the monetary transactions in the last paragraph, you could do so relatively easily without having to use a transaction by intelligently trapping application errors and maintaining state. However, consider that a transaction isn't limited in size. Imagine keeping track of 500 database changes manually! Also, suppose the server is turned off in the middle of your application's processing. You need to make sure that when the application is brought back online, it knows exactly where it stopped so that it can either reverse all the changes made or attempt to continue where it left off.

Fortunately, because transactions exist, you need not worry about any of these problems. By wrapping your database actions in a transaction, you can help ensure that your data remains correct and consistent. In the next few sections, you'll see how to use database transactions.

Transactions and ADO.NET

The ADO.NET `Connection` object is used to work with transactions. As you'll see in the next few sections, the `Connection` object is used to initiate the transaction. Any command objects that need to enlist in the transaction are then assigned to the transaction. The transaction object itself is used to save, roll back, and perform other actions on the transaction.

Starting a Transaction

In ADO.NET, you can start a database transaction by calling the `BeginTransaction()` method of the `Connection` object, as seen in Listing 18.1.

LISTING 18.1   Starting a New Transaction

```
'Create Connection
Dim conn as SqlConnection = new SqlConnection("Data Source=(local);" +
                                "Initial Catalog=northwind;UID=sa;PWD=;")

'Create Command
Dim cmd as SqlCommand = new SqlCommand()
cmd.Connection = conn

'Connection must be open to start transaction
conn.Open()

'Create Transaction and apply it to command object
Dim myTrans = conn.BeginTransaction("TransactionName")
```

In order to begin a new transaction, the Connection object must be open. If you attempt to start a new transaction without first calling the Open() method of the Connection object, an InvalidOperationException is thrown.

Notice that the BeginTransaction() method returns a SqlTransaction object. For the life of the transaction, you will use this object to manipulate the database transaction, as needed.

At this point, you might be tempted to start executing commands against the database. However, before you can send any queries to the database using this transaction, you must assign the transaction object to the Transaction property of the Command object as seen in the last line of Listing 18.1. This is slightly counterintuitive, because the Command object already has an associated Connection object assigned, and transactions operate over a connection. However, you must still remember this step.

Do not forget to assign the SqlTransaction object returned by the BeginTransaction() method to the Transaction property of the Command object. If you forget, an InvalidOperationException will be thrown by your code the first time you attempt to execute a query.

Now you're ready to make some database changes using the Command object. Feel free to be creative. You can even delete an entire table, if you like. Because you're executing all these changes in a transaction, it's very easy to roll back your changes and return to the table's original state.

Keep in mind that only changes made to the database through this `Connection` object will be in the transaction. Therefore, if you were to modify the data through any other means, such as SQL Enterprise Manager, those changes will not be rolled back.

Rolling Back a Transaction

As you process each of the individual database changes that comprise your database transaction, it's possible to undo or roll back any of the changes you've made to the database since beginning the transaction. For instance, alluding to the monetary transaction example from earlier this hour, if there is an error removing the funds from bank account A after placing the money in account B, you would definitely want to roll back the changes you've made and either retry the transaction at a later time, or flag the record for later examination.

To roll a transaction back to its original state, you just call the `Rollback()` method of the transaction object, as in Listing 18.2.

LISTING 18.2   Rolling a Transaction Back

```
<%@ Import Namespace="System.Data" %>
<%@ Import Namespace="System.Data.SqlClient" %>

<HTML>
<HEAD>
    <LINK rel="stylesheet" type="text/css" href="Main.css">
    <!-- End Style Sheet -->

    <script language="VB" runat="server" >
        Sub Page_Load(Source as Object, E as EventArgs)

        If IsPostBack then

          Dim sOutput as string

          'Create Connection
          Dim conn as SqlConnection = new SqlConnection("Data Source=" + _
                      "localhost;Initial Catalog=northwind;UID=sa;PWD=;")

          'Create Command
          Dim cmd as SqlCommand = new SqlCommand()
          cmd.Connection = conn
```

LISTING 18.2   continued

```
'Connection must be open to start transaction
conn.Open()

'Create Transaction and apply it to command object
Dim myTrans = conn.BeginTransaction("TransactionName")
cmd.Transaction = myTrans

'Show Database before modifications
GetAndBindData(datagrid1)

'Execute Database Change #1
ExecuteSQL(cmd, "UPDATE Fruits SET Quantity = 4 " + _
                "WHERE Name = 'Apple'")

'Execute Database Change #2
Try
    ExecuteSQL(cmd, "DELETE FROM FRUITS")
    Throw New Exception("A random horrible database error")
    myTrans.Commit()
Catch
    myTrans.Rollback()
End Try

'Requery to make sure changes are gone
GetAndBindData(datagrid7)

conn.Close()

Else
  '--- No post back ---
  'Just display the fruit table as it is
  GetAndBindData(datagrid1)


End If  'Postback

End Sub

Private Sub ExecuteSQL(cmd as SqlCommand, sSQL as string)

    cmd.CommandText = sSQL
    cmd.ExecuteNonQuery()

End Sub

Private Sub GetAndBindData( myDataGrid as _
                            System.Web.UI.WebControls.DataGrid )
```

18

LISTING 18.2   continued

```
                Dim conn as SqlConnection = new SqlConnection("Data Source=" + _
                            localhost;Initial Catalog=Northwind;UID=sa;PWD=; ")
                Dim cmd as SqlCommand = new SqlCommand("SELECT name, " + _
                                    "description, quantity FROM Fruits", conn)

                conn.Open()
                myDataGrid.DataSource = cmd.ExecuteReader()
                myDataGrid.DataBind()
                conn.Close()

            End Sub
        </script>

</HEAD>
<BODY>

<h1>Working With Transactions</h1>
<hr>



<form runat="server" id=form1 name=form1>
  <asp:label id=lblStatus runat="server" />

  <p>

  <input type="submit" Value="Run Queries">
  <table align="center" cellpadding=10 cellspacing=10>
    <tr>
      <td colspan=2 valign="center">
        <h3>Original Data:</h3>
        <asp:datagrid id=datagrid1 runat="server" />
        <br><br>
      </td>
    </tr>
    </tr>
      <td colspan=2>
        <h3>After rolling back transaction to beginning:</h3>
        <asp:datagrid id=datagrid7 runat="server" />
      </td>
    </tr>
  </table>

</form>
<hr>

</BODY>
</HTML>
```

Listing 18.2 creates a transaction, performs some database changes, and then rolls these changes back. On line 28, the transaction is started using the `BeginTransaction()` method of the `Connection` object. On the following line, the transaction object is assigned to the `Command` object. Any queries executed using the `cmd` `Command` object are performed under the umbrella of this transaction.

The database is then displayed before modifications using the `GetAndBindData()` method on line 32. On lines 34–36, the first database change is made, changing the quantity of apples to 4. Lines 37–43 perform the next database change. Then, an error is simulated using the `Throw()` method on line 39, causing the `Rollback()` method to run in the `Catch` code block on line 41. Had there been no error, the transaction would have been committed and all database changes made final. However, because the `Rollback()` method was called instead, all changes made under this transaction are reverted back to their previous state.

FIGURE 18.1

The appearance of the Web form in Listing 18.2 after submitting the form.

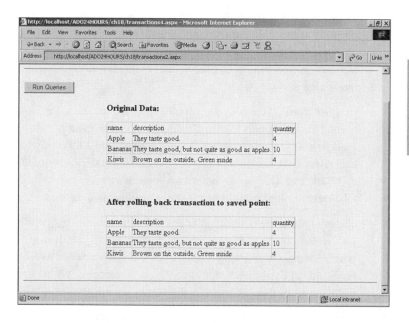

18

As you can see in Figure 18.1, the code in Listing 18.2 displays a Web form. After you click the button labeled Run Queries, a connection to the database is opened and a transaction started. Database change #1 is made, and then the second change is attempted. The second database change is wrapped in a `Try...Catch` block. This enables you to check for an error and handle that error gracefully. In this case, the transaction is rolled back, canceling any changes. Otherwise, the transaction is saved.

Committing a Transaction

In Listing 18.2, after all database modifications have been successfully performed, the transaction is saved by using the `Commit()` method of the transaction object. This ends the transaction and makes all database changes permanent.

Canceling a Transaction

If an error had occurred during the second database modification in Listing 18.2, the error would have been caught by the `Try...Catch` block and the `Catch` portion of the code would have been executed. In this case, the `Rollback()` method of the transaction object would have been called, reversing all changes made to the database, leaving it in its original state.

Saving a Transaction

When working with database transactions, it's possible to save the transaction at any point. However, the term "saving" when applied to transactions is a bit misleading. The process is more like bookmarking a site than saving a file. After saving at a point in a transaction, you can revert back to that point, canceling any changes you might have made after saving.

In other words, let's say you initiate a transaction, and save the transaction after updating several hundred fields in the database. Suppose that later, after several other database modifications, an error occurs. Rather than rolling all the way back to the beginning, you can save your transaction after the first batch of queries is executed. Then, later you can roll back your changes to that saved point. However, this method can be dangerous if any table relationships are missing, creating an unstable database.

To save a database transaction at any point, you need only call the `Save()` method of the transaction object, and pass it the name you would like to use to reference the saved point. Saving a transaction often makes more sense when working with hundreds or thousands of database changes in a single transaction. Without saving, you'd be forced to roll back all of these changes in the case of an error!

The example in Listing 18.3 demonstrates this concept. Just as in the previous example, a database connection is opened and a transaction initiated. Some changes are made to the data in the database, the transaction is saved, some more changes are made, and then the transaction is rolled back to the saved point. The transaction is then committed, finalizing all the changes made up to the saved point. Figure 18.2 shows the appearance of the Web form after submitting the form.

LISTING 18.3   Rolling a Transaction Back to a Saved Point

```
<%@ Page Debug="true" %>
<%@ Import Namespace="System.Data" %>
<%@ Import Namespace="System.Data.SqlClient" %>

<HTML>
<HEAD>
    <LINK rel="stylesheet" type="text/css" href="Main.css">
    <!-- End Style Sheet -->

    <script language="VB" runat="server" >
        Sub Page_Load(Source as Object, E as EventArgs)

            If IsPostBack then

                Dim sOutput as string

                'Create Connection
                Dim conn as SqlConnection = new SqlConnection("Data Source=" + _
                            "localhost;Initial Catalog=northwind;UID=sa;PWD=;")

                'Create Command
                Dim cmd as SqlCommand = new SqlCommand()
                cmd.Connection = conn

                'Connection must be open to start transaction
                conn.Open()

                'Create Transaction and apply it to command object
                Dim myTrans = conn.BeginTransaction("TransactionName")
                cmd.Transaction = myTrans

                'Show Database before modifications
                GetAndBindData(datagrid1)

                'Execute Database Change #1
                ExecuteSQL(cmd, "UPDATE Fruits SET Quantity = 2 " + _
                            "WHERE Name = 'Apple'")

                'Insert potentially hundreds of database changes here

                'Save Transaction
                myTrans.Save("SavePoint1")

                'Execute Database Change #2
                ExecuteSQL(cmd, "DELETE FROM FRUITS")

                'Oh no!  We've made a horrible mistake.
                'Rollback to saved point
```

18

LISTING 18.3 continued

```
        myTrans.Rollback("SavePoint1")

        'Commit earlier changes
        myTrans.Commit()

        'Requery
        GetAndBindData(datagrid7)

        conn.Close()

      Else

        '--- No post back ---
        'Just display the fruit table as it is
        GetAndBindData(datagrid1)

      End If  'Postback

    End Sub

    Private Sub ExecuteSQL(cmd as SqlCommand, sSQL as string)

        cmd.CommandText = sSQL
        cmd.ExecuteNonQuery()

    End Sub

    Private Sub GetAndBindData( myDataGrid as _
                                System.Web.UI.WebControls.DataGrid )

        Dim conn as SqlConnection = new SqlConnection("Data Source=" + _
                    "localhost;Initial Catalog=Northwind;UID=sa;PWD=;")
        Dim cmd as SqlCommand = new SqlCommand("SELECT name, " + _
                            "description, quantity FROM Fruits", conn)

        conn.Open()
        myDataGrid.DataSource = cmd.ExecuteReader()
        myDataGrid.DataBind()
        conn.Close()

    End Sub
  </script>

</HEAD>
<BODY>

<h1>Working With Transactions</h1>
```

LISTING 18.3 continued

```
<hr>

<form runat="server" id=form1 name=form1>
  <asp:label id=lblStatus runat="server" />

  <p>

  <input type="submit" Value="Run Queries" id=submit1 name=submit1>
  <table align="center" cellpadding=10 cellspacing=10>
    <tr>
      <td colspan=2 valign="center">
        <h3>Original Data:</h3>
        <asp:datagrid id=datagrid1 runat="server" />
        <br><br>
      </td>
    </tr>
    </tr>
      <td colspan=2>
        <h3>After rolling back transaction to saved point:</h3>
        <asp:datagrid id=datagrid7 runat="server" />
      </td>
    </tr>
  </table>

</form>
<hr>

</BODY>
</HTML>
```

Listing 18.3 is similar to the previous transaction code provided in Listing 18.2. Line 29 starts a transaction that is then assigned to the cmd Command object on the next line. The current state of the database is displayed using the GetAndBindData() method on line 33. A database change is then made on line 36, changing the quantity of apples from 2 to 4.

Shortly after on line 42, the transaction is saved using the Save() method of the transaction object. The following line of code then deletes all contents from the Fruit table. For the purposes of this example, that is undesirable. On line 49, the transaction is rolled back to the previous save point, before the deletion was performed. Line 52 uses the Commit() method to end the transaction and commit these database changes. Line 55 again shows the state of the database. As you can see in Figure 18.2, the quantity of apples is modified, but the results of the DELETE query were not saved.

18

FIGURE **18.2**

Saving a database transaction.

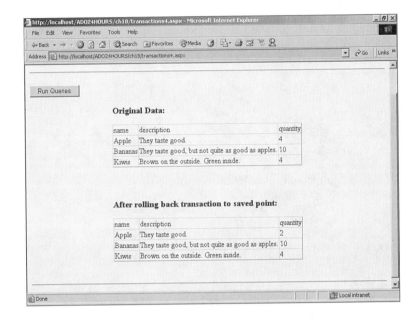

Transactions with Stored Procedures

Database transactions are by no means limited to ADO.NET. In fact, transactions are powered by the data source. That is to say, when you initiate a transaction inside ADO.NET, the data source (in this case Microsoft SQL Server) actually performs all the work.

To illustrate this point, the example in Listing 18.4 demonstrates how to perform a database transaction inside a stored procedure. It's very similar to an example used in a previous hour that adds an employee to the Employees table of the Northwind SQL Server database. This procedure also assigns a territory to the newly added employee as well, all rolled into a transaction.

To start a transaction inside a stored procedure in Microsoft SQL Server, you use the BEGIN TRAN keywords. To roll back a transaction, you use ROLLBACK TRAN and as you might have guessed, to commit a transaction, you use COMMIT TRAN.

LISTING 18.4   Rolling a Transaction Back to a Saved Point

```
CREATE PROCEDURE Employee_Add
(
    @LastName nvarchar(20),
    @FirstName nvarchar(10),
```

LISTING 18.4   continued

```
    @Title nvarchar(30),
    @BirthDate datetime,
    @HireDate datetime,
    @Address nvarchar(60),
    @City nvarchar(15),
    @PostalCode nvarchar(10),
    @TerritoryID nvarchar(20)
)

AS

    DECLARE @iCommunityProductAuditID int

    BEGIN TRAN

    -- add the main record
    INSERT INTO Employees
    (
        LastName,
        FirstName,
        Title,
        BirthDate,
        HireDate,
        Address,
        City,
        PostalCode
    )
    VALUES
    (
        @LastName,
        @FirstName,
        @Title,
        @BirthDate,
        @HireDate,
        @Address,
        @City,
        @PostalCode
    )

    IF @@ERROR <> 0
    BEGIN
      ROLLBACK TRAN
      RETURN @@ERROR
    END

        -- get EmployeeID
    declare @EmployeeID int
    SET @EmployeeID = @@IDENTITY
```

18

LISTING 18.4 continued

```
-- add employee to a territory
    INSERT INTO EmployeeTerritories
    (
        EmployeeID,
    TerritoryID
    )
VALUES
(
    @EmployeeID,
    @TerritoryID
)

IF @@ERROR <> 0
BEGIN
  ROLLBACK TRAN
  RETURN @@ERROR
END

COMMIT TRAN

RETURN @@ERROR
GO
```

The `Employee_Add` stored procedure in Listing 18.4 accepts a relatively large list of para-meters in lines 3–11. As you'll recall from Hour 15, "Working with Stored Procedures," these are the same as function arguments. Line 18 begins a transaction within the stored procedure. Lines 21–42 add a record into the Employees table using the values supplied in the parameters.

If any errors were encountered while performing the `INSERT` query, the transaction is rolled back using the `ROLLBACK TRAN` SQL statement in lines 44–48. In line 52, the auto-matically incremented identity number created for the newly added employee is assigned to the `@EmployeeID` variable. The `@EmployeeID` is then used in lines 55–64 to add a ter-ritory for that new employee to the EmployeeTerritories table. Again, lines 66–70 ensure that if any errors were encountered, the entire transaction is rolled back; this means that not only will the `EmployeeTerritories` entry be removed, but also the entry made for the new employee in the Employees table. On line 72, the transaction is commited.

Summary

In this hour, you've seen how to work with database transactions using ADO.NET. You saw how to start a transaction and assign that transaction to the `Command` object. You then saw how to revert transactions back to previous states and also how to finalize a transaction. Lastly, you saw how to perform a transaction directly in a stored procedure.

Q&A

Q Can I enlist multiple command operations in the same transaction?

A Certainly! All you need to do is create another Command object and assign it the same Connection object. Then remember to assign the SqlTransaction object to it as well.

Q What happens to my transaction if the server crashes while it is processing?

A This is dependent upon your data source. However, using Microsoft SQL Server 7.0 or 2000, all changes made during the life of your transaction will be rolled back. Almost any transactional data source should operate in the same manner.

Q What if I do not explicitly call the Commit() method to save the transaction?

A If you do not call the Commit() method, the database changes made during the life of the transaction will not be saved.

Q Are changes to database schema performed while in a transaction rolled back as well?

A Yes. If you were to create a table while participating in a transaction, and then decided to roll the transaction back, the table would be rolled back as well.

18

Workshop

These quiz questions are designed to test your knowledge of the material covered in this chapter. The answers to the quiz questions can be found in Appendix A, "Answers to Quizzes."

Quiz

1. Which method of the SqlTransaction object finalizes a transaction? How is this done in T-SQL?

2. In ADO.NET, a database transaction is started by using which object?

Exercise

Try to implement a simple financial transaction example, like the one mentioned in the introduction of this hour. Create two database tables, one for bank A and one for bank B. Then create a procedure that copies the checking and savings balance from one bank to another for a given AccountID. Make sure, of course, to use a transaction to perform the transfer.

HOUR 19

Using Automatically Generated Commands

Most application code (Web or otherwise) that accesses SQL Server data tends to be fairly simple in nature. Rarely is there the need to do complex table joins as the basis of your DataSet population, let alone as the basis of updates back to the database. In the cases where you are only dealing with single-table commands, you can leverage the CommandBuilder feature of .NET to generate the appropriate INSERT, UPDATE, and DELETE commands for this type of single-table processing automatically. There are some limitations to automatic code generation, but its efficiency and coding simplicity far outweigh these limitations. In addition, Visual Studio .NET Enterprise Architect provides much of the same type of code generation capability but does not use the CommandBuilder object. In both cases, Microsoft continues to try to make the programmer's job easy.

In this hour, you will learn the following topics:

- When automatically generated commands are created
- Coding examples using the CommandBuilder

- What to do when the original SELECT statement changes
- A brief look at Windows Form Designer–generated code

Automatically Generated Commands

A recent survey of a large Silicon Valley-based corporation's application code library yielded an interesting characteristic about their major intranet applications. This characteristic was that nearly 90% of the code acted (read, updated, inserted, or deleted) against only one table at a time. There were many reasons for this including performance (keeping tight, short transactions), concurrency issues (minimizing of locking), and a desire to keep application code very small and modular. This is very typical for most organizations. With this in mind, the advent of having code generated automatically if it meets certain criteria was made a reality in .NET.

As you analyze your coding requirements and find that you will meet these criteria, you can take advantage of having .NET generate much of your update, insert, and delete code for you. .NET uses an object called CommandBuilder to automatically generate the DeleteCommand, InsertCommand, and UpdateCommand of the DataAdapter. It is available for both the OLE DB and SQL data adapters (the SqlCommandBuilder class and the OleDbCommandBuilder class). From a benefits point of view, this translates directly into smaller, more easily maintained code throughout. Now, this is a really big benefit.

> The SqlDataAdapter and the OleDbDataAdapter do not automatically generate the SQL statements required to reconcile changes made to a DataSet with the associated data source. You must *explicitly* set the SelectCommand property of the data adapter to make this happen!

Automatically Generated Commands Criteria

To take advantage of the automatically generated commands capability, you must only be dealing with a single table at a time. The table must also have a unique primary key or unique column of some kind; otherwise, an InvalidOperation exception will be encountered and no automatically generated commands will be created. The generated code does not take into account any underlying relationships that might exist that logically relate tables such as foreign key constraints, and so on. The responsibility is on you to make sure you are not interfering with this type of situation.

The logic for this automatically generated code will also adhere to the optimistic concurrency model (see Chapter 14, "Managing ADO.NET Concurrency," for more detailed information on what the optimistic concurrency model is). In other words, the data that is read by the SelectCommand will not be locked for update and can be modified by any other user or application at any time. And, the update and delete code that is automatically generated will contain a WHERE clause that compares all of the original data values against what exists in the database. If it fails this comparison, the command will not succeed and will throw a DBConcurrencyException.

In the case of an update, if the row that it is targeting was deleted, the update will fail with the same DBConcurrencyException.

Speaking of the SelectCommand, the CommandBuilder must execute the SelectCommand in order to retrieve the necessary metadata to build the INSERT, UPDATE, and DELETE commands. So, this will be one extra query that must be executed (only a slight, but necessary nuisance).

If anything changes with the metadata after this initial SelectCommand retrieval (for example, you select a different column and want to update this value instead), you will have to refresh this metadata, which will also cause a refresh of the automatically generated UPDATE, INSERT, and DELETE code.

CommandBuilder has a bit of difficulty mapping output parameters that are identity columns (or autonumbers columns). In this case, you will not be able to use this feature and have to explicitly code the UPDATE command.

And last, but not least, if any column names or table names contain any special characters like periods, quotation marks, spaces, or other nonalphanumeric characters (even if delimited by brackets [ ]), this will cause the generated logic to fail. This would only affect perhaps .05% of the world. Most folks name their columns and tables in a fairly standard way.

This limitation does not apply to table names in the form of schema.owner.table, though.

Using the `CommandBuilder`

Normally when you go about updating, deleting, or inserting data via the DataSet, you fill the dataset, make your changes to the DataSet, and then issue an explicit update (DELETE or INSERT) command. Listing 19.1 shows a typical update process:

LISTING 19.1   The Update Process (19NormalUpd.vb)

```
Dim dbConn As SqlConnection = New SqlConnection("Data Source=localhost;
        Integrated Security=SSPI;Initial Catalog=northwind")
Dim CustomerAdapter As SqlDataAdapter = New SqlDataAdapter
```

19

LISTING 19.1   continued

```
        ("SELECT CustomerID, ContactName FROM Customers", dbConn)
CustomerAdapter.UpdateCommand=New SqlCommand
        ("UPDATE Customers SET ContactName=@ContactName " & _
        "WHERE CustomerID = @oldCustomerID", dbConn)

CustomerAdapter.UpdateCommand.Parameters.Add
        ("@ContactName", SqlDbType.NVarChar, 30, "ContactName")
Dim OldParms As SqlParameter
OldParms = CustomerAdapter.UpdateCommand.Parameters.Add
        ("@oldCustomerID", SqlDbType.NChar, 5, "CustomerID")
OldParms.SourceVersion = DataRowVersion.Original
Dim CustomerDataSet As DataSet = New DataSet()
CustomerAdapter.Fill(CustomerDataSet, "Customers")
Dim UpdtRow As DataRow = CustomerDataSet.Tables("Customers").Rows(0)
UpdtRow("ContactName")= "Donald Renato"
CustomerAdapter.Update(CustomerDataSet, "Customers")
```

However, if your update operation to the database meets all of the criteria that we out-
lined earlier, the code could be greatly simplified by taking advantage of the automatically generated code from the CommandBuilder. Listing 19.2 is the same update
processing but utilizing the SqlCommandBuilder instead. We will be able to remove the
UpdateCommand logic, the old parameter-saving logic, and yield a tighter, smaller code
result. You will see first the declaration of the SqlCommandBuilder for the
SqlDataAdapter. This will generate all of the needed INSERT, UPDATE, and DELETE commands automatically. Then, you simply open the connection, fill the dataset, update a
value in the dataset, and push the update back to the database
(CustomerAdapter.Update..). That's it.

LISTING 19.2   Updating Using the SqlCommandBuilder (19AGCUpd.vb)

```
Dim dbConn As SqlConnection = New SqlConnection("Data Source=localhost;
        Integrated Security=SSPI;Initial Catalog=northwind")
Dim CustomerAdapter As SqlDataAdapter = New SqlDataAdapter
        ("SELECT CustomerID, ContactName FROM Customers", dbConn)
Dim CustomerCMDBLDR As SqlCommandBuilder =
                            New SqlCommandBuilder (CustomerAdapter)
Dim CustomerDataSet As DataSet = New DataSet()
dbConn.Open()
CustomerAdapter.Fill(CustomerDataSet, "Customers")
Dim UpdtRow As DataRow = CustomerDataSet.Tables("Customers").Rows(0)
UpdtRow("ContactName")= "Donald Bertucci"
CustomerAdapter.Update(CustomerDataSet, "Customers")
dbConn.Close()
```

Showing What Was Automatically Generated

If you want, you can display the exact SQL code that the CommandBuilder has generated using the Get..Command() methods. Listing 19.3 is a code example of displaying the generated commands out to the console and the execution results of this display.

LISTING 19.3   Displaying the Generated Commands (19ShowUpd.vb)

```
Dim CustomerAdapter As SqlDataAdapter = New SqlDataAdapter
        ("SELECT CustomerID, ContactName FROM Customers", dbConn)
Console.Writeline(CustomerCMDBLDR.GetUpdateCommand().CommandText)
Console.Writeline(CustomerCMDBLDR.GetInsertCommand().CommandText)
Console.Writeline(CustomerCMDBLDR.GetDeleteCommand().CommandText)
```

The preceding code, when executed, displays the following results:

```
UPDATE Customers SET CustomerID = @p1 , ContactName = @p2 WHERE ( (CustomerID =
@p3) AND ((ContactName IS NULL AND @p4 IS NULL) OR (ContactName = @p5)) )
INSERT INTO Customers( CustomerID , ContactName ) VALUES ( @p1 , @p2 )
DELETE FROM  Customers WHERE ( (CustomerID = @p1) AND ((ContactName IS NULL AND
@p2 IS NULL) OR (ContactName = @p3)) )
```

If the SELECT Statement Changes

If the SELECT statement that was originally defined in your program needs to change for any reason, you run the risk of executing automatically generated code that does not match the current SELECT statement's metadata. For example, your application might need a different set of columns than were selected earlier, or the SELECT statement could be dynamically provided as an input from the user. If something has changed in this SELECT statement, you must make sure you regenerate the automatically generated code.

What really is happening is that the metadata has changed (the different SELECT statement) and any automatically generated code would be out of sync with this new metadata. The approach for keeping the SELECT statement's metadata in sync with the automatically generated code is to issue a Refresh command after any changes have been made to the SELECT statement.

Listing 19.4 is an example of code that issues a first SELECT statement (CustomerID and ContactName), updates data based on that SELECT statement's automatically generated code, then changes the SELECT statement (CustomerID and CompanyName), refreshes the automatically generated code, and proceeds with the next update based on the newly generated code. Very clean implementation!

19

LISTING 19.4   Refreshing the Automatically Generated Code (19RefreshUpd.vb)

```
Dim CustomerAdapter As SqlDataAdapter = New SqlDataAdapter
              ("SELECT CustomerID, ContactName FROM Customers", dbConn)
Dim CustomerCMDBLDR As SqlCommandBuilder = New SqlCommandBuilder
                                                      (CustomerAdapter)
Dim CustomerDataSet As DataSet = New DataSet()
dbConn.Open()
CustomerAdapter.Fill(CustomerDataSet, "Customers")
Dim UpdtRow As DataRow = CustomerDataSet.Tables("Customers").Rows(0)
UpdtRow("ContactName")= "Juliana Nicole"
CustomerAdapter.Update(CustomerDataSet, "Customers")
CustomerAdapter.SelectCommand.CommandText=
                        "SELECT CustomerID, CompanyName FROM Customers"
CustomerCMDBLDR.RefreshSchema()
CustomerDataSet.Tables.Remove(CustomerDataSet.Tables("Customers"))
CustomerAdapter.Fill(CustomerDataSet, "Customers")
Dim UpdtARow As DataRow = CustomerDataSet.Tables("Customers").Rows(0)
UpdtARow("CompanyName")= "ABCDE Company"
CustomerAdapter.Update(CustomerDataSet, "Customers")
dbConn.Close()
```

Windows Form Designer-Generated Code—VS .NET

Many places in Visual Studio .NET Enterprise Architect have been enhanced with automatic code generation. The area that corresponds to that of the CommandBuilder can be found when you create the DataAdapter for database access for a form when using the Windows Form Designer. You do not have to use the CommandBuilder object to set this capability. You simply choose to have the Data Adapter Configuration Wizard generate INSERT, UPDATE, and DELETE statements for you. These then become part of the Windows Form Designer–generated code used by the form you are building. They will also follow the optimistic concurrency model if you direct the wizard to do so. Figure 19.1 shows the Data Adapter Configuration Wizard with the Use SQL statements option checked and the Advanced SQL Generation Options dialog box. As you can see, these correspond exactly with what CommandBuilder would generate.

The next wizard dialog box (see Figure 19.2) reviews the list of tasks the Data Adapter Confirmation Wizard has performed, which includes the generation of the INSERT, UPDATE, and DELETE statements (just as we saw with the CommandBuilder object).

Then, if you jump back over to the Code Editor tab in the Windows Form Designer, as you can see in Figure 19.3, you will see a node that contains the "Windows Form Designer generated code". Expand this node and you can walk through all the generated INSERT, UPDATE, and DELETE code that was generated for you.

FIGURE 19.1

Data Adapter Configuration Wizard and the Advanced SQL Generation Options dialog box.

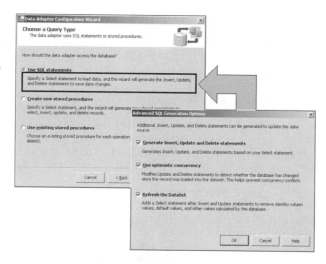

FIGURE 19.2

Data Adapter Configuration Wizard—View Wizard Results.

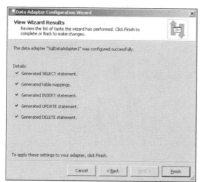

19

The generated code is quite extensive and pretty much bulletproof as well. Again, this example follows the optimistic concurrency model for updates. A snippet of code that was generated is shown in Listing 19.5.

LISTING 19.5 Generated Code (19Vsdesigner.vb)

```
'SqlInsertCommand1
        Me.SqlInsertCommand1.CommandText = "INSERT INTO Customers
             (CustomerID, CompanyName, ContactName, ContactTitle, Address" & _
        ", City, Region, PostalCode, Country, Phone, Fax) VALUES
                                 (@CustomerID, @CompanyName, " & _
        "@ContactName, @ContactTitle, @Address, @City, @Region,
             @PostalCode, @Country, @Phone, @Fax); " & _
        "SELECT CustomerID, CompanyName, ContactName,
                                         ContactTitle, Address," & _
```

LISTING 19.5   continued

```
"City, Region, PostalCode, Country, Phone, Fax
                FROM Customers WHERE (CustomerID = @CustomerID)"_

'SqlUpdateCommand1
       Me.SqlUpdateCommand1.CommandText = "UPDATE Customers
              SET CustomerID = @CustomerID, CompanyName = @CompanyName,
              ContactName = @ContactName, ContactTitle = @ContactTitle, " & _
       " Address = @Address, City = @" & _
       "City, Region = @Region, PostalCode = @PostalCode, Country = @Country,"&
       "Phone = @P hone, Fax = @Fax WHERE (CustomerID = @Original_CustomerID) " &
       "
       "AND (Address = @Original_Address OR @Original_Address IS NULL AND " &
       " Address IS NULL) AND (City = @Original_City OR " &        _
       "@Original_City IS NULL AND City IS NULL) " & _
       " AND (CompanyName = @Original _CompanyName) AND (ContactName = " &
       " @Original_ContactName OR @Original_ContactName" & _
       " IS NULL AND ContactName IS NULL) AND (ContactTitle = @Original" & " &
       "ContactTitle OR @Original_ContactTitle IS NULL AND ContactTitle" &
       " IS NULL) AND (Country = @Original_Country OR @Original " & _
       " _Country IS NULL AND Country IS NULL) AND (Fax = @Original" & _
       "_Fax OR @Original_Fax IS NULL AND Fax IS NULL) AND " &
       " (Phone = @Original_Phone OR @" & _
       "Original_Phone IS NULL AND Phone IS NULL) AND (PostalCode = " &
       " @Original_PostalCode OR @Original_PostalCode " & _
       " IS NULL AND PostalCode IS NULL) AND (Region = @Original" & _
       "_Region OR @Original_Region IS NULL AND Region IS NULL); " &
       " SELECT CustomerID, CompanyName, ContactName, ContactTitle " & _
       ", Address, City, Region, PostalCode, Country, " & _
       "Phone, Fax FROM Customers WHERE (CustomerID = @CustomerID)"
'SqlDeleteCommand1
       Me.SqlDeleteCommand1.CommandText = "DELETE FROM Customers " &
       WHERE (CustomerID = @Original_CustomerID) AND (Address = " & _
       "@Original_Address OR @Original_Address IS NULL AND Address " &
       " IS NULL) AND (City = @Original_City OR @Original_City " & _
       "IS NULL AND City IS NULL) AND (CompanyName = @Original_CompanyName)" &
       "AND (ContactName = @Original_ContactName OR @Original_Contact" & _
       "Name IS NULL AND ContactName IS NULL) AND (ContactTitle = " &
       "@Original_ContactTitle OR @Original_ContactTitle IS NULL " & _
       " AND ContactTitle IS NULL) AND (Country = @Original_Country " & _
       " OR @Original_Country IS NULL AND Country IS NULL) AND " & _
       "(Fax = @Original_Fax OR @Original_Fax IS NULL AND Fax IS NULL)" &
       " AND (Phone = @Original_Phone " & _
       "OR @Original_Phone IS NULL AND Phone IS NULL) AND" &
       " (PostalCode = @Original_Postal Code OR @Original_PostalCode " & _
       " IS NULL AND PostalCode IS NULL) AND (Region = @Original " & _
       " _Region OR @Original_Region IS NULL AND Region IS NULL)"
```

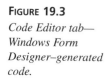

FIGURE 19.3

*Code Editor tab—
Windows Form
Designer–generated
code.*

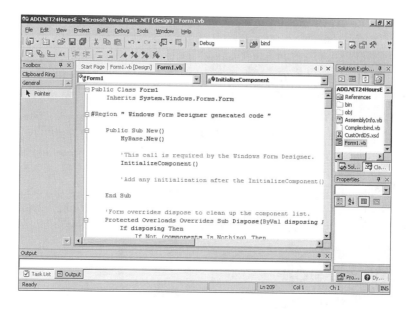

You can see the WHERE clause comparisons for guaranteeing your update or delete is being used (for optimistic concurrency). Just be glad that you don't have to code all of this yourself!

Summary

In this hour, you've seen the advantages of using automatically generated commands via the CommandBuilder object. Not only does this simplify coding, but it also makes your code much more consistent and easy to maintain. Even though you are limited to single-table data accesses when using this capability, you shouldn't run into that many cases where you can't take advantage of the CommandBuilder. Remember, the CommandBuilder is using the optimistic concurrency model. And luckily, when you are using the VS .NET Enterprise Architect, you can leverage off the same automatically generated code while building the DataAdapter instances for your forms development. Coding life just got a lot easier.

Q&A

Q How will I know when to use CommandBuilder or not?

A The data access requirements must correspond to the single-table limitation, the unique column or primary key requirement along with no related table

19

functionality that could cause data update discrepancies (like foreign key constraints, and so on). If you have met this criteria, save yourself a bunch of coding and use `CommandBuilder`!

Q Do I do the same type of coding for the `SqlDataAdapter` that I would do for the `OleDbDataAdapter`?

A Yes! There is basically no difference in the coding approach for either `DataAdapter`. Both can use the `CommandBuilder` capability.

Q What if I don't refresh the `SELECT` statement's metadata when the statement is changed?

A Unpredictable results will occur. Very often you will see the error of a new referenced column is not available. Be sure to refresh the metadata after any `SELECT` statement change!

Workshop

These quiz questions are designed to test your knowledge of the material covered in this chapter. The answers to the quiz questions can be found in Appendix A, "Answers to Quizzes."

Quiz

1. `CommandBuilder` will generate `UPDATE` and `DELETE` statements following which concurrency model?

   a. Pessimistic concurrency model

   b. Optimistic concurrency model

   c. Data update concurrency model

2. True or false: Automatically generated commands will be created for all `SelectCommands` coded in Visual Basic or C#.

3. What must be done following the change of a `SELECT` statement when using `CommandBuilder` to automatically generate code?

   a. Reassign `SELECT` variables

   b. Refresh metadata

   c. Close connection

   d. Open connection

4. True or false: The following `SELECT` statement is valid for using with `CommandBuilder`:

```
SELECT a.*, b.*
FROM Customers a, Orders b
WHERE a.CustomerID = b.CustomerID
```

5. The `SelectCommand` that will be used for the `CommandBuilder` must:

    a. Include a `SELECT Distinct` clause

    b. Contain all columns in the table

    c. Return at least one primary key or unique column

    d. Contain a `WHERE` clause with at least one filter

Exercise

Take (download) the original non-`CommandBuilder` sample code (19NormalUpd.vb) and manually convert it to use automatically generated commands with `CommandBuilder`. You can use either the `OleDBCommandBuilder` or `SqlCommandBuilder` objects.

After you have completed this conversion (and it works!), add in an insert and delete that also uses the automatically generated commands.

19

HOUR **20**

Working with Typed DataSets

ADO.NET code has made some great strides forward in the context of typing. One such major stride is in the ability to access the data held in the DataSet through a "strongly typed" metaphor. This may not seem like such a big deal at first glance, but when compared to the old "weakly typed" approach of vintage ADO, it is more than a pleasure to work with. In particular, you can now access the typed DataSet's tables and columns with more simplified and user-friendly code. Using typed DataSets also yields better code coming out of the chute because any previously unknown runtime typing issues come out at compile time and not at runtime (as runtime errors, nasty indeed!). Microsoft also throws in the XML Schema Definition tool (XSD.exe—as part of the .NET Framework SDK) that generates typed DataSets and has embedded the process of generating typed DataSets as standard practice in Visual Studio .NET. The rest is up to you.

In this hour, you will learn the following topics:

- A more detailed discussion of the typed DataSet
- How to generate typed DataSets with XSD.exe
- How to generate typed DataSets in VS .NET
- Using annotations with typed DataSets for even better code
- Typical programming with typed DataSets

The Typed DataSet

A typed DataSet is a class that derives from a DataSet class and inherits all the methods, events, and properties of DataSets. In other words, it looks and acts the same as a DataSet. A typed DataSet also provides strongly typed methods, events, and properties. All this translates to being able to access (in your code) the tables and columns by name, instead of using collection-based methods. In addition, Visual Studio .NET code editors use the typed DataSet to help automatically complete lines as you physically type a line of code. As previously stated, the strong typing of DataSets also contributes to catching type mismatch errors at compile time as opposed to at runtime. In the next section, we will be generating the XML schema directly from some SQL Server tables and creating typed DataSets for use in a coding example.

To generate a typed DataSet that can be used by many programs (and languages such as VB and C#), you must first start with an XML schema representation of the DataSet. This will be the .xsd XML file (XML Schema Definition). After this has been created, it can be turned into a typed DataSet and made available to programs that reference it properly (via a generated .dll). This .xsd schema of the DataSet must be compliant with the XML Schema definition language standards, available at http://www.w3.org/2001/XMLSchema and http://w3c.org.

After the XML Schema is generated, we will run it through the XSD.exe (XML Schema Definition) tool and create the typed class definitions in the appropriate language we would be using it with (such as VB or C#). We then compile the typed class definition as a library (.dll) to be used in our code. It's really that simple. All we then have to do is include the library (and Imports) in our VB code, and we can reference the strongly typed DataSet easily. Let's step through this process now. Later in this hour we will see how to do this using VS .NET Enterprise Architect as well.

Generating a Typed DataSet

As mentioned earlier, you must first generate some valid XML for the DataSet you
intend to create. Well, you must have a clue of what you need in this DataSet before you
can start this process. Your coding needs dictate this. If you need only a portion of the
Customers data, it is a pretty small DataSet definition. Figure 20.1 illustrates the
Customers table in the Northwind database. We will use all or portions of the Customer
data in our coding example. Listing 20.1 is the associated XML Schema Definition for
Customers (compliant with the XML Schema definition language standards).

LISTING 20.1   The XML Schema File for Customers DataSet

```
<?xml version="1.0" encoding="utf-8"?>
<xs:schema id="CustDataSet" xmlns=""
    xmlns:xs="http://www.w3.org/2001/XMLSchema"
    xmlns:msdata="urn:schemas-microsoft-com:xml-msdata">
  <xs:element name="CustDataSet" msdata:IsDataSet="true">
    <xs:complexType>
      <xs:choice maxOccurs="unbounded">
        <xs:element name="Customers">
          <xs:complexType>
            <xs:sequence>
              <xs:element name="CustomerID" type="xs:string" minOccurs="0" />
              <xs:element name="CompanyName" type="xs:string" minOccurs="0" />
              <xs:element name="ContactName" type="xs:string" minOccurs="0" />
              <xs:element name="ContactTitle" type="xs:string" minOccurs="0" />
              <xs:element name="Address" type="xs:string" minOccurs="0" />
              <xs:element name="City" type="xs:string" minOccurs="0" />
              <xs:element name="Region" type="xs:string" minOccurs="0" />
              <xs:element name="PostalCode" type="xs:string" minOccurs="0" />
              <xs:element name="Country" type="xs:string" minOccurs="0" />
              <xs:element name="Phone" type="xs:string" minOccurs="0" />
              <xs:element name="Fax" type="xs:string" minOccurs="0" />
            </xs:sequence>
          </xs:complexType>
        </xs:element>
      </xs:choice>
    </xs:complexType>
  </xs:element>
</xs:schema>
```

20

If you need a much more complex DataSet that includes perhaps Customers (all elements) and their associated orders (all elements), the XML coding is a bit longer. Figure
20.2 shows the relationship that must be traversed from the Customers table to the
Orders table. This also translates into a potential complex XML schema definition that

contains both customers and orders. Remember, it must allow you to traverse a relation-ship (from parent customers to their child orders) using one DataSet (as seen in Listing 20.2).

FIGURE 20.1

The Customers table.

LISTING 20.2   The XML Schema File for Customers and Orders DataSet

```xml
<?xml version="1.0" encoding="utf-8"?>
<xs:schema id="CustDataSet0" xmlns=""
    xmlns:xs="http://www.w3.org/2001/XMLSchema"
    xmlns:msdata="urn:schemas-microsoft-com:xml-msdata">
  <xs:element name="CustDataSet0" msdata:IsDataSet="true">
    <xs:complexType>
      <xs:choice maxOccurs="unbounded">
        <xs:element name="Customers">
          <xs:complexType>
            <xs:sequence>
              <xs:element name="CustomerID" type="xs:string" minOccurs="0" />
              <xs:element name="CompanyName" type="xs:string" minOccurs="0" />
              <xs:element name="ContactName" type="xs:string" minOccurs="0" />
              <xs:element name="ContactTitle" type="xs:string" minOccurs="0"/>
              <xs:element name="Address" type="xs:string" minOccurs="0" />
              <xs:element name="City" type="xs:string" minOccurs="0" />
              <xs:element name="Region" type="xs:string" minOccurs="0" />
              <xs:element name="PostalCode" type="xs:string" minOccurs="0"/>
              <xs:element name="Country" type="xs:string" minOccurs="0" />
              <xs:element name="Phone" type="xs:string" minOccurs="0" />
              <xs:element name="Fax" type="xs:string" minOccurs="0" />
            </xs:sequence>
          </xs:complexType>
        </xs:element>
        <xs:element name="Orders">
          <xs:complexType>
            <xs:sequence>
              <xs:element name="OrderID" type="xs:int" minOccurs="0" />
              <xs:element name="CustomerID" type="xs:string" minOccurs="0" />
```

LISTING 20.2   continued

```
            <xs:element name="EmployeeID" type="xs:int" minOccurs="0" />
            <xs:element name="OrderDate" type="xs:dateTime" minOccurs="0" />
            <xs:element name="RequiredDate" type="xs:dateTime" minOccurs="0"/>
            <xs:element name="ShippedDate" type="xs:dateTime" minOccurs="0" />
            <xs:element name="ShipVia" type="xs:int" minOccurs="0" />
            <xs:element name="Freight" type="xs:decimal" minOccurs="0" />
            <xs:element name="ShipName" type="xs:string" minOccurs="0" />
            <xs:element name="ShipAddress" type="xs:string" minOccurs="0"/>
            <xs:element name="ShipCity" type="xs:string" minOccurs="0" />
            <xs:element name="ShipRegion" type="xs:string" minOccurs="0" />
            <xs:element name="ShipPostalCode" type="xs:string" minOccurs="0"/>
            <xs:element name="ShipCountry" type="xs:string" minOccurs="0" />
          </xs:sequence>
        </xs:complexType>
      </xs:element>
    </xs:choice>
  </xs:complexType>
  </xs:element>
</xs:schema>
```

FIGURE 20.2

The Customers and Orders table relationships.

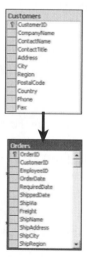

A quick-and-dirty way to generate the XML schema file definition for a DataSet is to utilize the WriteXMLSchema method of the DataSet and just generate it out to a physical file using the System.IO.StreamWriter object. The VB code example in Listing 20.3 defines what the DataSet should contain (Customers table data, all elements), fills the DataSet, and then writes out the XML schema for the DataSet into a physical file named Customers.xsd. Always use the "xsd" file type for XML Schema files.

20

LISTING 20.3   Generating the XML Schema File Definition (20xmlsch.vb)

```
dbConnection = new SqlConnection("server=localhost;
        Trusted_Connection=yes;database=northwind")
    dbSqlDataAdapter = new SqlDataAdapter
      ("select * from customers", dbConnection)
    CustDataSet = new DataSet()
    dbSqlDataAdapter.Fill(CustDataSet,"Customers")
    Dim xmlsch As System.IO.StreamWriter =
            New System.IO.StreamWriter("Customers.xsd")
    CustDataSet.WriteXmlSchema(xmlsch)
    xmlsch.Close()
```

If you wanted your `DataSet` to also include the Orders data (as seen in Figure 20.2), you could just create another `sqlDataAdapter` that defines the `SELECT` statement for the Orders table and fill this into your `DataSet` as well (as shown here):

```
SqlConnection("server=localhost;Trusted_Connection=yes;database=northwind")
    dbSqlDataAdapter1 = new SqlDataAdapter
            ("select * from customers", dbConnection)
    dbSqlDataAdapter2 = new SqlDataAdapter
            ("select * from orders", dbConnection)
    CustODataSet = new DataSet()
    dbSqlDataAdapter1.Fill(CustODataSet,"Customers")
    dbSqlDataAdapter2.Fill(CustODataSet,"Orders")
    Dim xmlsch As System.IO.StreamWriter =
            New System.IO.StreamWriter("CustomerO.xsd")
    CustODataSet.WriteXmlSchema(xmlsch)
    xmlsch.Close()
```

After the XML Schema file is created, you can use this with the XSD tool to generate the typed `DataSet`. Open up the physical file that was generated and make sure that you have the desired schema id name (`<xs:schema id= "CustDataSet"`) along with its associated element name value (`<xs:element name="CustDataSet"`) as you can see in Listing 20.4.

LISTING 20.4   Customer `DataSet` XML for generating a Typed `DataSet`
(Customers.xsd)

```
<?xml version="1.0" encoding="utf-8"?>
<xs:schema id="CustDataSet"  xmlns=""
xmlns:xs="http://www.w3.org/2001/XMLSchema"
xmlns:msdata="urn:schemas-microsoft-com:xml-msdata">
  <xs:element name="CustDataSet" msdata:IsDataSet="true">
    <xs:complexType>
      <xs:choice maxOccurs="unbounded">
        <xs:element name="Customers">
          <xs:complexType>
```

Using XSD.exe: The XML Schema Definition Tool

The XSD.exe (XML Schema Definition) tool is supplied to you in the .NET Framework SDK. The XSD tool can generate XML schema or Common Language Runtime classes from XDR, XML, and XSD files, or from classes in a runtime assembly. You will be providing the XML Schema file as input (Customers.xsd in this example) along with a few directives. The file extensions drive the XSD tool logic. So if you specify (and provide) an XML file, XSD.exe will infer a schema from the data in the file and produce an associated schema file (.xsd). If you specify (and provide) an XSD file (schema file), XSD.exe will generate source code for runtime objects that correspond to the XML Schema. For our purpose the important directives are:

- /d[ataset]—Instructs XSD.exe to generate a typed DataSet.

- /l[anguage]—Instructs XSD.exe on what language to use (VB or CS or JS). Default language is CS (C#).

- /n(amespace):*namespace*—Specifies the runtime namespace for the generated types. The default namespace is Schemas.

The output (results) of the XSD.exe command will be the corresponding typed DataSet class code for the language specified. An example of generating the typed DataSet class code from our Customers.xsd XML Schema file would be (from the DOS prompt):

```
D:> xsd.exe /d /l:VB customers.xsd /n:XSDSchema.Northwind
Microsoft (R) Xml Schemas/DataTypes support utility
[Microsoft (R) .NET Framework, Version 1.0.3617.0]
Copyright (C) Microsoft Corporation 1998-2001. All rights reserved.
Writing file 'D:\ADOSAMPLE\customers.vb'.
```

The resulting Customers.VB source code is quite extensive, and it is recommended that this code should not be changed. Here are the first few lines from the code:

```
'------------------------------------------------------------
' <autogenerated>
'     This code was generated by a tool.
'     Runtime Version: 1.0.3617.0
'     Changes to this file may cause incorrect behavior and will be lost if
'     the code is regenerated.
' </autogenerated>
'------------------------------------------------------------
Option Strict Off
Option Explicit On
Imports System
Imports System.Data
Imports System.Runtime.Serialization
Imports System.Xml
'This source code was auto-generated by xsd, Version=1.0.3617.0.
```

20

```
Namespace XSDSchema.Northwind
    <Serializable(), _
    System.ComponentModel.DesignerCategoryAttribute("code"), _
    System.Diagnostics.DebuggerStepThrough(), _
    System.ComponentModel.ToolboxItem(true)> _
    Public Class CustDataSet
        Inherits DataSet
        Private tableCustomers As CustomersDataTable
. . .
```

Use the /t:library directive when compiling this code so that a corresponding library
(.dll) is generated for later use. Following our example, you would specify (at the DOS
prompt):

```
D:> vbc.exe  /t:Library customers.vb  /r:System.dll  /r:System.Data.dll
                    /r:System.Xml.dll
Microsoft (R) Visual Basic .NET Compiler version 7.00.9447
for Microsoft (R) .NET Framework version 1.00.3617
Copyright (C) Microsoft Corporation 1987-2001. All rights reserved.
```

Now the typed DataSet is available to use in your code by including the namespace
(Imports for VB, Using for C#) and the appropriate /r: reference for the .dll (library).
The following is an example of compiling a sample VB program followed by some sam-
ple code lines of that VB program:

```
D:> vbc.exe 20usetyped.vb /r:System.dll /r:System.Data.dll /r:System.Xml.dll
                    /r:customers.dll
Microsoft (R) Visual Basic .NET Compiler version 7.00.9447
for Microsoft (R) .NET Framework version 1.00.3617
Copyright (C) Microsoft Corporation 1987-2001. All rights reserved.
```

The preceding example compiled the VB program code shown in Listing 20.5.

LISTING 20.5   Visual Basic Program Code—Typed DataSets (20UseTyped.vb)

```
Imports System
Imports System.Data
Imports System.Data.SqlClient
Imports Microsoft.VisualBasic
Imports XSDSchema.Northwind
namespace HowTo.ADONET24.Samples
public class usetypedDS
  public shared sub Main()
    Dim mytypedds as usetypedDS = new usetypedDS()
    mytypedds.Run()
  end sub
  public sub Run()
    try
      Dim CSDataSet As CustDataSet = New CustDataSet()
```

LISTING 20.5   continued

```
    Dim CustomerAdapter As SqlDataAdapter =
     New SqlDataAdapter("SELECT CustomerID, CompanyName, ContactName " &
          "FROM Customers WHERE CustomerID like 'B%' " &
          "ORDER BY          CustomerID",
          "server=localhost;Trusted_Connection=yes;database=northwind;")
    CustomerAdapter.Fill(CSDataSet, "Customers")
    Dim CustRow As CustDataSet.CustomersRow
    For each CustRow in CSDataSet.Customers
        Console.Writeline("Customers Selected: " + CustRow.ContactName)
    Next
    Console.WriteLine ("Much simpler code")
   catch e as Exception
    ' Display the error.
    Console.WriteLine(e.ToString())
   end try
  end sub
 end class
end namespace
```

Looking at the preceding code, you can readily see that using the typed DataSet has simplified the code and has improved how the code reads as well. Specifically, it's now much easier to reference the CustDataSet (the typed DataSet we created):

```
Dim CSDataSet As CustDataSet = New CustDataSet()
```

Also we can use all of the inherited methods and properties directly:

```
Dim CustRow As CustDataSet.CustomersRow
```

and

```
Console.Writeline("Customers Selected: " + CustRow.ContactName)
```

Now the hard work of generating the typed DataSet has been done and it can be used over and over accordingly. Go ahead and execute the sample program to verify its capability.

20

Using Annotations with a Typed DataSet

Please note that default reference names are given to the objects in the DataSet, such as CustomersRow for the DataRow object name and Customers for the DataRowCollection object name. This might be fine, but things can be made even simpler and clearer by using annotations with a typed DataSet. Plus, it's not very hard.

Annotations will allow you to modify the names of the elements in your typed DataSet without modifying the underlying schema.

Our coding preference is to be able to reference the DataRow object name as just "Customer" (instead of CustomerRow) and the DataRowCollection object name as "Customers". This will make coding even simpler.

The following code is part of an annotated version of the original customers.xsd XML Schema file we used in generating our typed DataSet. To use annotations, you must include a special xmlns reference in your XML Schema file (**xmlns:codegen="urn:schemas-microsoft-com:xml-msprop"**). Then, each annotation uses the **codegen=** in its specification.

```
<?xml version="1.0" encoding="utf-8"?>
<xs:schema id="CustDataSet"
    xmlns:codegen="urn:schemas-microsoft-com:xml-msprop"
    xmlns=""
    xmlns:xs="http://www.w3.org/2001/XMLSchema"
    xmlns:msdata="urn:schemas-microsoft-com:xml-msdata">
  <xs:element name="CustDataSet" msdata:IsDataSet="true">
    <xs:complexType>
      <xs:choice maxOccurs="unbounded">
        <xs:element name="Customers"
          codegen:typedName="Customer"
          codegen:typedPlural="Customers">
          <xs:complexType>
            <xs:sequence>
              <xs:element name="CustomerID"
                   type="xs:string" minOccurs="0" />
```

Then we just repeat the process of generating this as a typed DataSet as we did earlier. The VB code (20UsedTyped.vb) that we used earlier can now be coded as follows:

(20UsedTypedA.vb)

```
Imports System
Imports System.Data
Imports System.Data.SqlClient
Imports Microsoft.VisualBasic
Imports XSDSchema.Northwind
namespace HowTo.ADONET24.Samples
public class usetypedDSA
   public shared sub Main()
      Dim mytypedds as usetypedDSA = new usetypedDSA()
      mytypedds.Run()
   end sub
   public sub Run()
      try
         Dim CSDataSet As CustDataSet = New CustDataSet()
         Dim CustomerAdapter As SqlDataAdapter =
```

```
        New SqlDataAdapter("SELECT * FROM Customers " &
           "WHERE CustomerID like 'B%' ORDER BY CustomerID",
           "server=localhost;Trusted_Connection=yes;database=north
➡wind;")  ·
        CustomerAdapter.Fill(CSDataSet, "Customers")
        Dim Customer As CustDataSet.Customer
        For each Customer in CSDataSet.Customers
            Console.Writeline("Customers Selected: " +
Customer.ContactName)
        Next
        Console.WriteLine ("Much more readable code")
      catch e as Exception
        ' Display the error.
        Console.WriteLine(e.ToString())
      end try
    end sub
  end class
end namespace
```

And, adding new customer code is as easy as

```
Dim NewCust As CustDataSet.Customer =
CSDataSet.Customers.NewCustomer()
NewCust.CustomerID = "BERTU"
NewCust.CompanyName = "Bertucci's Pizza"
CSDataSet.Customers.AddCustomer(newCust)
```

Updating customer data is as easy as

```
CSDataSet.Customers("BERTU").ContactName = "Donald Renato"
```

Typed DataSets in Visual Studio .NET

In Visual Studio .NET, you will frequently be adding typed datasets to forms or components to manipulate data, bind controls to the dataset, and so on. Remember, when you add a dataset, you are really creating an instance of the typed DataSet class on your form or component. The dataset must be in your project for you to use it. Just as you did before, you will have to generate this typed dataset somehow. There are a few places where the typed dataset can come from. The first is by generating it in another form or component in your project. Or, you could create it manually (as we did earlier) and pull it into your project to use. And lastly, you can create a reference to an XML Web service or another component that returns a dataset. In all cases, we will want to generate it as a typed dataset. The best way to get the hang of generating the needed typed dataset in VS .NET is to build a tiny forms application. Let's quickly step through an example that will query customer contact names for customers in the Customers table of the Northwind SQL Server database.

20

Create a New Project in VS .NET

1. Create a new project in VS .NET by choosing File, New, and then choosing the Project option.

2. When the New Project dialog box appears, choose Visual Basic Projects (or Visual C# Projects) and Windows Applications. Name this project "ADO.NET24hours" as you can see in Figure 20.3.

FIGURE 20.3

Visual Studio .NET New Projects dialog box.

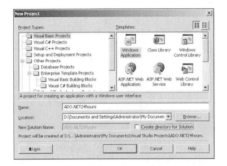

3. This creates a default form for you to start from.

Add the Data Connection and Data Adapter

We will be accessing the Customers table in SQL Server's Northwind database. So, first we will need to create a data connection and a data adapter to Microsoft SQL Server.

1. From the Data tab of the Toolbox, drag a SQLDataAdapter object into your form.

FIGURE 20.4

Visual Studio .NET Form with Data Toolbox SqlDataAdapter *object selected.*

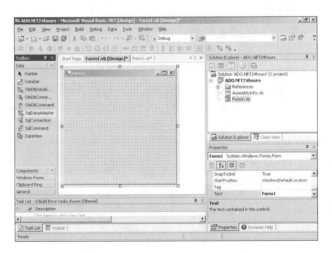

2. This will automatically invoke the Data Adapter Configuration Wizard. Both the data connection and the data adapter can be fully configured here.

   a. The wizard starts with the Choose Your Data Connection dialog box. If you already have a connection defined in your project, it will be placed in the dialog box; otherwise, choose to create a new connection and specify the appropriate connection information (test the connection as well).

FIGURE 20.5

Data Adapter Wizard—Choose Your Data Connection dialog box.

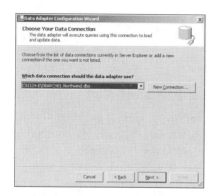

   b. You will then have to decide to supply SQL statements, build a new stored procedure, or give the name of an existing stored procedure for the data access. In our example we will use the Use SQL Statements option.

   c. You will be presented with a Generate the SQL Statements dialog box where you will simply type in a valid SQL statement or you can use the Query Builder option to formulate the SQL query. For this example, just type in the following query:

```
SELECT CustomerID, ContactName FROM Customers
WHERE (CustomerID = @param1)
```

   It should also be noted that for SqlDataAdapters, you will use a named parameter (@param....) for any values that are to be substituted into the WHERE clause. The OleDBDataAdapter's SQL statements would use a "?". This dialog box should look like what is shown in Figure 20.6.

   d. Lastly, the wizard will show you the tasks it has done and indicate whether the SqlDataAdapter has been configured successfully.

After the SqlDataAdapter and DataConnection objects have been configured and added to the form, you must first generate a typed DataSet and then add an instance of this DataSet to the form.

20

FIGURE 20.6

Data Adapter Wizard—Generate the SQL Statements dialog box.

Generate the Typed `DataSet`

You can generate a typed `DataSet` from either a predefined XML Schema (as we did manually before) or from a `DataSet` you have already created with the Component Designer. Because we already have a good Customers.xsd (XML schema), we will use this approach (for consistency).

1. Choose Project, Add Existing Item and locate the .xsd file you will be using as the basis of your dataset creation (Customers.xsd). We have placed a copy in the ADO.NET24hours folder.

2. When you have located the .xsd file, choose Open and the file will be placed in your Solution Explorer.

3. Double-click on this Customers.xsd entry in the Solution Explorer window. Immediately it will appear in the Component Designer as you can see in Figure 20.7.

FIGURE 20.7

Visual Studio .NET Component Designer for Customers.xsd.

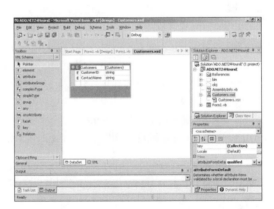

4. Choose Schema, Generate DataSet and you will see the customers.vb entry added in the Solution Explorer. A typed `DataSet` has been generated and placed below the customers.xsd schema file in the Solution Explorer. You haven't added this dataset to your form yet; that comes next.

You could have just as easily created a typed `DataSet` from the `SqlDataAdapter` side as well. After the `SqlDataAdapter` is added to the designer, you could have chosen the Data menu and the Generate DataSet option. The resulting typed `DataSet` would be what was specified in the SQL statement for the data adapter.

Add an Instance of the `DataSet` to the Form

You must now add an instance of the typed `DataSet` to the form. Simply drag and drop a `DataSet` object from the Data tab of the toolbox and place it in the form. As you can see in Figure 20.8, you must choose whether it should be a "typed" or "untyped" dataset. Simply choose for it to be typed and click OK.

FIGURE 20.8

The Add Dataset dialog box for a new instance of a `DataSet` for the form.

You have now completed everything you need to do to populate the `DataSet` from a valid SQL Server connection.

Add Some Controls to Display the Data

The next step is to complete the small form example to include a couple of text boxes and a control button. From the Windows Forms tab of the Toolbox, add the following:

- `Textbox`—With a name of `txtCustParameter` and `text` is blank.
- `Textbox`—With a name of `txtContactName` and `text` is blank.
- `Button`—With a name of `btnGet` and `text` of "Get Contact".

Go ahead and add labels in front of each text box so that it looks like the form in Figure 20.9.

Figure 20.9

Add text boxes, button, and labels to the form.

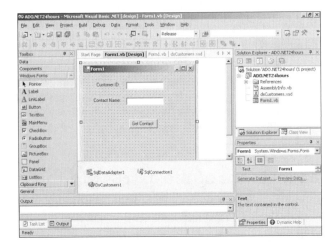

Add Code to Populate the `DataSet`

Now we are ready to complete the application by adding the code to fill the dataset based on the parameterized value we get from the `txtCustParameter` text box. This will be plugged into the SQL statement and executed to fill the `DataSet` (and displayed in the `txtContactName` text box).

Just double-click on the Get Contact button to create a method for the `Click` event. You will have to add code to the handler to set the value of the single parameter required by the SQL statement (from `txtCustParameter`), make a call to the dataset's `Clear` method to clear the dataset between iterations, and call the data adapter's `Fill` method, passing the reference to the dataset and the parameter value for the query. The following code is added:

```
SqlDataAdapter1.SelectCommand.Parameters("@param1").Value =
     txtCustParameter.Text
Customers1.Clear()
SqlDataAdapter1.Fill(Customers1)
```

Bind the Text Box to the `DataSet`

Nothing is left to do other than bind the text box to the `DataSet` and run the application.

1. From the Forms designer, select the `txtContactName` text box and press F4. This will position you to the properties window for this text box.

2. Expand the (DataBindings) node in the properties list and its text property.

3. Expand the Customers1 and Customers nodes and select the ContactName from the list as seen in Figure 20.10.

FIGURE 20.10

The (Databindings) node of the text box property.

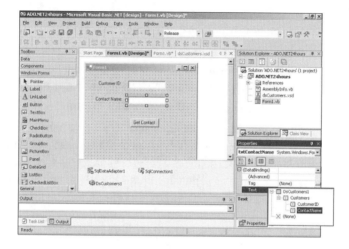

Test It!

That's it. Now just hit the F5 key and test your application by putting in a CustomerID value that is in the Customers table. Try the value "ALFKI". In Figure 20.11 you can see the form retrieving a valid contact name from the Customers database successfully.

FIGURE 20.11

Form execution— retrieving valid contact name from Customers.

20

Summary

In this hour, you've been completely inundated with typed DataSet creation and usage. We have gone from extracting XML schema files with the WriteXmlSchema method, to generating typed DataSets manually with the XSD tool and dynamically in Visual Studio .NET Enterprise Architect. Using typed DataSets should move you greatly toward simplifying coding and making it much more user-friendly (for you and others who have to maintain the code you write), and you will find fewer runtime typing issues across the board, adding to the stability of your applications.

Q&A

Q What is the best way to create a typed `DataSet`?

A Two paths exist for you to generate typed `DataSets`. One path is the manual approach using the XSD tool. The other path is dynamically using the Generate Dataset option in Visual Studio .NET. Both are equal in their results.

Q Should I code my own XSD schema files for datasets?

A You can do this, but remember, this XML schema must comply to the standard XML schema definitions as described at `http://w3c.org`. It is much easier to have Visual Studio .NET, use the `WriteXmlSchema` method, or use the XSD tool to generate this for you. You can then edit this slightly to suit your needs.

Workshop

These quiz questions are designed to test your knowledge of the material covered in this chapter. The answers to the quiz questions can be found in Appendix A, "Answers to Quizzes."

Quiz

1. What is the directive of XSD that generates the dataset?

   a. `/n` directive

   b. `/d` directive

   c. `/l` directive

2. True or false: You can only generate a typed `DataSet` using the XSD XML Schema Definition tool?

3. How can the manually created typed `DataSet` be referenced in my VB code?

   a. Imports an `/r` directive with library (.dll)

   b. `/l` language directive at compile time

   c. `/n` directive at compile time

4. What is used to create more user-friendly names for `DataSet` objects in the XML Schema file for a `DataSet`?

    a. Annotations on the `<XS:element name ...>`

    b. Comments, preceded by `<>`

    c. New tag definitions of `<XS:User-Friendly term >`

Exercise

Part I: Go back and modify the 20xmlsch.vb program to include orders along with customers. Compile and execute it so that it produces a corresponding XML Schema file (.xsd).

Part II: Modify the 20UsedTyped.vb program to use this new Typed `DataSet` and to traverse orders for each customer.

20

HOUR 21

Optimizing Data Access Using Tiered Development

In the preceding hour, you saw how to take advantage of the strongly typed nature of the Microsoft .NET Framework by using a typed `DataSet` to perform data access to make your code more readable. In this hour, you'll see how to implement tiered development practices in your applications.

In this hour, you'll learn how to

- Create an assembly that will perform database access
- Return Product List data through your assembly to a product listing screen
- Use a custom class to return detailed product information

What Is Tiered Development?

A number of different application design paradigms exist. However, one of the most important and influential is the notion of tiered development practices. Tiered development refers to the idea of separating an application into logical and physical layers with each layer serving a single purpose. There's no limit to the number of layers an application could have, so this style of development is often referred to as N-tier development (where N can be any positive integer).

For instance, consider most of the examples you have seen in this book so far. These examples are all good instances of two-tier design. The Web form or Windows form serves as the presentation layer because its primary job is to display content to the user and gather user input. Most of these examples connect directly to a data source. By storing the data, the data source provides the second tier in the application.

Two-tier application design works well for small applications that will require little maintenance throughout the lifetime of the application. When designing Web applications prior to ASP.NET, performance was more of a consideration because all script in ASP is interpreted. These performance considerations are mostly gone with ASP.NET because everything, including the Web form itself, is compiled. However, the fact remains that having SQL statements strewn throughout the presentation tier of your application makes your code hard to read, manage, and upgrade.

Additionally, the two-tier development model leaves the business logic of your application spread out in the presentation layer, almost certainly with the same business logic repeated on multiple pages. (Business logic refers to the business rules modeled by your application. For instance, not allowing a user to purchase over 100 items in a single order would be a good example of a business rule.) If the business logic in your application changes, it would be difficult for anyone but the original programmer to locate and change all of the necessary business logic code instances.

The larger the application, the more these problems are exacerbated.

A solution to this problem is to insert an additional tier between the presentation layer and the database layer. The job of this layer is to encapsulate business logic and perform data access. In Microsoft .NET, this tier is implemented as an assembly. In the next few sections, you'll see how to implement a simple middle tier for some previous examples in this book.

How Many Tiers Are Enough?

This is an easy question to answer, but difficult to gauge sometimes, in practice. Your application should have as many tiers as conditions require.

For instance, consider the scenario of upgrading a two-tier application to a three-tier application by moving business logic and data access from the presentation layer to the new middle layer. An alternate way to do this is to split this new middle layer into two layers. One layer implements only business logic; the other layer only performs the physical database access for the business logic layer.

Many large applications are designed with this methodology. Though it requires some extra work, the effort is rewarded with a replaceable database layer. In other words, if you need to switch your database back end from Oracle to Microsoft SQL Server 2000 (in case your application grows larger and needs to scale out, for instance), you only need to write a new database access layer and use it to replace the old one.

However, this example is unnecessarily complex in order to explain the concepts in this chapter.

FIGURE 21.1

The .NET tiered development model.

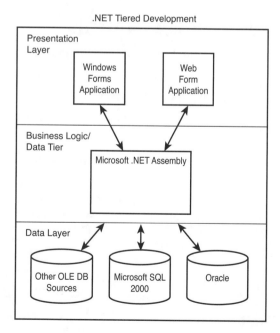

21

Implementing Tiered Development

As mentioned, tiered development is implemented in Microsoft .NET by using an assembly. An assembly is analogous to a component in Microsoft's previous development platforms. An assembly contains objects and methods and compiles to a DLL. The assembly can be referenced and used by your Web or Windows form.

In the next few sections, you're going to see how to implement an additional tier in some of the examples from Hour 11, specifically the product list screen and the product details screen. The original examples are not provided in this chapter, so now might be a good time to go back and review the purpose and implementation of these screens in Hour 11.

Planning Your Approach

As you recall, the product list screen displayed a list of all products in the Northwind database and the product details screen displayed detailed product information for a single product. As mentioned earlier, all data access and business logic (if any) will be removed from the Web forms and placed into an assembly. The Web forms will then call the assembly to get data, rather than directly calling the database itself.

Creating Your Own Assembly

To create a new assembly in your application, perform the following steps:

1. In your Web project directory, create a new directory called components. This directory will contain the code that makes up the assembly.

2. Create a new file called ProductsDB.vb. This file will contain the code implementing the middle tier.

The classes that will be necessary for our middle layer are organized into namespaces. A namespace is just a code container; an organizational device. You're already familiar with namespaces—remember that System.Data.SqlClient is just a namespace with various classes implementing data access to SQL Server.

3. Place the code from Listing 21.1 into the ProductsDB.vb file to create the new namespace.

LISTING 21.1   Providing a Product Listing Through the ProductsDB Assembly

```
Imports System
Imports System.Configuration
Imports System.Data
Imports System.Data.SqlClient

Namespace ADO24HRS

End Namespace
```

In the next section, you'll see how to add some classes into this namespace that will perform the data access for the product list page.

Creating Your Own Classes

The next step is to add a class to the ADO24HRS namespace in the ProductsDB.vb file. The new class, named ProductsDB, can be seen in Listing 21.2. This class name does not have to match the filename. However, because all of the objects you will be working with are products, ProductsDB is a logical choice.

The first Web form we will use to implement this middle tier is the product list Web form. If you recall, its job is to retrieve a list of all products in the database and then display them using a DataList control. Therefore, the name of the method that will perform the data access is called GetAllProducts. This method is also present in Listing 21.2. As you can see, it performs the same data access tasks currently being performed from the product list Web form.

LISTING 21.2   Providing a Product Listing Through the ProductsDB Assembly

```
Imports System
Imports System.Configuration
Imports System.Data
Imports System.Data.SqlClient

Namespace ADO24HRS


    Public Class ProductsDB


        Public Function GetAllProducts() As SqlDataReader

            'Create Instance of Connection and Command Objects
            Dim conn as New SqlConnection( _
```

21

LISTING 21.2   continued

```
                    ConfigurationSettings.AppSettings("ConnectionString"))
        Dim cmd as New SqlCommand("Products_GetAll", conn)

        'Mark the Command as a Stored Procedure
        cmd.CommandType = CommandType.StoredProcedure

        'Return Results
        conn.Open()
        Return cmd.ExecuteReader(CommandBehavior.CloseConnection)

    End Function


    End Class

End Namespace
```

Instead of having a connection string present every time you make a call to the database, it makes a lot of sense to place the connection string into some sort of global constant for your application. In the case of this component layer in a Web forms application, the connection string is stored in a section of the Web.Config file called AppSettings and then retrieved from that single location each time it is used. This makes it much easier to make changes to the connection string.

Compiling the AD024HRS Namespace

Before we can use this new assembly, it must be compiled. This can be done most easily through the use of a batch file (or, if you are using Visual Studio .NET, just build your project). Place the following code into a file named mk.bat in the same component directory as your ProductsDB.vb file:

```
vbc /t:library /out:..\bin\ProductsDB.dll /r:System.dll /r:System.Web.dll
➡/r:System.Xml.dll /r:System.Data.dll ProductsDB.vb
```

The preceding line of code calls the Visual Basic .NET compiler (vbc.exe) and compiles the ProductsDB.vb file into a usable assembly. It compiles the file directly to the /bin directory of the Web forms application.

After you've placed the preceding code into the mk.bat file, execute the batch file either from a DOS prompt or by double-clicking on the file from Windows Explorer. You will not see any error messages if you double-click on the batch file from Explorer.

In order to use the compiled assembly, a bin folder must be present in the application root for your Web forms project. In most cases, this means that the bin directory must be located in the main directory of your Web project.

After running the mk.bat file, check the bin directory of your Web project and make sure a file named ProductsDB.dll is present. This is your compiled assembly.

Wiring Up the Product List Page to the ProductsDB Assembly

With the assembly now in place and accessible by the pages in your application, you can remove the old data access code from the product list and replace it with the code in Listing 21.3. Alternatively, you can just create a new Web form in your application and place the code from Listing 21.3 in the new Web form.

LISTING 21.3   Retrieving Product Data through an Assembly

```
<% @Page Language="VB" %>
<%@ Import Namespace="System.Data" %>
<%@ Import Namespace="System.Data.SqlClient" %>

<HTML>
<HEAD>
    <LINK rel="stylesheet" type="text/css" href="Main.css">
    <!-- End Style Sheet -->

    <script language="VB" runat="server" >
        Sub Page_Load(Source as Object, E as EventArgs)

            LoadGridData( products )

        End Sub

        Private Sub LoadGridData( _
                        myDataList as System.Web.UI.WebControls.DataList )

            'Declare new instance of ProductsDB
            Dim products as New ADO24HRS.ProductsDB()

            myDataList.DataSource = products.GetAllProducts()
            myDataList.DataBind()

        End Sub
    </script>

</HEAD>
```

21

LISTING 21.3 continued

```
<BODY>

<h1>Product List</h1>
<hr>

<form runat="server" id=form1 name=form1>

<asp:DataList id="products" RepeatColumns="2"
        AlternatingItemStyle-backcolor="#DDDDDD"
        SelectedItemStyle-backcolor="CadetBlue"
        runat="server">
    <ItemTemplate>
        <table border="0" width="300">
          <tr>
              <td width="25">
                   
              </td>
              <td width="72" valign="middle" align="right">
                <a href='productdetails.aspx?productID=
➡<%# DataBinder.Eval(Container.DataItem, "ProductID") %>'>
                    <img src='/ADO24HOURS<%# DataBinder.Eval(
➡Container.DataItem, "ImagePath") %>' width="72" height="72" border="0">
                </a>
              </td>
              <td width="150" valign="middle">
                <a href='ProductDetails.aspx?productID=
➡<%# trim(DataBinder.Eval(Container.DataItem, "ProductID")) %>'>
                    <%# DataBinder.Eval(Container.DataItem,
➡"ProductName") %></a><br>
                <b>Price: </b>
                    <%# DataBinder.Eval(Container.DataItem,
➡"UnitPrice", "{0:c}") %><br>
                <b>Units In Stock: </b>
                    <%# DataBinder.Eval(Container.DataItem,
➡"UnitsInStock") %>
                <br>
                </a>
              </td>
          </tr>
        </table>
    </ItemTemplate>
</asp:DataList>

</form>
<hr>

</BODY>
</HTML>
```

As you can see, the code in Listing 21.3 is not much different from the original example in Hour 11. Instead of using ADO.NET directly, the new middle layer performs all data access. As you can see in lines 20–24 of Listing 21.3, the Web form now only needs to create an instance of the `ProductsDB` class and then call the `GetAllProducts()` method of that class. This method returns a `SqlDataReader`, which is indistinguishable from a `SqlDataReader` created directly in the Web form. You can use it to bind to the `DataList`. When this page is run, it will look much like the one in Figure 21.2.

Notice that you're returning a `SqlDataReader` object from the new data access layer. If you recall, the `SqlDataReader` is a forward-only, read-only view of data that maintains a connection to the database for as long as it is open. Because you're opening a database connection for the `SqlDataReader` in an assembly, you must take special action to ensure that the connection is closed when the `SqlDataReader` is done. If you look at the `Return` statement in the `GetAllProducts()` method, you'll notice that we're calling the `ExecuteReader()` method with a special option. `CommandBehavior.CloseConnection` makes sure the database connection is closed after the `SqlDataReader` is done with its connection.

FIGURE 21.2

The appearance of the product list Web form loaded with data from an assembly.

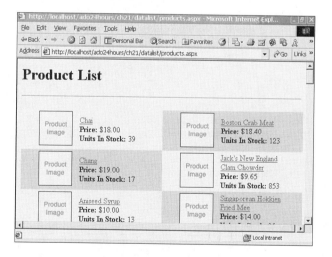

Using Custom Objects Instead of Single Rows of Data

If you look at the Web form in Listing 21.3 in the preceding section, you'll notice that the Web form links to a page that will provide more details for the selected product. This is referred to as a master-detail set of Web form screens. When implementing the product detail screen, you have a number of options.

You can retrieve a single row of data from your data source as in a `SqlDataReader` or a `DataSet`. However, this creates some unnecessary overhead. Why generate an entire `DataSet` or `DataReader` object for just a single row of data?

A more efficient method of retrieving data in this case is to create a custom class in your assembly, and then use an instance of that class to send data back to the Web form. This will require some special coding in your stored procedure, data layer, and Web form.

The first change you'll notice is that the stored procedure (seen in Listing 21.4) doesn't actually return any records. It returns a set of six values to the data layer using output parameters. For a review of stored procedures and output parameters, please see Hour 15, "Working with Stored Procedures."

LISTING 21.4   Retrieving Product Data Through an Assembly

```
CREATE PROCEDURE Product_Get
(
    @ProductID int,
    @ProductName nvarchar(40) OUTPUT,
    @QuantityPerUnit nvarchar(20) OUTPUT,
    @UnitPrice money OUTPUT,
    @UnitsInStock smallint OUTPUT,
    @Discontinued bit OUTPUT,
    @ImagePath nvarchar(50) OUTPUT
)

AS

SELECT
    @ProductName = ProductName,
    @QuantityPerUnit = QuantityPerUnit,
    @UnitPrice = UnitPrice,
    @UnitsInStock = UnitsInStock,
    @Discontinued = Discontinued,
    @ImagePath =ImagePath
FROM
    Products
WHERE
    ProductID = @ProductID
```

The next step is to add a method to your data layer in order to access the data. Add the `GetProductDetails()` method in Listing 21.6 to the `ProductsDB` class in the ADO24HRS namespace from Listing 21.2. The only difference between this data access method and other methods you've seen is that this one doesn't return a `DataSet` or a `SqlDataReader`. It returns an object of type `ProductDetails`. This object is defined by the code in Listing 21.5. The class consists of six variables that will be used to package the results from the stored procedure and transfer to the Web form. Make sure to add the code from Listing 21.5 to your ADO24HRS namespace as well.

LISTING 21.5   The `ProductDetails` Custom Class

```
Public Class ProductDetails

    Public ProductName As String
    Public QuantityPerUnit As String
    Public UnitPrice As Decimal
    Public UnitsInStock As Int16
    Public Discontinued as Boolean
    Public ImagePath As String

End Class
```

LISTING 21.6   Retrieving Product Data Through an Assembly

```
Public Function GetProductDetails(ByVal productID As Integer) _
                                            As ProductDetails

    'Create Instance of Connection and Command Objects
    Dim conn as New SqlConnection( _
            ConfigurationSettings.AppSettings("ConnectionString"))
    Dim cmd as New SqlCommand("Product_Get", conn)

    'Mark the Command as a Stored Procedure
    cmd.CommandType = CommandType.StoredProcedure

    ' Add Parameters to SPROC
    Dim parameterProductID As SqlParameter = _
                    New SqlParameter("@ProductID", SqlDbType.Int, 4)
    parameterProductID.Value = productID
    cmd.Parameters.Add(parameterProductID)

    Dim parameterProductName As SqlParameter = _
            New SqlParameter("@ProductName", SqlDbType.NVarChar, 40)
    parameterProductName.Direction = ParameterDirection.Output
    cmd.Parameters.Add(parameterProductName)

    Dim parameterQuantityPerUnit As SqlParameter = _
            New SqlParameter("@QuantityPerUnit", SqlDbType.NVarChar, 20)
    parameterQuantityPerUnit.Direction = ParameterDirection.Output
    cmd.Parameters.Add(parameterQuantityPerUnit)
```

21

LISTING 21.6   continued

```
        Dim parameterUnitPrice As SqlParameter = _
                    New SqlParameter("@UnitPrice", SqlDbType.Money, 8)
        parameterUnitPrice.Direction = ParameterDirection.Output
        cmd.Parameters.Add(parameterUnitPrice)

        Dim parameterUnitsInStock As SqlParameter = _
                New SqlParameter("@UnitsInStock", SqlDbType.SmallInt, 2)
        parameterUnitsInStock.Direction = ParameterDirection.Output
        cmd.Parameters.Add(parameterUnitsInStock)

        Dim parameterDiscontinued As SqlParameter = _
                    New SqlParameter("@Discontinued", SqlDbType.SmallInt, 2)
        parameterDiscontinued.Direction = ParameterDirection.Output
        cmd.Parameters.Add(parameterDiscontinued)

        Dim parameterImagePath As SqlParameter = _
                New SqlParameter("@ImagePath", SqlDbType.NVarChar, 50)
        parameterImagePath.Direction = ParameterDirection.Output
        cmd.Parameters.Add(parameterImagePath)

        ' Open the connection and execute the Command
        conn.Open()
        cmd.ExecuteNonQuery()
        conn.Close()

        'Create and Populate ProductDetails Struct using
        'Output Params from the SPROC
        Dim myProductDetails As ProductDetails = New ProductDetails()

        myProductDetails.ProductName = _
                    Convert.ToString(parameterProductName.Value).Trim()
        myProductDetails.QuantityPerUnit = _
                Convert.ToString(parameterQuantityPerUnit.Value).Trim()
        myProductDetails.UnitPrice = _
                        Convert.ToDecimal(parameterUnitPrice.Value)
        myProductDetails.UnitsInStock = _
                        Convert.ToInt16(parameterUnitsInStock.Value)
        myProductDetails.Discontinued = _
                Convert.ToBoolean(parameterDiscontinued.Value)
        myProductDetails.ImagePath = _
                    Convert.ToString(parameterImagePath.Value).Trim()

        Return myProductDetails

    End Function
```

Now the data layer for the product details Web form is done! All that remains is to add the necessary code to the Web form that will actually display the information. In the next

example, you'll create the product details Web form, and wire it up to the
GetProductDetails() method in the ProductsDB class. Listing 21.7 contains the code
for the product details Web form.

LISTING 21.7   Retrieving Product Data Through an Assembly

```
<% @Page Language="VB" %>
<%@ Import Namespace="System.Data" %>
<%@ Import Namespace="System.Data.SqlClient" %>

<HTML>
<HEAD>
    <LINK rel="stylesheet" type="text/css" href="Main.css">
    <!-- End Style Sheet -->

    <script language="VB" runat="server" >
        Sub Page_Load(Source as Object, E as EventArgs)

            'Get OrderID
            Dim ProductID As Integer = Int32.Parse(Request.Params("ProductID"))

            LoadData( ProductID )

        End Sub

        Private Sub LoadData( productID as Int32 )

            'Declare new instance of ProductsDB
            Dim products as New ADO24HRS.ProductsDB()

            'Declare new instance of custom class
            Dim myProductDetails as ADO24HRS.ProductDetails

            'Fill custom class with data
            myProductDetails = products.GetProductDetails( productID )

            lblProductName.Text = myProductDetails.ProductName
            lblQuantityPerUnit.Text = myProductDetails.QuantityPerUnit
            lblUnitPrice.Text = myProductDetails.UnitPrice.ToString()
            lblUnitsInStock.Text = myProductDetails.UnitsInStock.ToString()
            ProductImage.Src = "/ADO24HOURS" + myProductDetails.ImagePath

            if( myProductDetails.Discontinued ) then
                lblDiscontinued.Visible = false
            end if

        End Sub
    </script>
```

21

LISTING 21.7   continued

```
  </HEAD>
<BODY>

<h1>View Product Details</h1>
<hr>

<form runat="server">

<table cellpadding=5>
  <tr>
    <td>
      <img id="ProductImage" height=144 width=144 runat="server">
    </td>
    <td valign="center">
      <strong><asp:label id="lblProductName" runat="server" /></strong>
      <br>
      Quantity Per Unit: <asp:label id="lblQuantityPerUnit" runat="server" />
      <br>
      In Stock:
      <strong><asp:label id="lblUnitsInStock" runat="server" /></strong>
      <br>
      Price Per Unit:<asp:label id="lblUnitPrice" runat="server" />
      <br>

      <strong>
      <asp:label id="lblDiscontinued" Color="red" runat="server" />
      </strong>
    </td>
  </tr>
</table>
Here would typically go a detailed product description.
</form>
<hr>

</BODY>
</HTML>
```

Accessing the product data is done a little bit differently than in the preceding example in this hour because you're accessing the public members of a class, rather than binding directly to a `SqlDataReader` object. In the `LoadData()` method in Listing 21.7, a new instance of the `ProductsDB` class is created. Then an instance of the `ProductDetails` class is created. Finally, the data from the `GetProductDetails()` method is loaded into the `ProductDetails` class. Then the individual members of the class are used to assign values to the correct labels on the page. Figure 21.3 shows the Web form when loaded in a Web browser.

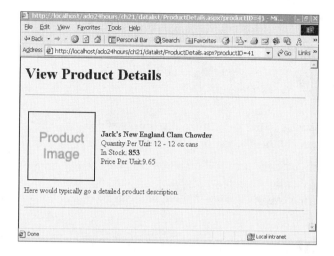

Figure 21.4 represents where the data moves in each of the examples in this chapter. This can be hard to keep track of, at first. However, the benefits to code readability and manageability far outweigh the extra time and effort necessary to implement additional physical layers in your application.

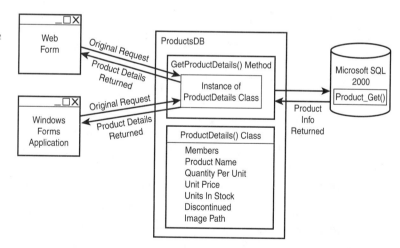

Summary

In this hour, you've seen an introduction to tiered development methodologies using ASP.NET and ADO.NET. First, you saw how to implement an additional application layer using a simple `SqlDataReader` example to display a list of products. Then, you saw

how to return a custom class with database values, rather than using a single-row
DataTable. In the next hour, you'll see how to handle an application's database modifications using three-tier development practices.

Q&A

**Q Because N-tier development requires additional layers, will I see a decrease in
performance for my application?**

A No, there's no noticeable decrease in performance associated with implementing
another tier in your application using the methods in this chapter. This model has
been proven to work well, even under heavy load from an application.

Workshop

These quiz questions are designed to test your knowledge of the material covered in this
chapter. The answers to the quiz questions can be found in Appendix A, "Answers to
Quizzes."

Quiz

1. What is the purpose of adding additional layers to your application?
2. Name the option you can use when calling the ExecuteReader() method of the
   Command object to make sure that the DataReader closes its connection to the database when it is done.

Exercise

Upgrade the orders.aspx and orderdetails.aspx examples from Hour 11 to use a middle
tier to access data. Remember that both of these examples use a SqlDataReader to
retrieve information from the database, so your middle-tier code will be very similar to
the first example (product list) in this chapter.

You should create a new class in the ADO24HRS namespace called OrdersDB in order to
implement the new screens. Keep in mind that a namespace can span several files (that
is, you can copy the ProductsDB.vb file created in this chapter to a file called
OrdersDB.vb, replace the product methods with ones for the order screens, and compile
it in the same way).

Hour **22**

Modifying Data in an N-Tier Application

In the preceding hour, you saw how to implement three-tier data access into your applications to improve the manageability and readability of your code. In this hour, those concepts will be reinforced as you see some ways to update and add new data to your data source using three-tier development methods.

In this hour, you'll learn how to

- Build a Product Update screen
- Build a Product Add screen

Updating Product Data

In the preceding hour, you saw how to create a set of screens that displays a list of products and enables you to click on a particular product to see the detailed product information. The next few sections of this hour reinforce the same three-tier style of development by implementing an administrative section.

The stored procedure that will actually update the product information in the database is straightforward and provided in Listing 22.1. As you can see, it accepts the product values as parameters and passes those parameters to an UPDATE query. When the query is done, the number of records updated by the query is passed back to the calling method. This can be used to ensure that the update had no errors. Because we're updating a single product at a time, the number of rows modified should always be "1" if the query is successful.

LISTING 22.1 The Product_Update Stored Procedure

```
CREATE PROCEDURE Product_Update
(
    @ProductID int,
    @ProductName nvarchar(40),
    @QuantityPerUnit nvarchar(20),
    @UnitPrice money,
    @UnitsInStock smallint,
    @ImagePath varchar(256),
    @Discontinued bit,
    @RowsAffected int OUTPUT
)
AS

UPDATE
    Products
SET
    ProductName = @ProductName,
    QuantityPerUnit = @QuantityPerUnit,
    UnitPrice = @UnitPrice,
    UnitsInStock = @UnitsInStock,
    ImagePath = @ImagePath,
    Discontinued = @Discontinued
WHERE
    ProductID = @ProductID
```

With the stored procedure created, the next step is to create the necessary middle-tier method that will perform the update. Place the code from Listing 22.2 into the ProductsDB.vb file. For more details on creating a component layer, please see the relevant sections in the preceding hour.

LISTING 22.2 The UpdateProducts Middle-Tier Method

```
Public Function UpdateProducts( ProductID as Int32, _
                                ProductName as string, _
                                QuantityPerUnit as string, _
                                UnitPrice as string, _
```

LISTING 22.2   continued

```
                                    UnitsInStock as Int16, _
                                    ImagePath as string, _
                                    Discontinued as Boolean ) as Int32

    'Create Instance of Connection and Command Objects
    Dim conn as New SqlConnection( _
            ConfigurationSettings.AppSettings("ConnectionString"))
    Dim cmd as New SqlCommand("Product_Update", conn)

    'Mark the Command as a Stored Procedure
    cmd.CommandType = CommandType.StoredProcedure

    ' Add Parameters to SPROC
    Dim parameterProductID As SqlParameter = _
                    New SqlParameter("@ProductID", SqlDbType.Int, 4)
    parameterProductID.Value = productID
    cmd.Parameters.Add(parameterProductID)

    Dim parameterProductName As SqlParameter = _
            New SqlParameter("@ProductName", SqlDbType.NVarChar, 40)
    parameterProductName.Value = ProductName
    cmd.Parameters.Add(parameterProductName)

    Dim parameterQuantityPerUnit As SqlParameter = _
        New SqlParameter("@QuantityPerUnit", SqlDbType.NVarChar, 20)
    parameterQuantityPerUnit.Value = QuantityPerUnit
    cmd.Parameters.Add(parameterQuantityPerUnit)

    Dim parameterUnitPrice As SqlParameter = _
                    New SqlParameter("@UnitPrice", SqlDbType.Money, 8)
    parameterUnitPrice.Value = Convert.ToDecimal(UnitPrice)
    cmd.Parameters.Add(parameterUnitPrice)

    Dim parameterUnitsInStock As SqlParameter = _
            New SqlParameter("@UnitsInStock", SqlDbType.SmallInt, 2)
    parameterUnitsInStock.Value = Convert.ToInt16(UnitsInStock)
    cmd.Parameters.Add(parameterUnitsInStock)

    Dim parameterImagePath As SqlParameter = _
            New SqlParameter("@ImagePath", SqlDbType.NVarChar, 50)
    parameterImagePath.Value = ImagePath
    cmd.Parameters.Add(parameterImagePath)

    Dim parameterDiscontinued As SqlParameter = _
            New SqlParameter("@Discontinued", SqlDbType.Bit, 1)
    parameterDiscontinued.Value = Discontinued
    cmd.Parameters.Add(parameterDiscontinued)

    Dim parameterRowsAffected As SqlParameter = _
```

22

LISTING 22.2   continued

```
                     New SqlParameter("@RowsAffected", SqlDbType.Int, 4)
            parameterRowsAffected.Direction = ParameterDirection.Output
            cmd.Parameters.Add(parameterRowsAffected)

            conn.Open()
            cmd.ExecuteNonQuery()
            conn.Close()

            Return Convert.ToInt32(parameterRowsAffected.Value)

        End Function
```

After you've added the preceding code into the ProductsDB.vb file, don't forget that you must recompile the namespace. You must manually recompile your namespace after each change.

As you can see, the `UpdateProducts()` method in Listing 22.2 accepts seven arguments that describe a product. Lines 9–15 set up the `Connection` and `Command` objects. Then, lines 17–51 create the set of stored procedure input parameters. The last parameter, found in lines 53–56, sets up the output parameter that we'll use to ensure our query was successful.

With the middle tier and data layers firmly in place, you can easily work on the presentation layer. Rather than create an entirely new product list screen, you can use the Products.aspx Web form from the preceding hour in Listing 21.3 with a few changes. At the end of the `DataList`'s `ItemTemplate`, place the code in Listing 22.3. This will create a new link for each product on the product list screen. Clicking these links will navigate to the ProductEditor.aspx Web form that you will create next. You can see the additional link created in Figure 22.1. Notice that the hyperlink generated by the `DataGrid` passes the ProductID to the producteditor.aspx page in the querystring. This is the mechanism the product editor uses to identify which product is being modified.

LISTING 22.3   Adding an Additional Link to the Products.aspx DataList

```
<a href='producteditor.aspx?productID=
➥<%# DataBinder.Eval(Container.DataItem, "ProductID") %>'>
    edit product
</a>
```

FIGURE 22.1

Each product in the Product List screen now contains an additional link: edit product.

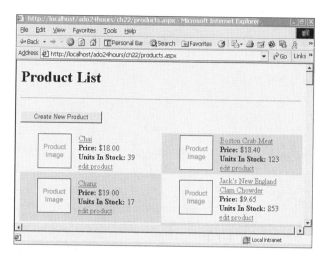

The code for the ProductEditor.aspx Web form is provided in Listing 22.4. Notice that it is much like the ProductDetails.aspx screen. Instead of displaying the detailed product information in label Web controls, however, it uses editable text boxes. Note that the LoadData methods for these two screens are almost identical. When the ProductEditor.aspx Web form loads, it retrieves the product information using the exact same techniques as the ProductDetails.aspx uses.

LISTING 22.4   The ProductEditor.aspx Web Form

```
<% @Page Language="VB" %>
<%@ Import Namespace="System.Data" %>
<%@ Import Namespace="System.Data.SqlClient" %>

<HTML>
<HEAD>
    <LINK rel="stylesheet" type="text/css" href="Main.css">
    <!-- End Style Sheet -->

    <script language="VB" runat="server" >
        Sub Page_Load(Source as Object, E as EventArgs)

            'Get ProductID and store in Viewstate
            Dim ProductID As Integer = Int32.Parse(Request.Params("ProductID"))
            if ProductID <> "" then
                ViewState("ProductID") = ProductID
            end if

            if IsPostBack then
```

LISTING 22.4   continued

```
                UpdateData( Convert.ToInt32(ViewState("ProductID")) )

        end if

        LoadData( ProductID )

End Sub

Private Sub UpdateData( productID as Int32 )

    Dim iResults as Int32

    Dim product as new ADO24HRS.ProductsDB()
    iResults = product.UpdateProducts( _
                productID, _
                txtProductName.Text, _
                txtQuantityPerUnit.Text, _
                txtUnitPrice.Text, _
                txtUnitsInStock.Text, _
                txtImagePath.Text, _
                chkDiscontinued.Checked )

    if iResults = 1 then
        lblOutput.Text = "Record successfully updated!"
    else
        lblOutput.Text = "There was a problem updating the record"
    end if

End Sub

Private Sub LoadData( productID as Int32 )

    'Declare new instance of ProductsDB
    Dim products as New ADO24HRS.ProductsDB()

    'Declare new instance of custom class
    Dim myProductDetails as ADO24HRS.ProductDetails

    'Fill custom class with data
    myProductDetails = products.GetProductDetails( productID )

    txtProductName.Text = myProductDetails.ProductName
    txtQuantityPerUnit.Text = myProductDetails.QuantityPerUnit
    txtUnitPrice.Text = myProductDetails.UnitPrice.ToString()
    txtUnitsInStock.Text = myProductDetails.UnitsInStock.ToString()
    ProductImage.Src = "/ADO24HOURS" + myProductDetails.ImagePath
    txtImagePath.Text = myProductDetails.ImagePath.ToString()
    chkDiscontinued.Checked = myProductDetails.Discontinued
```

LISTING 22.4   continued

```
            End Sub
        </script>

</HEAD>
<BODY>

<h1>Edit Product Details</h1>
<hr>

<form runat="server" id=form1 name=form1>

<asp:label id="lblOutput" runat="server" />

<table cellpadding=5>
  <tr>
    <td>
      <img id="ProductImage" height=144 width=144 runat="server">
    </td>
    <td valign="center">
      <table>
        <tr>
          <td>
            <strong>Product Name: </strong>
          </td>
          <td>
            <asp:TextBox id="txtProductName" runat="server" />
          </td>
        </tr>
        <tr>
          <td>
            Quantity Per Unit:
          </td>
          <td>
            <asp:TextBox id="txtQuantityPerUnit" runat="server" />
          </td>
        </tr>
        <tr>
          <td>
            Units In Stock:
          </td>
          <td>
            <asp:TextBox id="txtUnitsInStock" runat="server" />
          </td>
        </tr>
        <tr>
          <td>
            Price Per Unit:
          </td>
        </td>
```

LISTING 22.4 continued

```
      <td>
        <asp:TextBox id="txtUnitPrice" runat="server" />
      </td>
    </tr>
    <tr>
      <td>
        Image Path:
      </td>
      <td>
        <asp:TextBox id="txtImagePath" runat="server" />
      </td>
    </tr>
    <tr>
      <td>
        Product Discontinued:
      </td>
      <td>
        <asp:CheckBox id="chkDiscontinued" runat="server" />
      </td>
    </tr>
    <tr>
      <td>
         
      </td>
      <td>
        <input type="submit" value="Submit Changes">
      </td>
    </tr>
  </table>
  </td>
  </tr>
</table>

</form>
<hr>

</BODY>
</HTML>
```

After you click on one of the new Edit Product links on the product listing screen, the ProductEditor.aspx Web form from Listing 22.4 loads. It appears much like the screen in Figure 22.2.

You can use the Product Editor to make changes to existing product information, such as the product name, quantity in stock, and price. After you make changes to the selected product and submit the form, the Web form gathers the product information and passes it

22

to the UpdateProducts() method of the ProductsDB class, found in Listing 22.2. As you saw earlier, that method then passes that product information to the Product_Update stored procedure from Listing 22.1. The Product_Update method executes an UPDATE SQL query, which saves the product data. After this is completed, the stored procedure passes the number of rows affected by the query back to the UpdateProducts() method. The UpdateProducts() method passes this value back to the Web form, which uses the value to either confirm for the user that the product was updated successfully, or inform the user that something went wrong.

FIGURE 22.2

The appearance of the Product Editor.

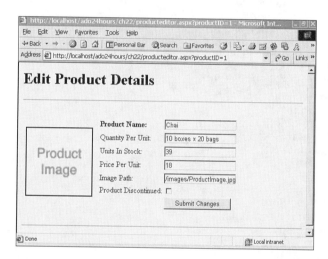

Adding Product Data

Though the ProductEditor.aspx Web form can now be used to update product information, there's still no way to add new products into the database. In this section, you'll see how to modify the existing Product Editor to also handle the case where a user needs to enter a new product. You could create an entirely new screen to handle product additions, but because this new screen would be very similar to the existing Product Editor, it makes sense to just modify the existing code to handle both cases.

The stored procedure Product_Add in Listing 22.5 performs the actual addition of new product data into the database. Notice that the parameters are nearly the same as for the Product_Update stored procedure in Listing 22.1. However, there are a few differences. Because Product_Add is creating a new entry in the products table, a new ProductID is generated instead of being passed in as an argument. This newly created ProductID is then returned to the component layer. You can check that value to ensure that the new product was actually inserted into the database. You know that if the value of the ProductID is not greater than 0, the insert was unsuccessful.

LISTING 22.5 The Product_Add Stored Procedure

```
CREATE PROCEDURE Product_Add
(
    @ProductName nvarchar(40),
    @QuantityPerUnit nvarchar(20),
    @UnitPrice money,
    @UnitsInStock smallint,
    @ImagePath varchar(256),
    @Discontinued bit,
    @ProductID int OUTPUT
)
AS

INSERT INTO Products
(
    ProductName,
    QuantityPerUnit,
    UnitPrice,
    UnitsInStock,
    ImagePath,
    Discontinued
)
VALUES
(
    @ProductName,
    @QuantityPerUnit,
    @UnitPrice,
    @UnitsInStock,
    @ImagePath,
    @Discontinued
)

SELECT @ProductID = @@IDENTITY
```

With the stored procedure created, the next step is to create the component layer method that will use the stored procedure in Listing 22.5 to add the new product record. The new AddProduct() method is provided in Listing 22.6.

LISTING 22.6 The ProductEditor.aspx Web Form

```
Public Function AddProduct( _
                           ProductName as string, _
                           QuantityPerUnit as string, _
                           UnitPrice as string, _
                           UnitsInStock as Int16, _
```

LISTING 22.6   continued

```
                                    ImagePath as string, _
                                    Discontinued as Boolean ) as Int32

    'Create Instance of Connection and Command Objects
    Dim conn as New SqlConnection( _
                ConfigurationSettings.AppSettings("ConnectionString"))
    Dim cmd as New SqlCommand("Product_Add", conn)

    'Mark the Command as a Stored Procedure
    cmd.CommandType = CommandType.StoredProcedure

    ' Add Parameters to SPROC
    Dim parameterProductName As SqlParameter = _
                New SqlParameter("@ProductName", SqlDbType.NVarChar, 40)
    parameterProductName.Value = ProductName
    cmd.Parameters.Add(parameterProductName)

    Dim parameterQuantityPerUnit As SqlParameter = _
            New SqlParameter("@QuantityPerUnit", SqlDbType.NVarChar, 20)
    parameterQuantityPerUnit.Value = QuantityPerUnit
    cmd.Parameters.Add(parameterQuantityPerUnit)

    Dim parameterUnitPrice As SqlParameter = _
                    New SqlParameter("@UnitPrice", SqlDbType.Money, 8)
    parameterUnitPrice.Value = Convert.ToDecimal(UnitPrice)
    cmd.Parameters.Add(parameterUnitPrice)

    Dim parameterUnitsInStock As SqlParameter = _
                New SqlParameter("@UnitsInStock", SqlDbType.SmallInt, 2)
    parameterUnitsInStock.Value = Convert.ToInt16(UnitsInStock)
    cmd.Parameters.Add(parameterUnitsInStock)

    Dim parameterImagePath As SqlParameter = _
                New SqlParameter("@ImagePath", SqlDbType.NVarChar, 50)
    parameterImagePath.Value = ImagePath
    cmd.Parameters.Add(parameterImagePath)

    Dim parameterDiscontinued As SqlParameter = _
                New SqlParameter("@Discontinued", SqlDbType.Bit, 1)
    parameterDiscontinued.Value = Discontinued
    cmd.Parameters.Add(parameterDiscontinued)

    Dim parameterProductID As SqlParameter = _
                    New SqlParameter("@ProductID", SqlDbType.Int, 4)
    parameterProductID.Direction = ParameterDirection.Output
    cmd.Parameters.Add(parameterProductID)
```

LISTING 22.6   continued

```
            conn.Open()
            cmd.ExecuteNonQuery()
            conn.Close()

            Return Convert.ToInt32(parameterProductID.Value)

        End Function
```

Finally, you'll need to make a few edits to the ProductEditor.aspx Web form in order to enable the form to handle adding a new product. The two changes are in Listings 22.7 and 22.8. Add the AddNew() method in Listing 22.7 either just before or just after the existing UpdateData() method. This is the method that will call the component layer AddProduct() method from Listing 22.6.

Likewise, replace the old Page_Load() event on the ProductEditor.aspx Web form with the one in Listing 22.8. Page_Load() has been modified to handle the case where the ProductID passed to it is 0. If the ProductID is 0, the form assumes it should load a blank form and enable the user to add a new product record to the database.

LISTING 22.7   The ProductEditor.aspx Web Form

```
Private Sub AddNew( )

    Dim iResults as Int32

    Dim product as new ADO24HRS.ProductsDB()
    iResults = product.AddProduct( _
            txtProductName.Text, _
            txtQuantityPerUnit.Text, _
            txtUnitPrice.Text, _
            txtUnitsInStock.Text, _
            txtImagePath.Text, _
            chkDiscontinued.Checked )

    if iResults > 1 then
        lblOutput.Text = "Record successfully added!"
    else
        lblOutput.Text = "There was a problem adding the record."
    end if

End Sub
```

LISTING 22.8   The ProductEditor.aspx Web Form

```
Sub Page_Load(Source as Object, E as EventArgs)

    'Get ProductID and store in Viewstate
    Dim ProductID As Integer = Int32.Parse(Request.Params("ProductID"))
    if ProductID <> "" then
        ViewState("ProductID") = ProductID
    end if

    if IsPostBack then
        if ProductID <> 0 then
            UpdateData( Convert.ToInt32(ViewState("ProductID")) )
        else
            AddNew()
        end if
    end if

    if ProductID <> 0 then
        'Load existing product information
        LoadData( ProductID )
    else
        'Prepare form for new data
        ProductImage.Visible = False
        header.InnerText = "Add New Product"
    end if

End Sub
```

The last task you need to perform is to add a button or hyperlink anywhere inside the
server-side form tags in products.aspx. A sample button is provided in Listing 22.9.

LISTING 22.9   The Create New Product Button Added to Products.aspx

```
<asp:button id="cmdNewProduct" OnClick="cmdNewProduct_OnClick"
            Text="Create New Product" runat="server" />
```

Then, when the user clicks on the new button, redirect them to the ProductEditor.aspx
Web form with the ProductID set to 0. This sample code is provided in Listing 22.10.

LISTING 22.10   The Create New Product Button Added to Products.aspx

```
Private Sub cmdNewProduct_OnClick( Source as Object, E as EventArgs )
    Response.Redirect("ProductEditor.aspx?ProductID=0")
End Sub
```

Now, when the ProductEditor.aspx Web form is loaded using this button, your screen will look like the one in Figure 22.3, ready to enter a new product.

FIGURE 22.3

The appearance of the Product Editor screen ready to accept a new product.

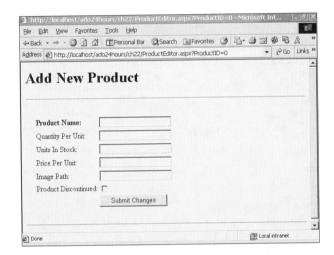

Summary

In this hour, you've seen how to engineer a set of screens for adding and updating product information, using ADO.NET and three-tier development practices. First you saw how to implement a new ProductEditor.aspx Web form to handle the update capabilities. Then you saw how to add additional functionality to create new products.

Q&A

Q Where can I find more information about building N-tier applications?

A At the time this book was published, there were no good N-tier .NET development books. However, several exist for other platforms including COM and Visual Basic 6.0. One good book on the topic is *Building N-Tier Applications with COM and Visual Basic(r) 6.0* by Ash Rofail and Tony Martin, published by John Wiley & Sons. If you're familiar with the technology used, the N-tier concepts will be easy to follow.

Workshop

These quiz questions are designed to test your knowledge of the material covered in this chapter. The answers to the quiz questions can be found in Appendix A, "Answers to Quizzes."

Quiz

1. Identity and briefly explain the purpose of each of the application layers used in the examples in this hour.

2. What is the term used to describe the relationship between a screen that lists a set of items, and a screen used to edit individual items from that list?

Exercise

Create a Web form that will enable users to update existing employee information or add new employee records to the Employees table of the Northwind database. Use the examples provided in this hour and the last hour as a guide.

HOUR **23**

Optimizing Data Access

As the number of users of an application (Web or Windows forms) increases, the performance of the application is limited by its slowest part. The slowest piece of an application at any given time is referred to as the application's "bottleneck." There will almost always be a bottleneck in your application because one component or another will always be slower than the others. In this hour, you'll see some effective techniques you can use to ensure that the data access portion of your application isn't the bottleneck.

In this hour, you'll learn

- Some tips to improving your ADO.NET code for faster data access
- How to use the tracing functionality in ASP.NET to locate bottlenecks in your application
- How to use the SQL Query Analyzer to improve the speed of your database queries

Optimizing ADO.NET Code

Several ways exist to increase the performance of ADO.NET code in your Web or Windows forms applications. In this section, you'll see some direct improvements you can make to your ADO.NET code to improve the speed of your data access.

DataReader Versus DataSet

As you know, you have two different ways of retrieving data from your data source using ADO.NET. You can use a `DataAdapter` object to fill a `DataSet` with data, and then work with the data in the `DataSet` or display it on a form using a `DataGrid` or other mechanism for display. In a number of cases, you need a `DataSet`: You might need to perform calculations or otherwise work on several items within the `DataSet` at once. However, if you're just displaying data, the `DataReader` object is a more appropriate choice.

The `DataReader` opens a read-only, forward-only view of your data, with no more than one row of data in memory at one time. By using a `DataReader` to bind to your controls, you will incur the lowest amount of system overhead. By using a `DataReader` object instead of the `DataSet`, you can definitely improve the performance of your site. For small sets of data, this difference is barely noticeable. However, as the amount of data increases, the performance gains realized by the `DataReader` become more evident. In a quick test using 500 rows of data, the `DataSet` took twice as long as the `DataReader` to retrieve the result set and display it on the Web form. In the same test using 1,000 rows of data, the `DataSet` took several times longer than the `DataReader` and consumed a much greater amount of memory. However, keep in mind that certain actions are unavailable when using a `DataReader`, such as automatic paging using the `DataGrid`.

Managing Database Connections

Automatic connection pooling is provided by the data providers. A different connection pool is created for each connection string used in an application. In addition to this automatic connection pooling, you can speed up your code by keeping your connection to the database open during several queries that happen in rapid succession rather than opening and closing the connection between each call to the database.

Choose Your Data Provider Wisely

Your choice of data provider can have very significant effects on the performance of your application. Always choose a managed provider to connect to your data source, if one is available. One example of a managed provider is the `System.Data.SqlClient` namespace, which is a managed provider for Microsoft SQL Server versions 7.0 and up.

If no managed provider is available, your next best choice for performance is probably to use the `System.Data.OleDb` managed provider to access your data source through OLE DB. Though this adds one level of indirection in accessing your data when compared to using a direct managed provider such as the one for SQL, using OLE DB still provides relatively fast data access.

Lastly, if no OLE DB provider is available for your data source, you can use the ODBC managed provider available separately from the Microsoft .NET Framework SDK. You can download it for free from the download section at http://www.microsoft.com. ODBC is the slowest option of those listed here, but it also supports a much wider range of data sources.

Use "SELECT *" Sparingly

To simplify your database queries, you might be tempted to use "SELECT *" to return all available database columns in a query. Though this command makes your code easier to read, you could return a large amount of data that you don't need. Specify only the column names that you plan to use.

Automatically Generated Commands

For applications that require high performance, do not use automatically generated commands. The DataAdapter needs to make additional calls to the server in order to generate the commands. This additional overhead can needlessly slow down your application.

ASP.NET Tracing

ASP.NET provides an extremely handy tool for discovering bottlenecks in your application. Specify trace="true" in the Page directive of your Web form as in the following line:

```
<% @Page debug="true" trace="true" Language="VB" %>
```

The next time you load your Web form, you will notice that ASP.NET has automatically printed out a wealth of information for you below your form. In addition to the entire control tree for your form, all server variables and request values, you can see exactly how long each stage of the page's life cycle took. You can see this in Figure 23.1.

The last two columns in the Trace Information section provide the exact (probably more exact than you care to know) amount of time the page object took to load, by stage. So, you can see from Figure 23.1 that the page took approximately 2.86 seconds to load, and approximately 2.78 seconds was spent in the PreRender event.

It's possible to add entries into this list of trace information. By calling Trace.Write() and passing it the category name and your message, not only can you check the value of a particular variable at any given time, but you can also use it to time your events. Look

at the code in Listing 23.1. At the beginning of the `LoadDataGrid()` method, a message is
sent to the `Trace` object denoting the start of data access. After all data access is complete, another message is sent.

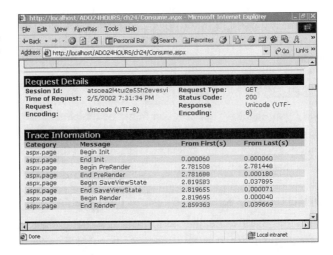

Similarly, the `DataBind()` method of the `DataGrid` is wrapped, as well. Now, when you
load the Web form, it will display these trace entries. You can see the new entries in
Figure 23.2.

LISTING 23.1   Using Trace Functionality to Locate Bottlenecks in an ASP.NET
Application

```
<% @Page debug="true" trace="true" Language="VB" %>
<%@ Import Namespace="System.Data" %>
<%@ Import Namespace="System.Data.SqlClient" %>

<HTML>
<HEAD>
    <LINK rel="stylesheet" type="text/css" href="Main.css">
    <!-- End Style Sheet -->

    <script language="VB" runat="server" >
        Sub Page_Load(Source as Object, E as EventArgs)

            LoadDataGrid(orders)

        End Sub

        Private Sub LoadDataGrid( _
```

LISTING 23.1   continued

```
                     myDataGrid as System.Web.UI.WebControls.DataGrid)

    Trace.Write("LoadDataGrid", "Start Data Access")

    Dim conn as New SqlConnection("Initial Catalog=Northwind;" + _
                        "Server=(local);UID=sa;PWD=;")
    Dim cmd as New SqlCommand("SELECT * FROM Suppliers", conn)

    Dim adapter as SqlDataAdapter = new SqlDataAdapter(cmd)
    Dim dsSuppliers as New DataSet()

    conn.Open()
    adapter.Fill(dsSuppliers)
    conn.Close()

    Trace.Write("LoadDataGrid", "End Data Access")

    Trace.Write("LoadDataGrid", "Begin Data Bind")

    orders.DataSource =  dsSuppliers
    orders.DataBind()

    Trace.Write("LoadDataGrid", "End Data Bind")

  End Sub
  </script>

</HEAD>
<BODY>

<h1>Tracing Data Access</h1>
<hr>

<form runat="server" id=form1 name=form1>
  <asp:DataGrid id="orders" runat="server"></asp:DataGrid>
</form>
<hr>

</BODY>
</HTML>
```

You've seen most of the code in Listing 23.1 many times. However, notice the
Trace="true" property specified in the page directive on line 1. This turns on tracing for
the Web form. As mentioned before, this will automatically generate a great deal of
information located below your form. One such section, shown in Figure 23.2, is named
Trace Information. By using the Trace object shown on line 20, you can display your

own messages in this section. In addition to enabling you to find bottlenecks in your application, the `Trace` object is also a terrific way to debug by outputting variable values.

FIGURE **23.2**

Using trace information to locate bottlenecks in an application.

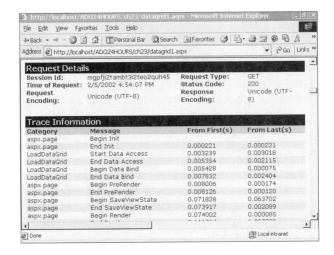

From Figure 23.2, you can see that accessing the data in the Web form took .002115 seconds and the binding of the data lasted for .002404 seconds. Tracing can help you efficiently discover which methods are performing slowly.

Most often, you'll discover that the source of a slow data access method is actually a badly performing database query. In the next section, you'll see how to improve the performance of your database queries using the SQL Query Analyzer tool.

Improving Your Queries with the SQL Query Analyzer

As you've seen from some of the examples in this book thus far, the Query Analyzer is a handy tool that enables you to send queries to the database and display the results. This makes it an effective debugging tool, particularly in debugging queries embedded in stored procedures.

However, the Query Analyzer also offers several options that will help you to greatly increase the performance of your queries.

> A note to more experienced readers: The Query Analyzer does things you should be doing anyhow... but if you haven't, it's a great way to get them done.

Before attempting to use the Query Analyzer, let's create a large test table.

Loading the Database with Sample Data

Add the `LoadTestData` stored procedure in Listing 23.2 to your Northwind database. This table will be used for testing purposes in this hour. `LoadTestData` creates a table containing a number of common fields. It then proceeds to add @rowcount number of data rows to the table, passed in as the only parameter.

LISTING 23.2   An Example of the `RequiredField` Control

```
CREATE PROCEDURE LoadTestData
(
    @rowcount bigint
)
AS

if exists (select * from dbo.sysobjects
            where id = object_id(N'[dbo].[TestData]') and
                OBJECTPROPERTY(id, N'IsUserTable') = 1)
drop table [dbo].[TestData]

CREATE TABLE [dbo].[TestData] (
    [TestID] [int] IDENTITY (1, 1) NOT NULL ,
    [Name] [varchar] (40) COLLATE SQL_Latin1_General_CP1_CI_AS NOT NULL ,
    [Address] [varchar] (50) COLLATE SQL_Latin1_General_CP1_CI_AS NOT NULL ,
    [Address2] [varchar] (50) COLLATE SQL_Latin1_General_CP1_CI_AS NULL ,
    [City] [varchar] (30) COLLATE SQL_Latin1_General_CP1_CI_AS NOT NULL ,
    [State] [char] (2) COLLATE SQL_Latin1_General_CP1_CI_AS NOT NULL ,
    [Zip] [varchar] (10) COLLATE SQL_Latin1_General_CP1_CI_AS NOT NULL ,
    [Description] [varchar] (500) COLLATE SQL_Latin1_General_CP1_CI_AS NULL
) ON [PRIMARY]

declare @identity bigint
select @identity = 0

WHILE ( @identity < @rowcount )

BEGIN
```

LISTING 23.2   continued

```
INSERT INTO TestData
(
    [Name],
    Address,
    City,
    State,
    Zip,
    [Description]
)
VALUES
(
    'Jason Lefebvre',
    '11 Longfellow St.',
    'Pawtucket',
    'RI',
    'Zip',
    'The quick brown fox jumps over the lazy dog.  The quick brown fox jumps
➥over the lazy dog.  The quick brown fox jumps over the lazy dog.'
)
select @identity = @@IDENTITY
END
```

After the LoadTestData stored procedure from Listing 23.2 is in the Northwind database, open an instance of the SQL Query Manager. On my machine, I loaded three million rows to ensure a good test. This created approximately 1.7 gigabytes of data. You'll probably want to create significantly fewer rows—on the order of 100,000 rows or so.

Showing the Query Execution Plan

Now that you have the sample data loaded into your database, enter a simple query that returns the name, address, and city of the record at TestID of 70000. You'll find that the query does not perform very well. In fact, this query took almost two full minutes to complete! This would definitely appear to slow down our ADO.NET code.

Fortunately, the Query Analyzer can shed some light on why the query is running slowly. Click on the Query menu item and then select Display Estimated Execution Plan. Then, run the query again. You'll notice an additional tab labeled Execution Plan at the bottom of the screen. After the query is done running, you can click on that tab to see how SQL Server spent its time processing your query. By hovering your mouse over an item in the plan, you can see detailed information for that part of the query. You can see this in Figure 23.3.

FIGURE 23.3

Viewing a SQL Server execution plan.

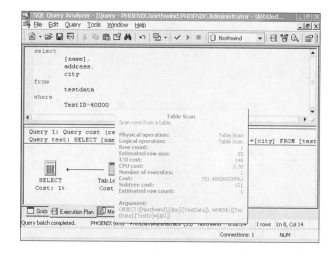

In this instance, the query is spending almost all of its time performing a table scan. This usually means that there is a problem with a table's index. Fortunately, the Query Analyzer can help us fix those as well.

Analyzing Table Indexes

Follow these steps to have the Query Analyzer examine the indexes of a table.

1. Choose the Query menu again and select the Index Tuning Wizard. Click Next in the introductory screen that loads (shown in Figure 23.4).

FIGURE 23.4

The Index Tuning Wizard.

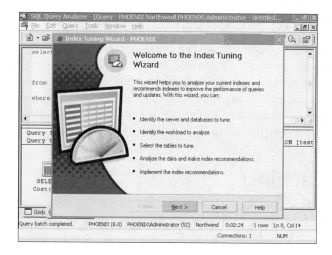

2. Accept all defaults on the next two screens you're prompted with by clicking Next.

3. As shown in Figure 23.5, the wizard then prompts you to select the tables you would like to tune. Check the box to the left of "TestData" and select Next. The Index Tuning Wizard then analyzes the table.

FIGURE 23.5

Choosing a table to analyze.

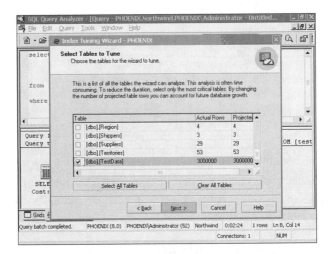

After the Index Tuning Wizard is done analyzing a table, it will load a list of recommendations. Accept all recommendations by clicking Finish, and then rerun the earlier query. It should perform significantly faster than last time.

Simulating Application Traffic

Often, small changes to your code can have a large effect on the performance of your application. Unfortunately, it's difficult to know exactly where these bottlenecks will occur. One of the best ways of finding out how your application will perform with a large set of concurrent users is to simulate that exact situation. Microsoft provides a free tool called the Microsoft Web Application Stress Tool for generating user load. You can download it from http://webtool.rte.microsoft.com/.

Data Caching

Data caching is another feature provided by ASP.NET that can significantly increase the speed of your data access code, by not retrieving the same data repetitively. In ASP.NET, the cache is implemented using the Cache object. Because it works just like any dictionary object, it's easy to use. The following line of code will store a DataSet in the Cache object with the name "Categories":

```
Cache("Categories") = dsCategories
```

It can be read out of the cache later with the following code:

```
myDataSet = Ctype(Cache("Categories"), DataSet)
```

To implement data caching in your Web application, first check to see if the DataSet is stored in the cache. If it is, use the cached version. Otherwise, load the DataSet data from the database and then store the DataSet in the cache for the next call. Listing 23.3 demonstrates how to store a DataSet in the cache.

LISTING 23.3   Using the ASP.NET Cache Object

```
public sub GetCategoryData()

  'if the dataset exists in the cache
  if Page.Cache("Categories") <> "" then
     'Return the cached DataSet
     return Ctype(Page.Cache("Categories"), DataSet)
  'otherwise, retrieve DataSet from database
  else
     'Create ADO.NET connection and command objects
     SqlConnection conn = new SqlConnection( _
        ConfigurationSettings.AppSettings("ConnectionString"))
     SqlCommand cmd = new SqlCommand("SELECT * " + _
                                        "FROM Categories", conn)

     'Create DataAdapter and DataSet objects
     Dim myAdapter as SqlDataAdapter = new SqlDataAdapter(cmd)
     Dim ds as DataSet = new DataSet()

     'Open connection to database
     conn.Open()

     'Fill the DataSet
     myAdapter.Fill(ds, "Categories")

     'Close connection to database
     conn.Close()

     'Place the dataset in the cache
     context.Cache("AllDomains") = ds

     'Return the dataset
     Return ds

end sub
```

Summary

In this hour, you learned some practical techniques for improving the speed and effectiveness of your application's data access. First, you saw some general techniques for tweaking ADO.NET to achieve faster data access. Then, you learned how to use the `Trace` object in ASP.NET to locate potential bottlenecks in your application. By using the SQL Query Analyzer, you can find out exactly why a database query is running slowly, and also some ways to improve the speed of the query. Lastly, data caching was used to reduce the number of repetitive calls to the database.

Q&A

Q Where can I learn more about tweaking application performance?

A At the time this book was published, there were very few resources for improving the performance of Microsoft .NET applications. However, one way to improve application performance is to make small changes to your code and then test, noting the performance gain or loss. Don't be afraid to get your hands dirty and have fun. Also, though not yet published at the time this book was published, *Performance Tuning Microsoft .NET Applications* from Microsoft Press seems very promising, written by a team of professionals at Microsoft who improve application performance for a living.

Workshop

These quiz questions are designed to test your knowledge of the material covered in this chapter. The answers to the quiz questions can be found in Appendix A, "Answers to Quizzes."

Quiz

1. For best performance, of the `DataAdapter` and `DataReader` objects, which would you use to bind database data to a pageable `DataGrid` object to display the results of a query on a form?

2. Name one way you can improve the responsiveness of your queries using the Microsoft SQL Query Analyzer.

Exercise

Choose a previous exercise from any of the hours in this book. Analyze the code generated for the exercise and look for ways the code could be improved, using the concepts from this chapter. If you're using ASP.NET, use the `Trace` object to keep track of how much time your improvements have saved.

Hour 24

Transmitting DataSets Using Web Services

One of the most interesting and talked-about features of the Microsoft .NET Framework is the ability to quickly and easily create Web services. A Web service enables developers to access remote methods and data using open standard protocols for transport and packaging. Web services use port 80 (the standard HTTP port) and XML to send and package data respectively.

By utilizing Web services, you can transmit data from any given host on the Internet to any other given host because Web services use TCP/IP to transport data. This enables you to build truly distributed applications without having to worry much about making sure the two hosts can communicate successfully. Best of all, Web services are easy to create and consume. If you can build a Web form, you can build a Web service.

In this hour, you'll learn how to

- Create a Web service that transmits a `DataSet`
- Create a Web form that consumes the `DataSet`

Sending a DataSet Using Web Services

To create a Web service, create a file in your Web project entitled suppliers.asmx. The .asmx extension tells the .NET Framework that this file should be treated as a Web service. Copy and paste the code from Listing 24.1 (or Listing 24.2 if you prefer C#) into the file and save. That's it! You've created your first Web service, which you can view in a browser by navigating directly to the suppliers.asmx URL.

Let's take a moment to the look at the Web service itself. Notice that the very first line of the file is a WebService directive. Up to this point, you have only seen a Page directive in that location. Notice also that the class of the Web service is provided in the WebService directive.

Next, several necessary namespaces are imported, just the same as in any Web form in this book. Then the Suppliers class is defined. The class inherits from the WebService class. The only difference is the WebMethod attribute specified before the publicly defined method. This specifies that the method is accessible as a Web method. The method is then defined. A DataSet is created and loaded with data from the Suppliers table in the Northwind database.

LISTING 24.1 A Web Service That Returns All Suppliers in the Northwind Database in Visual Basic .NET

```vb
<%@ WebService Language="VB" Class="Suppliers" %>

Imports System.Web.Services
Imports System.Data
Imports System.Data.SqlClient

Public Class Suppliers
        Inherits WebService

    <WebMethod ()> _
    public function GetAllSuppliers() as DataSet

        Dim conn as New SqlConnection("Initial Catalog=Northwind;" + _
                                "Server=(local);UID=sa;PWD=;")
        Dim cmd as New SqlCommand("SELECT * FROM Suppliers", conn)

        Dim adapter as SqlDataAdapter = New SqlDataAdapter(cmd)
        Dim dsSuppliers as New DataSet()

        conn.Open()
        adapter.Fill(dsSuppliers, "Suppliers")
        conn.Close()
```

LISTING 24.1   continued

```
            Return dsSuppliers

        End function

    End Class
```

LISTING 24.2   A Web Service That Returns All Suppliers in the Northwind
Database in C#

```csharp
<%@ WebService Language="C#" Class="Suppliers" %>

using System.Web.Services;
using System.Data;
using System.Data.SqlClient;

public class Suppliers: WebService
{
    [ WebMethod() ]
    public DataSet GetAllSuppliers()
    {
        SqlConnection conn = new SqlConnection("Initial Catalog=Northwind;" +
                                "Server=(local);UID=sa;PWD=;");
        SqlCommand cmd = new SqlCommand("SELECT * FROM Suppliers", conn);

        SqlDataAdapter adapter = new SqlDataAdapter(cmd);
        DataSet dsSuppliers = new DataSet();

        conn.Open();
        adapter.Fill(dsSuppliers, "Suppliers");
        conn.Close();

        return dsSuppliers;
    }
}
```

The GetAllSuppliers() method in Listings 24.1 and 24.2 is the same data access code
that you've seen many times throughout this book. A DataSet of all the suppliers in the
Northwind database is generated. The DataSet is then returned as the output of the function. Web services transport data using XML. Because DataSets are represented internally as XML, you do not need to do anything else! The DataSet will automatically
transmit.

When you navigate to the suppliers.asmx URL, you will see a screen like the one in
Figure 24.1. It contains some information about Web services in general and shows you

all the public methods supported by the current Web service. Note that in this case, the only public method is GetAllSuppliers().

FIGURE 24.1

An automatically generated information screen for your Web service.

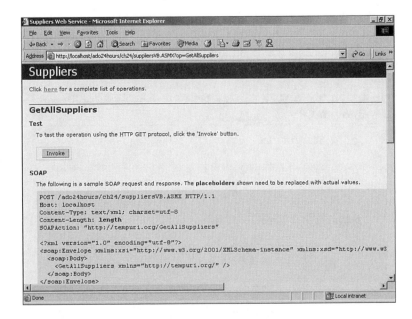

By clicking on the GetAllSuppliers() method, you will navigate to a screen like the one in Figure 24.2. This screen gives more detailed information about the GetAllSuppliers() method, including a sample SOAP request and response. These define exactly what type of data the Web service expects to receive and send in a call to this method.

If you click on the Invoke button to test the Web service, you will navigate to a screen like the one in Figure 24.3. This is the actual information returned by the Web service. If you look closely at the data, you'll see that it is the XML representation of a dataset. Because Web services transmit data packaged in XML, it's pretty handy that datasets are XML entities!

Now that you've created the Web service and ensured that it works by performing the tests, it's time to create a Web form that will use the DataSet returned from a remote machine to bind to a DataGrid.

FIGURE 24.2

Automatically generated information for calling your Web service.

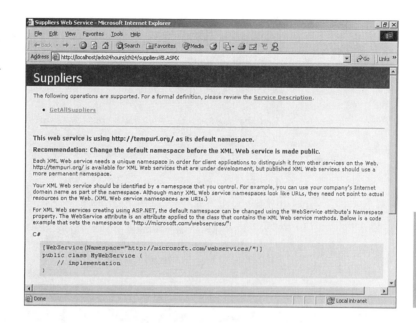

FIGURE 24.3

Invoking the GetAllSuppliers() Web service.

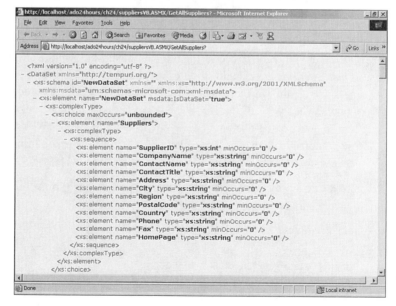

What Is SOAP?

SOAP (Simple Object Access Protocol) is currently a hot topic in the development world, and for good reason. After all, it's the underlying protocol to Web services, which according to Microsoft is much of the drive behind its .NET strategy.

Generally speaking, SOAP is a protocol designed to facilitate the transfer of data, wrapped in XML over HTTP. SOAP defines the format of the Web service request, as seen at the bottom of Figure 24.1. In addition, SOAP defines the organization and format of the data returned, as you can see by invoking a Web service as in Figure 24.3.

Though it's always a good idea to understand how things work "under the hood," you don't need to understand SOAP to use Web services. The Microsoft .NET Framework handles all the details for you. Because SOAP is an XML-based (and thus human-readable) protocol, you can examine the SOAP request and response in detail to find out what went wrong.

Consuming a `DataSet` from a Web Service

Consuming a `DataSet` using Web services is trickier than creating the Web service itself. There are a number of actions you must perform in order.

First, for your code to access the remote objects and methods, you must build a proxy class. A proxy class is a local set of methods that match the remote methods. Its purpose is to handle the work of actually calling the Web service and receiving the data. In other words, when you call the Web service in your code, you are actually calling the methods in the proxy class. The proxy class connects to the remote Web service on your behalf and automatically parses the payload of XML data returned from the service into values that your application can use directly.

To create a proxy class, go to a command prompt and run the following line of code to generate a Visual Basic .NET proxy class:

```
wsdl /language:vb http://localhost/ado24hours/ch24/suppliersvb.asmx
➥namespace:Northwind
```

or this one to generate a C# proxy class:

```
wsdl /language:cs http://localhost/ado24hours/ch24/suppliersCS.asmx
➥namespace:Northwind
```

The wsdl.exe utility connects to the Web service, analyzes its properties and methods, and constructs the local proxy class mentioned earlier.

> The wsdl.exe utility connects to the remote machine to create the proxy class. You must have TCP/IP connectivity to port 80 of the machine hosting the Web service for the utility to work.

After you've run the utility, it generates either a .cs or .vb file, depending on the language you've chosen. The next step is to compile the proxy class. This is done using the standard C# or Visual Basic .NET compiler. To compile the proxy class in C#, type the following line into a command prompt:

```
csc /Target:library Suppliers.cs
```

To compile using Visual Basic .NET, use the following:

```
vbc /Target:library suppliers.vb /r:system.dll r:system.data.dll
➥/r:system.xml.dll /r:system.web.services.dll
```

After you've compiled the proxy class into a DLL assembly, place that DLL into the /bin directory of your Web application. Now the remote Web method is accessible to any Web form in your project.

The last remaining step is to create a Web form that will make use of the remote method. The GetAllSuppliers method returns a list of suppliers, so you can bind this list to a DataGrid for display on the Web form. The DataSet object returned from the Web service is no different than any returned from a direct call to our data source.

In Listing 24.3, notice that you must import the Northwind namespace in order to have access to the Suppliers class. An instance of the Suppliers class is created in the LoadDataGrid() method. Then the GetAllSuppliers( ) method is called just as if it were a local method.

LISTING 24.3   Consuming the GetAllSuppliers() Web Service

```
<% @Page debug="true" Language="VB" %>
<%@ Import Namespace="System.Data" %>
<%@ Import Namespace="System.Data.SqlClient" %>
<%@ Import Namespace="Northwind" %>
```

LISTING 24.3   continued

```
<HTML>
<HEAD>
    <LINK rel="stylesheet" type="text/css" href="Main.css">
    <!-- End Style Sheet -->

    <script language="VB" runat="server" >
        Sub Page_Load(Source as Object, E as EventArgs)

            LoadDataGrid(orders)

        End Sub

        Private Sub LoadDataGrid( _
                        myDataGrid as System.Web.UI.WebControls.DataGrid)

            Dim mySuppliers as new Suppliers()

            orders.DataSource = mySuppliers.GetAllSuppliers()
            orders.DataBind()

        End Sub
    </script>

</HEAD>
<BODY>

<h1>Consuming Suppliers DataSet</h1>
<hr>

<form runat="server" id=form1 name=form1>
    <asp:DataGrid id="orders" runat="server"></asp:DataGrid>
</form>
<hr>

</BODY>
</HTML>
```

If you are using Visual Studio .NET to consume a DataSet from a Web service, you must perform one additional step. You must also add the Web reference to your project. To do this, right-click on References and choose Add Web Reference as shown in Figure 24.4.

This will load the Add Web Reference browser as shown in Figure 24.5. Enter the URL of your suppliers.asmx Web service into the Address box. After you click Add Reference, you'll be able to reference the methods of the supplier's Web service.

FIGURE 24.4

Adding a Web reference to a Visual Studio .NET project.

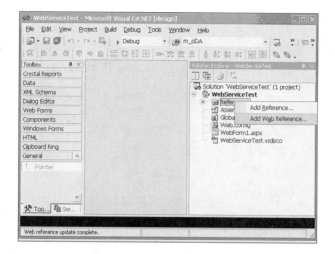

FIGURE 24.5

The Add Web Reference browser.

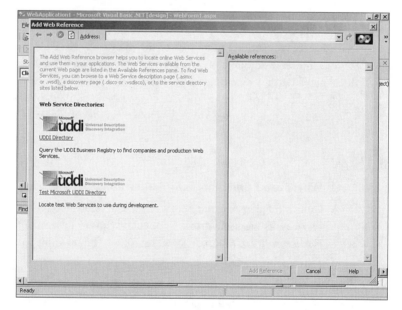

When the Web form in Listing 24.3 loads, you will see a screen like the one in Figure 24.6.

24

FIGURE 24.6

Consuming the DataSet *returned by the* GetAllSuppliers() *Web service.*

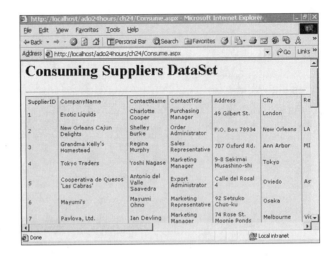

Summary

Web services are an important part of the Microsoft .NET Framework. You can use them to transmit large amounts of data between any two connected hosts on the Internet or local network, thus enabling easily distributed applications. In this hour, you saw how to create a Web service that returns a DataSet of all suppliers in the Northwind database. Then you saw how to integrate that Web service into a local application.

Q&A

Q Where can I find more information about Web services?

A Quite a number of good books have been published recently on the subject of Web services, as the topic grows in popularity every day. An excellent book on the topic is *Microsoft .NET Web Services* by Robert Tabor, from Sams Publishing.

Q Can any object be sent over Web services?

A Yes, but not necessarily automatically. To transmit custom classes or data types, you will need to tell the framework how to convert the object to XML. This is referred to as XML serialization. The Microsoft .NET Framework automatically serializes almost all simple data types. For more information, see XML serialization in the Microsoft .NET Framework SDK documentation.

Q Are Web services reliable?

A The answer is "it depends." Web services use XML and HTTP, both of which are battle-tested and proven protocols themselves. From this perspective, you can rely on the fact that you'll have few problems with Web services themselves, as long as they are accessible.

However, Web services are only as reliable as their weakest link. If you are invoking a Web service located on a server in your company's domain, it is likely to be very reliable—and if the Web service does go down, most likely your organization has an IT staff you can notify. However, consider the number of times transient Internet conditions have prevented you from accessing a favorite Web site. There are many points of failure between any two machines on the Internet that are entirely out of your control. Therefore, any Web services provided by hosts on the Internet are by their very nature unreliable and not fit for use in mission-critical applications.

Remember that when the Nimda virus reached its peak number of infections, the amount of additional Internet traffic generated by the virus caused sites to be unavailable or slow to load for several days. This poor performance would be reflected directly by any application making use of a remote Web service.

24

Workshop

These quiz questions are designed to test your knowledge of the material covered in this chapter. The answers to the quiz questions can be found in Appendix A, "Answers to Quizzes."

Quiz

1. What is the purpose of a proxy class?
2. What is the file extension used by a Web service in the Microsoft .NET Framework?

Exercise

Choose a Northwind table of your choice and expose it as a `DataSet` through a Web service. Then, consume the Web service from a Web form.

Appendix A

Hour 1

Quiz Answers

1. b. The DataSet is the object that can contain several DataTables and store relationship and constraint information.
2. True.
3. The System.Data namespace contains these classes.

Hour 2

Quiz Answers

1. True.
2. The easiest way to add a DataTable to a DataSet is to call the Add() method of the DataTable collection of the DataSet object.

Hour 3

Quiz Answers

1. a. The INSERT command enables you to add new records to a database table.

2. The WHERE portion of a SQL query uses an expression to filter the records returned by the query.

Hour 4

Quiz Answers

1. The foreign key column may only contain values from the primary key column of the parent table. In other words, if the CustomerID column of a customer table and order table are the primary and foreign key respectively, the CustomerID column of the order table may only contain values from the CustomerID column of the customer table.

2. This depends entirely on your data source. In most cases, you will get an error message telling you not to delete a parent object without first deleting its children. Microsoft SQL Server 2000 supports "cascading deletes." When active, SQL Server will automatically delete the child rows for you.

Hour 5

Quiz Answers

1. The SqlConnection object is used to connect to Microsoft SQL Server version 7.0 and higher using a managed provider that "talks" directly to SQL Server. The OleDbConnection object connects to OLE DB sources.

2. False. Connections to the database are not automatically closed.

Hour 6

Quiz Answer

1. The Fill() method of the DataAdapter object is used to place query results into a DataSet.

2. First, you must create an instance of the Connection object and properly configure it. Then you must associate this connection with the Command object. One way of

doing this is to set the `Connection` object to the `Connection` property of the `Command` object. Then, after you open your connection, you can execute your query and retrieve the results.

3. False. You can't mix objects from one managed provider with another to retrieve data.

Hour 7

Quiz Answers

1. The `ExecuteNonQuery()` object is used to execute commands against the data source that will not return any records. Therefore, it is ideal to use in situations where you want to modify or delete database data.

2. False. If you execute a query using `ExecuteNonQuery()` that will return data, it will result in the data from your database query being lost, but no error will occur.

Hour 8

Quiz Answers

1. True. There is never any more than one database record in memory while the `DataReader` is open and retrieving data. This makes it very lightweight compared to the `DataAdapter`, particularly when a large number of records are being returned.

2. The `DataAdapter` stores the results of a database query into a `DataSet` object. The `DataReader` opens a pipe directly from the database to the data's destination.

Hour 9

Quiz Answers

1. c. `ListBox` controls use the `DisplayMember` and `DataSource` properties to bind data.

2. False. The complete opposite. It is the `BindingContexts` object that sits on top of all the `CurrencyManagers` for a form. Multiple forms have multiple `BindingContexts` objects.

3. True. However, it is usually easier to bind controls to data in a `DataSet` that contains the relationship as opposed to having to programmatically load from each and join them in your code.

A

4. c. (databinding).Text property. Specify down to the individual column that is to be bound to the control.

5. True. You can bind to both traditional data sources as well as almost any structure that contains data. There just has to be a way to populate the data somehow.

6. a, b, and c. All of these. In fact, any collection that implements the Ilist interface.

Hour 10

Quiz Answers

1. The GetXml() method returns the DataSet object in XML form.

2. A DiffGram is an XML document containing both the original data source values and any updated values from the DataSet, as well. This enables you to serialize a DataSet to XML form, and then restore it and still be able to apply the changes to the data back to the data source.

Hour 11

Quiz Answers

1. The DataGrid list control is used to display data in a table.

2. The DataList is used to display organized groups of information about a single entity.

3. True.

4. True.

Hour 12

Quiz Answers

1. True. The Repeater control has a set of templates that can be used to format data using HTML.

2. The RepeatColumn property of the DataList is used to specify the number of columns generated by the control.

3. False. Though it is possible to implement paging using the Repeater control, it is not native to the control and thus cannot be done automatically. To implement paging, use the DataGrid object.

Hour 13

Quiz Answers

1. a. Processing error conditions from a Try block. Any exception in the Try block will transfer control to the Catch block for determination.

2. False. If utilized, this capability can retain errors on each row in the dataset.

3. True. In general, it is good practice to close a connection. Doing so in a Finally block is good practice if the open connection was in the corresponding Try block.

4. a, b, and c. You have the flexibility to set errors at all three levels. What's more, if you set an error at the row level, you can test the table for errors at higher levels (for example, at the table level using the HasErrors method).

5. False. You can utilize the DiffGram structure to encapsulate the data, schema, and data row error information.

6. c. RowUpdated is the most widely used event because it reflects the outcome of the updates against the data source after they have been completed. This usage is especially common when looking for optimistic concurrency violations.

Hour 14

Quiz Answers

1. a and b. Both locks on data resources and database connections must be maintained in pessimistic concurrency.

2. a. In general, you will need to compare original values (that you read from the data source) to current values in the data source before the data can be updated. If any of the comparison fails (indicating that the row was updated by someone else), you have encountered an optimistic concurrency violation.

3. False: Pessimistic concurrency is not designed for fast scalable applications in .NET because of the expensive need to hold connections and locks.

4. c. DiffGrams are an excellent XML structure to use when having to implement optimistic concurrency between varying systems. All that you need to test for optimistic concurrency violations is embedded in these block structures.

A

Hour 15

Quiz Answers

1. True. A stored procedure can contain any valid set of SQL statements for your data source.

2. Parameters enable you to pass data into and out of a stored procedure, in addition to the ability to return the results of a database query in a resultset.

Hour 16

Quiz Answers

1. Tblimp.exe is the application that imports type libraries into your managed code.

2. ADO.NET is strongly typed and disconnected. ADO is not strongly typed and by default maintains a connection to the database as long as the recordset object is open.

Hour 17

Quiz Answers

1. a. When you open a connection to the database. If there is a matching connection string in the connection pool, it will draw on it. Otherwise, it will create a new one (and establish the minimum pool size entries).

2. False. In .NET, connection pooling is on as the default (pooling = "true").

3. c. Close the connection to the database. This will release the connection back to the connection pool for subsequent use. If you do not explicitly close the connection, it will not be available to use.

4. a. The entire connection string. Even the smallest difference in the coding of a conceptually equivalent connection string will cause it not to match an entry in the connection pool.

5. d. .NET CLR Data—performance object and its associated pool connection counters.

Hour 18

Quiz Answers

1. The `Commit()` method of the `SqlTransaction` object finalizes a transaction and commits all database changes made during the life of the transaction. To achieve the same when working with T-SQL, you would use `COMMIT TRAN`.

2. The `BeginTransaction()` method of the `Connection` object is used to start a transaction.

Hour 19

Quiz Answers

1. b. The optimistic concurrency model, which means that other users can update data that has been selected by your application and your application must check for this before committing your updates.

2. False. You must explicitly activate this capability by using the `CommandBuilder` object.

3. b. Refresh metadata. This is done using the `.Refreshschema()` method. You would then clear out (`.Remove`) the `DataSet` and fill it again for further processing.

4. False. The `SelectCommand` to be used with `CommandBuilder` must not span multiple tables.

5. c. Return at least one primary key or unique column. The `UPDATE` and `DELETE` statements must be able to locate the exact data row for update/delete to ensure integrity.

Hour 20

Quiz Answers

1. b. The `/d[ataset]` directive tells the XSD tool to generate a typed `DataSet` class code from the supplied .xsd schema file.

2. False. You can generate typed `DataSets` both manually with the XSD tool and dynamically in Visual Studio .NET.

3. a. You can use the Imports reference in your code and supply the `/r:` reference for the typed dataset class (.dll) you generated.

A

4. a. Annotations are available to add more user-friendly references to `DataSet` objects and do not change the physical `DataSet` schema.

Hour 21

Quiz Answers

1. The purpose of adding additional layers to your application is to improve the readability and manageability of your code.

2. The option is called `CommandBehavior.CloseConnection`.

Hour 22

Quiz Answers

1. The examples in this hour were divided into three layers. The Web form was the presentation layer in the application, collecting and displaying product information. The second layer is our business logic/data access tier. In this application, this tier is provided by our compiled assembly that contains the ProductsDB class. Lastly, the SQL database is the last tier, and stores the product data.

2. The term master-detail is used to describe the relationship between a list of items and the corresponding screen that enables you to edit those individual items.

Hour 23

Quiz Answers

1. This is a trick question. Because you would be unable to page through data with a `DataReader` object, you should use the `DataAdapter` to return a `DataSet`.

2. First, you can use the Query Analyzer to display SQL Server's execution plan for your query. You can use this plan to discover how you could better structure the query. Additionally, you can also use the Query Analyzer to analyze the indexes of your table. Often, the Query Analyzer will suggest index improvements that can greatly improve the speed of your queries.

Hour 24

Quiz Answers

1. The purpose of a proxy class is to create a set of local methods that perform the footwork involved with retrieving data from a remote Web service. Without a proxy class, you would be unable to compile the remote methods into your application

2. The Web service file extension is .asmx in the Microsoft .NET Framework.

A

INDEX

How can we make this index more useful? Email us at indexes@samspublishing.com

How can we make this index more useful? Email us at indexes@samspublishing.com

How can we make this index more useful? Email us at indexes@samspublishing.com

X

Y-Z